Lecture Notes in Computer Science 8568

Commenced Publication in 1973
Founding and Former Series Editors:
Gerhard Goos, Juris Hartmanis, and Jan van Leeuwen

Editorial Board

T0212148

Davide Di Ruscio   Dániel Varró (Eds.)

Theory and Practice of Model Transformations

7th International Conference, ICMT 2014
Held as Part of STAF 2014
York, UK, July 21-22, 2014
Proceedings

 Springer

Volume Editors

Davide Di Ruscio
University of L'Aquila
Department of Information Engineering, Computer Science and Mathematics
Via Vetoio, 67010 L'Aquila, Italy
E-mail: davide.diruscio@univaq.it

Dániel Varró
Budapest University of Technology and Economics
Department of Measurement and Information Systems
Magyar tudósok krt. 2, 1117 Budapest, Hungary
E-mail: varro@mit.bme.hu

ISSN 0302-9743   e-ISSN 1611-3349
ISBN 978-3-319-08788-7   e-ISBN 978-3-319-08789-4
DOI 10.1007/978-3-319-08789-4
Springer Cham Heidelberg New York Dordrecht London

Library of Congress Control Number: 2014942443

LNCS Sublibrary: SL 2 – Programming and Software Engineering

Typesetting: Camera-ready by author, data conversion by Scientific Publishing Services, Chennai, India

Printed on acid-free paper

Springer is part of Springer Science+Business Media (www.springer.com)

Foreword

Software Technologies: Applications and Foundations (STAF) is a federation of a number of leading conferences on software technologies. It was formed after the end of the successful TOOLS federated event (http://tools.ethz.ch) in 2012, aiming to provide a loose umbrella organization for practical software technologies conferences, supported by a Steering Committee that provides continuity. The STAF federated event runs annually; the conferences that participate can vary from year to year, but all focus on practical and foundational advances in software technology. The conferences address all aspects of software technology, from object-oriented design, testing, mathematical approaches to modelling and verification, model transformation, graph transformation, model-driven engineering, aspect-oriented development, and tools.

STAF 2014 was held at the University of York, UK, during July 21-25, 2014, and hosted four conferences (ICMT 2014, ECMFA 2014, ICGT 2014 and TAP 2014), a long-running transformation tools contest (TTC 2014), eight workshops affiliated with the conferences, and (for the first time) a doctoral symposium. The event featured six internationally renowned keynote speakers, and welcomed participants from around the globe.

The STAF Organizing Committee thanks all participants for submitting and attending, the program chairs and Steering Committee members for the individual conferences, the keynote speakers for their thoughtful, insightful, and engaging talks, the University of York and IBM UK for their support, and the many ducks who helped to make the event a memorable one.

July 2014   Richard F. Paige

Preface

This volume contains the papers presented at ICMT2014: the 7th International Conference on Model Transformation held during July 21-22, 2014, in York as part of the STAF 2014 (Software Technology: Applications and Foundations) conference series. ICMT is the premier forum for researchers and practitioners from all areas of model transformation.

Model transformation encompasses a variety of technical spaces, including modelware, grammarware, dataware, and ontoware, a variety of model representations, e.g., based on different types of graphs, and a variety of transformation paradigms including rule-based transformations, term rewriting, and manipulations of objects in general-purpose programming languages.

The study of model transformation includes foundations, structuring mechanisms, and properties, such as modularity, composability, and parameterization of transformations, transformation languages, techniques, and tools. An important goal of the field is the development of high-level model transformation languages, providing transformations that are amenable to higher-order model transformations or tailored to specific transformation problems.

The efficient execution of model queries and transformations by scalable transformation engines on top of large graph data structures is also a key challenge in different application scenarios. Novel algorithms as well as innovative (e.g., distributed) execution strategies and domain-specific optimizations are sought in this respect. To achieve impact on software engineering in general, methodologies and tools are required to integrate model transformation into existing development environments and processes.

This year, ICMT received 38 submissions. Each submission was reviewed by at least three Program Committee members. After an online discussion period, the Program Committee selected to accept 14 papers as part of the conference program. These papers included regular research papers, tool papers, and experience reports orginized into five sessions on model transformation testing and analysis, tracing and reverse engineering of transformations, and foundations and applications of model synchronization. We were honored to host Jean Bézivin as a keynote speaker of ICMT 2014, who gave an invited talk on "Software Modeling and the Future of Engineering."

Many people contributed to the success of ICMT 2014. We would like to truly acknowledge the work of all Program Committee members and reviewers for the timely delivery of reviews and constructive discussions given the very tight review schedule. We are also indebted to Philip Langer (Vienna University of Technology) serving as the web chair of ICMT 2014. Finally, the authors themselves constitute the heart of the model transformation community and their enthusiasm and hard work is a also key contribution.

May 2014   Davide Di Ruscio
                                                          Daniel Varro

Organization

Program Committee

Achim D. Brucker	SAP AG, Germany
Jordi Cabot	Inria-École des Mines de Nantes, France
Antonio Cicchetti	Mälardalen University, Sweden
Tony Clark	Middlesex University, UK
Benoit Combemale	IRISA, Université de Rennes 1, France
Krzysztof Czarnecki	University of Waterloo, Canada
Juan de Lara	Universidad Autonoma de Madrid, Spain
Gregor Engels	University of Paderborn, Germany
Jesus Garcia-Molina	Universidad de Murcia, Spain
Holger Giese	Hasso Plattner Institute, University of Potsdam, Germany
Martin Gogolla	University of Bremen, Germany
Jeff Gray	University of Alabama, USA
Reiko Heckel	University of Leicester, UK
Zhenjiang Hu	National Institute of Informatics, Japan
Ludovico Iovino	University of L'Aquila, Italy
Ethan K. Jackson	Microsoft Research, USA
Gerti Kappel	Vienna University of Technology, Austria
Dimitris Kolovos	University of York, UK
Thomas Kühne	Victoria University of Wellington, New Zealand
Jochen Küster	FH Bielefeld, Germany
Ralf Lämmel	Universität Koblenz-Landau, Germany
Tihamér Levendovszky	Vanderbilt University, USA
Richard Paige	University of York, UK
Marc Pantel	IRIT/INPT, Université de Toulouse, France
Alfonso Pierantonio	University of L'Aquila, Italy
István Ráth	Budapest University of Technology and Economics, Hungary
Bernhard Rumpe	RWTH Aachen University, Germany
Houari Sahraoui	DIRO, Université de Montréal, Canada
Andy Schürr	TU Darmstadt, Germany
Jim Steel	University of Queensland, Australia
Perdita Stevens	University of Edinburgh, UK
Markus Stumptner	University of South Australia, Australia

Additional Reviewers

Invited Talk
(Abstract)

Software Modeling and the Future of Engineering

Jean Bézivin

Independent Consultant in Software Modeling and
Retired Professor of Computer Science
University of Nantes, France
jbezivin@gmail.com

Abstract. In the past fifty years the world of engineering has considerably changed. From computer-assisted to software-intensive, most classical and emerging domain engineering fields now heavily draw on some forms of Software Model Engineering (SME) shortly called "Software Modeling". Starting from a general map of engineering fields, the talk will first outline this important evolution and the progressive shift of SME from the mere support of code production and maintenance to the much broader spectrum of a central practice in most of these current domain engineering fields. In other words the focus of software modeling is rapidly changing from software engineering to engineering software. But what is exactly SME? Historically its definition has been rather fluctuating. The last iteration, since 2000, did not even produce a unique characterization. On the contrary, SME may be viewed as composed as a set of different facets, some of them not even mutually compatible. The talk will describe these various segments of SME, their objective, market, usage characteristics and hopefully convergence of goals. One of these segments, the management of abstract correspondences between models (and of transformations, their operational counterparts) will be for example more particularly detailed and its importance outlined. All these observations will allow to conclude that, at this point of its history and in this state of maturity, software modeling may be seen as an essential contribution to the future of engineering and an outstanding long-term research opportunity.

Table of Contents

Model Transformation Testing

Foundations of Model Synchronization

Applications of Model Synchronization

Tracing and Reverse Engineering of Transformations

On the Usage of TGGs for Automated Model Transformation Testing

Martin Wieber, Anthony Anjorin, and Andy Schürr

Technische Universität Darmstadt,
Real-Time Systems Lab,
Merckstraße 25, 64283 Darmstadt, Germany
{martin.wieber,anthony.anjorin,andy.schuerr}@es.tu-darmstadt.de

Abstract. As model transformations are fundamental to model-driven engineering, assuring their quality is a central task which can be achieved by testing with sufficiently adequate and large test suites. As the latter requirement can render manual testing prohibitively costly in practice, a high level of automation is advisable. Triple Graph Grammars (TGGs) have been shown to provide a promising solution to this challenge as not only *test case generators*, but also generic *test oracles* can be derived from them. It is, however, unclear if such generated test suites are indeed adequate and, as different strategies can be used to steer the test generation process, a systematic means of comparing and evaluating such test suites and strategies is required.

In this paper, we extend existing work on TGG-based testing by (i) presenting a generic framework for TGG-based testing, (ii) describing a concrete instantiation of this framework with our TGG tool eMoflon, and (iii) exploring how the well-known technique of *mutation analysis* can be used to evaluate a set of test generation strategies by analyzing the generated test suites.

1 Introduction

Model transformations represent a fundamental paradigm in Model-Driven Engineering (MDE), and therefore, quality assurance of transformations is a crucial task and subject to active research. A viable strategy to improve the quality of and trust in model transformations is *testing*, which requires not only a sufficient amount of *adequate* test data, but also a suitable test *oracle* for test evaluation [4]. Manual testing quickly becomes infeasible for real-world applications, so *automating* the test derivation is also an important challenge [27].

String grammar-based test case generation [21] is a well-established technique used in grammar development [25] and compiler testing [20]. In the approach, test inputs (representing words of a language) are generated by consecutively applying the rules of a grammar. A similar approach exists in the MDE domain, where *graph grammars* can be used to generate (test) models [9,28,10]. For a comprehensive testing process, however, a *test oracle* is also required to decide whether the output of the System Under Test (SUT) is correct.

D. Di Ruscio and D. Varró (Eds.): ICMT 2014, LNCS 8568, pp. 1–16, 2014.

Triple Graph Grammars (TGGs) [26] can be used in this context [18,17], as they comprise two graph grammars (for source and target) connected by a third correspondence graph grammar. Applying a sequence of TGG rules thus results in a pair of a *source* and a *target model*, connected by the *correspondence model*. A TGG represents a declarative, rule-based specification of a language of consistent triples of connected source, target and correspondence models, which can be used to test a system by generating consistent triples with the rules of the TGG. The source (resp. target) model of each generated triple serves as input for the SUT, while the target (resp. source) model is regarded as a valid output to which the result of the SUT can be compared to. Consequently, the TGG is used not only for test generation, but also solves the oracle problem.

It remains, however, an open question if the derived test suites are indeed adequate. As with any grammar-based generation technique, this is influenced by the concrete derivation strategy used to guide and limit the generation process. In this paper, we demonstrate how the well-known technique of *mutation analysis* [8,24] can be used to systematically compare and evaluate such strategies for TGG-based test generation in terms of adequacy, and report on first results. Our overall contribution is threefold, as we

(1) Present an abstract framework for TGG-based test generation and evaluation, which can be used to classify current and future approaches (Sect. 2, 3).
(2) Describe (in Sect. 4) a concrete instantiation of the framework based on the eMoflon tool (www.emoflon.org). In comparison to the MoTE tool [17], eMoflon supports additional TGG features such as negative application conditions (NACs), bidirectional attribute constraints and *relation-like* (non-uniquely defined) mappings of one input to several legal outputs. These enable more expressive TGGs [19] and, thus, a richer test generation framework (including aligned rule coverage strategies);
(3) Show (with several experiments) how mutation analysis can be used to systematically evaluate the generated test suites and, indirectly, the applied strategies (Sect. 5).

2   A TGG-Centric Test Approach

Figure 1 depicts a generic, TGG-based testing framework as a UML component diagram. The architecture is tool, technology, and platform independent. We use this architecture in the following to explain the general approach, as well as to classify and compare concrete instantiations. A TGG specification of the considered model-to-model transformation serves as the basis of the framework. The specification is created with a *TGG tool* ① such as eMoflon, and serves as input for a *test generator* ②, which is the central component of this framework. The test generator produces test cases (as pairs of test models and expected results) by repeated application of TGG rules, and uses two auxiliary functional blocks:(i) a *traversal strategy* ②.① that guides the generation process by selecting the rules to be applied, and (ii) a *stop criterion* ②.② that controls when to end this process based on a *sufficiency* notion. The generated test stimuli are input to the

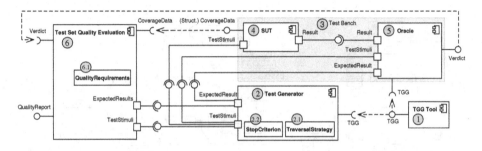

Fig. 1. Components of a generic TGG-based testing framework

components forming the *test bench* ③. Test bench related tasks are to(i) invoke the *SUT* ④ with the test stimuli, (ii) produce and maintain coverage data collected from the *SUT* if required, and (iii) pass the resulting output of the SUT to the *oracle* ⑤ for evaluation. The oracle determines whether a test fails or passes in form of a *verdict*. The verdict can be based on the output of the SUT, the expected results and test stimuli provided by the test generator, and the TGG specification. Finally, we include a *test set quality evaluation* component ⑥ to determine the quality of the generated test suite based on relevant pieces of information. Its inputs might comprise the test stimuli, the expected results, the verdict of the oracle (for being able to take the quality of the verdicts and the trustability of the oracle into account), and the coverage data. The evaluation also uses predefined *quality requirements* ⑥.① as a benchmark.

3 Design Choices and Variability in the Approach

Having introduced the general architecture, we now continue with a discussion of several *variation points* concerning concrete implementation of the framework (for testing and test generation). Figure 2 depicts two *feature models* we derived for this purpose: one for the testing task *setup* (left-hand side) and one for the *framework* (right-hand side). Feature models are a well-accepted means of describing a *family* of related *products* in terms of their commonalities and variability [5]. A *feature*, visualized by a box labelled with the corresponding name, represents a specific characteristic of the family of *products*. Features are organized hierarchically, whereby child features can only be selected if their parent feature is selected. Child features can be either *optional*, meaning that products could comprise any of these features, or *mandatory*, meaning that all valid products must have this feature. Child features can also be grouped into *alternative* or *non-empty selection groups*, the former (latter) indicating that exactly (at least) one feature has to be chosen. Additionally, we introduce an (informal) *influences relation* among the features, which indicates that the (de-)selection of the source feature influences the selection *or* deselection of the target feature. To preserve legibility, we only include a small amount of such connections.

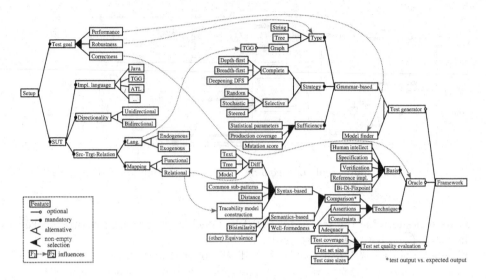

Fig. 2. Feature model describing variability in the *Setup* and the *Framework*

3.1   Variability Regarding the Setup

The testing task setup is mainly characterized by(i) the *test goal*, and (ii) the *SUT* with its most relevant properties (for other/more properties cf., e.g., [7]). Potential test goals include(i) *performance* – can the SUT handle *large* (e.g., element count) or *complex* (e.g., highly connected) input models, (ii) *robustness* – can the SUT cope with invalid input models (w.r.t. the languages induced by the metamodel or the TGG), and (iii) *correctness* – does the SUT implement the specified behavior.

Although the framework follows a specification-based (black-box) testing approach, design choices are still influenced by properties of the SUT. For example, the chosen *transformation language* has a strong influence on the available validation/verification techniques. The *directionality* of the SUT has an impact on required test models. Bidirectionality enables additional options to derive a test verdict (e.g., by performing a round-trip transformation and comparing the final result to the original start model). Another related aspect of the SUT concerns its *source-target-relation*. Whether a transformation is *exogenous* (source and target languages are different) or *endogenous* (identical source and target metamodels) influences, e.g., the decision if TGGs are suitable for testing. Design choices concerning the oracle are also influenced by whether a SUT realizes a function-like (one to one) or a relation-like (one to many) mapping.

3.2   Variability Regarding the Framework

Concrete implementations of the framework can differ w.r.t. the *test generator*, the *oracle*, and means of *quality evaluation*. We continue by discussing potential options and suggesting a corresponding (incomplete) classification.

Test Generator. Test models can be generated in many ways, e.g., by using a problem-specific generator or generic model finders. We suggest to distinguish two classes of test generators:(i) *grammar-based* test generators, and (ii) *model finders* such as *Alloy*.[1] Grammar-based test generators depend on the *grammar type*, a *generation strategy* to select and apply the rules, and a *sufficiency criterion*, to decide when to stop generating new "words" of the language. For robustness testing, it should be possible to generate invalid models (models that are not part of the language), which is why there is a connection between the features "Robustness" and "Type". The transformation language also has some influence on the choice of grammar type, e.g., TGG-based testing is more natural for exogenous than endogenous transformations. Model finders tend to suffer from the *combinatorial explosion* problem (cf. [11] for an Alloy-specific analysis) which might render them unsuitable for performance testing.

Oracle. Comparing actual and expected output models is only one of several oracle options (cf., e.g., [22]) whereby a concrete decision is strongly influenced by the test goal of the setup. The verdict of an oracle can be based on different *sources of truth* (Fig. 2):(i) human intuition, (ii) a specification of the transformation (not necessarily formal or related to TGGs), (iii) proven properties of the result (obtained through formal verification), (iv) an existing reference implementation, and (v) checking for a (round-trip) fixpoint in bidirectional transformations. Several *techniques* can be used to check the result against the expectations, such as *syntax-based* comparison via *(model) differencing* tools. For relation-like transformation semantics, however, a potentially infinite set of valid output-models exists for a single input model, which is difficult to handle with differencing-based oracles. Other options could be more feasible, such as(i) searching for *common sub-patterns* in the actual and the expected result, (ii) defining a *distance* with an upper bound as a metric to capture similarities (e.g., the number of distinct differences), or, (iii) in case a TGG is used, a *traceability model construction* to decide if input and output pairs can be extended to a consistent triple of the language defined by the TGG.

Test Set Quality Evaluation. As exhaustive testing is almost never feasible, objective quality indicators for test sets are required to limit testing effort. There are various options (non-complete list):(i) (relative) *adequacy* (the ability to detect artificially incorporated bugs from a mutation analysis), (ii) test *coverage* (achieved coverage of structural or specification elements when running the tests), (iii) *test set size* (#test cases), and (iv) *test case sizes* (#elements).

4 A Concrete Instantiation with eMoflon

We continue by presenting our implementation of the framework with eMoflon, and categorizing it according to Sect. 2. In addition to this we also introduce a running example: a tool integration scenario in which a library system (*source domain*) and a reference management tool (*target domain*) are synchronized.

---

[1] http://alloy.mit.edu

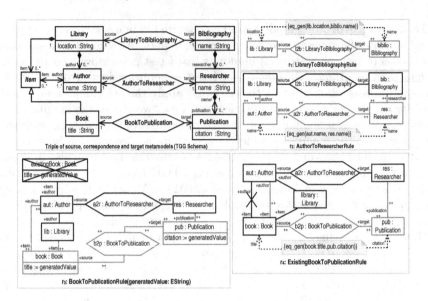

Fig. 3. TGG schema and TGG rules r_1 - r_4 for the running example

4.1 Running Example

The following example showcases relevant TGG features and is later on used for the case study in Sect. 5. The data structures to be synchronized are represented as *metamodels* which describe the concepts and relations in a domain as classes and associations between classes. The source metamodel, depicted to the top-left of Fig. 3, defines a `Library` containing `Authors` and `Items`. An `Author` can have arbitrarily many `Items` (only `Books` are shown for presentation purposes). Note that `Items` can belong to multiple authors, cf. the corresponding `item-author` association. The target metamodel comprises a `Bibliography` containing `Researchers`. The latter can have arbitrarily many `Publications`. Note that a `Publication` belongs to exactly one `Researcher`. Classes can have properties such as the `location` of a `Library` or the `name` of a `Researcher`. The two metamodels are connected by a *correspondence* metamodel that specifies which source and target elements correspond to each other, e.g., `Library` and `Bibliography` via the `LibraryToBibliography` correspondence type. This triple of metamodels is referred to as a *TGG schema*. *TGG rules* are patterns consisting of objects and links typed according to the TGG schema.

Rule r_1: `LibraryToBibliographyRule` (top-right of Fig. 3) specifies that libraries correspond to bibliographies and are created together (axiom rule). *Created* elements in TGG rules are green, with a "++" markup. The rule r_2: `AuthorToResearcherRule` specifies that authors and researchers are created together, but it also requires a *context*, namely the library and corresponding bibliography, into which the author and researcher are added. Context elements are black (with no markup) and must already have been created by other rules.

Rules r_1 and r_2 make use of bidirectional *attribute constraints* [3] to specify how attributes of different elements are related to each other. The constraint eq_gen(lib.location,biblio.name), for example, states that the location of the library and the name of the corresponding bibliography are to be equal.

Rules r_3: BookToPublicationRule and r_4: ExistingBookToPublication-Rule (Fig. 3, bottom) specify how books and publications are added. Rule r_3 makes use of a *Negative Application Condition* (NAC), depicted as the crossed out element existingBook, to ensure that the rule is only applicable if the author aut has not published a book with the same title. eMoflon supports such NACs to ensure that global constraints (in this case, no author can publish more than one book with the same title) are not violated (note that the title of the new book is provided as a *rule parameter*, supplied or generated at run time). Similarly, r_4 enables shared authorship of books (by several authors) and ensures that respective publications are assigned to each of the researchers. Another NAC is used in this case to prevent equally named books.

4.2   Design Rationale

We have implemented the components of Fig. 1 as part of our *eMoflon* tool suite. The design choices and specific characteristics (cf. Fig. 2) w.r.t. our concrete implementation are discussed in the following.

Handling Relational Specifications. Using TGGs as specification language induces a consistency *relation* over model pairs: such pairs are in relation to each other if a connecting correspondence model can be derived with the given rules. This consistency relation is not necessarily a *function*. For instance, consider our running example: As it is impossible to ascertain in the target domain how many authors worked together on the same book (publications are never shared), the backward transformation has a degree of freedom when translating publications of different authors with the same citation. These publications can either be transformed to the same book according to r_4, or to a new book for each author according to r_3 (different authors are free to publish books with the same title), meaning that the consistency relation is *non-functional* in the backward direction.

Coping with non-functionality is a challenge for a test (generation) framework. The oracle must take this degree of freedom into account, i.e., the valid output models for a given input model can be a set containing multiple elements. If one (or both) of the metamodels define types that have no respective counterpart in the opposite domain, then the set of valid output models is even unbounded in size; one can always construct another valid result from a given result by adding an instance of one of these types. We suggest (and have implemented) the following solution:

(a) After using the rules of the TGG to generate pairs of input and valid output models, we use a model-diff tool – *EMFCompare* of the Eclipse Modelling Framework (EMF) – to deduce a set of the discovered valid output models for every input model by grouping all output models for the same input. Note that this is a one-time effort during test creation.

(b) As the complete set of valid output models for an input model can in general be infinite, our default oracle only uses the deduced sets as a preliminary check for efficiency reasons: If the produced output model is in the deduced set then the test is reported as passed. This can be based, e.g., on EMF-Compare or a less rigid approximation (e.g., hash-based).

(c) If the produced output model is not in the set, an attempt is made to extend the input model and produced output model to a consistent triple by creating an appropriate correspondence model. The produced output model is "correct" with respect to the TGG *iff* this construction is possible. This algorithm for *correspondence construction* is automatically derivable from the TGG rules but must be rerun every time the tests are executed.

Exploiting NACs for Generating Robustness Tests. A grammar-based test generation approach typically generates words of the described language and is *not* directly suitable for robustness testing, which requires invalid test stimuli. One could manipulate (and falsify) the rules of the grammar to generate invalid words, but this seems rather arbitrary and would most likely lead to inconsistencies in the specification.

As the NACs which our TGG tool supports correspond *exactly* to global negative constraints in the source and target metamodels – i.e., the NACs only ensure that the rules do not violate these constraints [2] – we take the following approach: In case we encounter a potential rule application that is prohibited only by the NACs of the rule, it is possible to systematically generate invalid input models by ignoring the NACs and applying the rule nevertheless. Using such models for robustness testing corresponds clearly to checking how a SUT handles models that violate the set of constraints in a domain. For our running example, such invalid models include libraries with authors who have published multiple books sharing the same title, or published the same book twice. Our test generator ② is able to detect NACs in a TGG rule, create a version of the rule without the NACs, and allow the traversal strategy ②.① to decide whether robustness tests should be generated or not.

Handling Generation of Attribute Values. A non-trivial challenge when deriving test models lies in generating attribute values that are consistent with the specification. The attribute constraints supported by eMoflon, such as eq_gen in the running example, are used to generate consistent attribute values. They can be extended and refined as required (in Java) [3]. For the example, string values are generated randomly (but can also be repeated with a certain probability to provoke interesting situations such as books with the same title).

SUT Invocation. Our test generation framework can be used to test arbitrary (bi- and unidirectional) model transformations that take instances of the source/target metamodel as input and produces instances of the second metamodel as output. We generate test stubs (Java classes) with methods that must be implemented to invoke the SUT (cf. ④ in Fig. 1).

Coverage Strategies. The traversal strategy ②.① used by the test generator to explore the "derivation tree" can easily be implemented and adjusted by the user. A base class Strategy provides a set of template methods that are invoked by the test generator. The strategy is queried at every decision point in the test generation process and can filter and sort the current list of *applicable* TGG rules and corresponding matching locations. Currently, we provide default implementations for depth-first and breadth-first search strategies, as well as random traversal strategies. As default stop criterion ②.②, one can choose between upper bounds on:(i) the number of the generated test cases, (ii) the maximal run time (time out), (iii) the number of rule applications, (iv) certain combinations of the previous options, and (v) coverage of user-specified rule sequences.

Supported Technologies and Standards. eMoflon takes a generative approach, meaning that standard EMF-compatible Java code is generated for all components of the framework. The test generator and test bench represent executable components and the framework can be extended by means of Java inheritance to customize traversal strategies, stop criteria, SUTs, quality requirements etc. JUnit is required because sets of JUnit tests are created and run for the generated input models. We use the *de facto* modelling standard EMF/Ecore and, thus, any SUT that accepts such instance models as input and produces such models as output can be tested (adapters have to be used otherwise).

Bootstrapping with Graph Transformations. eMoflon is developed with eMoflon and our test generation framework is no exception to this. Our *compiler* that takes a TGG specification as input and derives a test generator ② as output, is implemented as a (higher order) model transformation specified completely with unidirectional programmed graph transformations.

5   Evaluation and Case Study

After describing the quality evaluation component ⑥ of Fig. 1 in general, we now give some hints towards its implementation and usage to evaluate: (a) the usefulness of this black-box testing approach in general, (b) the generated test suites in terms of mutation scores, (c) the influence of traversal strategies and stop criteria on test suite quality, and (d) feasible oracle options.

5.1   Assessing Test Suite Quality

We begin with the main technique to evaluate adequacy, namely mutation analysis, before describing the setup of the case study.

Mutation Analysis and Adequacy. Mutation analysis is a well-established means to evaluate a test suite's *adequacy* or, in other words, its flaw detection capability. The idea behind it is to systematically introduce single defects into the SUT each resulting in a *mutant* of the SUT. The sorts of the defects are implementation language dependent and should reflect "typical" errors made in real world situations. If the test suite contains at least one test that leads to an unexpected or wrong output (by oracle judgment), the mutant is recognized and said to be *killed* by the test suite. The *mutation score* of a test suite is the ratio of discovered to generated mutants, ranging from 0 to 1. An inherent challenge of the approach stems from mutants that are equivalent to the SUT w.r.t. input/output behavior. Comparing mutation scores is still possible, but for an absolute grading the scores should be adjusted by removing such SUT-equivalent mutants. A more interfering effect on the analysis stems from imperfect oracles (model comparison can be considered imperfect here) which classify SUTs and equivalent mutants differently and erroneously kill mutants (*false positives*). This can bias mutation scores by over- or underrating adequacy.

Setup. For our evaluation we use the running example with two SUTs: (a) A handwritten Java implementation, and (b) a (programmed) graph transformation (eMoflon) implementation (independent of the TGG rules). We refer to the first as Java and to the second as GraTra. Both SUTs implement the forward (source-to-target) and the backward (target-to-source) direction of the mapping.

It is important to note here that GraTra is *not* derived from the TGG specification. Although this is indeed possible, testing such automatically derived implementations would equate to testing the TGG tool itself (that provides the derivation) and is a very different task.

A related point to clarify is why it makes sense to consider other (manual) implementations of the TGG specification if it is possible to automatically derive an implementation. There are multiple arguments for doing this from the field of model-based testing (the TGG is considered here to be the test model), including: (i) the TGG is often an abstraction of the required transformation and focuses on the current details that are to be tested, (ii) a manual implementation is typically much more efficient (runtime and memory consumption), and (iii) the target platform might not be supported by the chosen TGG tool.

We derived a total of 31 mutants (10 for the forward direction, 21 for the backward direction) for Java, and 14 mutants (6 for forward, 8 for backward) for GraTra. Mutants were *generated* for GraTra and *handcrafted* in case of Java (e.g., by inverting Boolean conditions, introducing off-by-one errors, etc.). We refrained from using Java mutation frameworks because the vast majority of the resulting defects were too "low level" meaning they did not consider model and transformation semantics thus breaking the transformation right from the start. Mutation operators for GraTra basically relax or restrict the application conditions of the declarative rewriting rules (e.g., by altering the node types or by converting nodes to NAC elements; cf. [24] for a set of generic operators). During experimentation it became apparent that several mutants were in fact equivalent to the solution (7 in case of (a), 4 in case of (b)). We left them in the mutant set, however, to check if oracles produce false positive results.

Concerning test suite derivation, we implemented the following strategy/stop-criterion combinations to generate a total of four suites:(1) *all rule pairs* (**AP**) – breadth-first search for rule application sequences that cover all possible pairs of rules excluding axiom rule r_1, which is only allowed as the initial rule (result: 9 model triples); (2) *every rule once* (**ERO**) – breadth-first search for the shortest application sequence that ends with a given rule for all rules (result: 4 model triples, as we have 4 rules); (3) *rule dependencies* (**RD**) – breadth-first search for a rule application sequence that fulfills a given, problem-specific coverage requirement $\langle r_1, *, r_2, *, r_3, *, r_4 \rangle$ beginning with application of r_1, ending with

Table 1. Mutation analysis results (2 SUTs × 2 directions × 3 oracles vs. 4 test sets)

			AP					ERO					RD					TMD					#Mutants		
SUT	Direction	Oracle	true positives	false positives	mut_score	PPV	weighted mut_score	true positives	false positives	mut_score	PPV	weighted mut_score	true positives	false positives	mut_score	PPV	weighted mut_score	true positives	false positives	mut_score	PPV	weighted mut_score	equivalent	non-equivalent	total
Java	FWD	EmfCompare	10	0	1	1	1	9	0	0.9	1	0.9	9	0	0.9	1	0.9	10	0	1	1	1			
		Hash comp.	10	0	1	1	1	8	0	0.8	1	0.8	8	0	0.8	1	0.8	10	0	1	1	1	0	10	10
		Link creation	10	0	1	1	1	9	0	0.9	1	0.9	9	0	0.9	1	0.9	10	0	1	1	1			31
	BWD	EmfCompare	14	5	1	0.737	0.737	12	5	0.857	0.706	0.605	12	5	0.857	0.706	0.605	14	7	1	0.667	0.667			
		Hash comp.	12	5	0.857	0.706	0.605	10	5	0.714	0.667	0.476	10	5	0.714	0.667	0.476	12	7	0.857	0.632	0.541	7	14	21
		Link creation	13	0	0.929	1	0.929	10	0	0.714	1	0.714	10	0	0.714	1	0.714	13	0	0.929	1	0.929			
GraTra	FWD	EmfCompare	5	0	1	1	1	5	0	1	1	1	4	0	0.8	1	0.8	5	0	1	1	1			
		Hash comp.	5	0	1	1	1	5	0	1	1	1	4	0	0.8	1	0.8	5	0	1	1	1	1	5	6
		Link creation	5	0	1	1	1	5	0	1	1	1	5	0	1	1	1	5	0	1	1	1			14
	BWD	EmfCompare	5	0	1	1	1	4	0	0.8	1	0.8	4	0	0.8	1	0.8	5	0	1	1	1			
		Hash comp.	5	0	1	1	1	4	0	0.8	1	0.8	4	0	0.8	1	0.8	5	0	1	1	1	3	5	8
		Link creation	5	0	1	1	1	4	0	0.8	1	0.8	4	0	0.8	1	0.8	5	0	1	1	1			

application of r_4; the '$*$' stand for arbitrary intermediate sequences of rule applications. This requirement encodes the interdependency of the TGG rules, i.e., r_2 *depends* on the context created by r_1 and so forth (result: 1 model triple); (4) *timeout and max. depth* (**TMD**) – a depth-first traversal limited by a max. depth of 20 rule applications and a 3 s timeout (result: 174 model triples). From each model triple, a forward and a backward test was created.

5.2   Mutation Analysis Results

Table 1 summarizes the results of the mutation analysis for the two SUTs (upper half dedicated to Java, lower half to GraTra). Each result set is subdivided into forward (FWD) and backward (BWD) direction each comprising values for the three oracles EmfCompare, hash comparison, and (correspondence) link creation. The columns (captioned **AP**, **ERO**, ...) group the results for each of the four generated test suites. For better interpretability, we included the absolute numbers of *true positives* and *false positives*. True and false negatives are omitted for brevity (their resp. values can be calculated from the positive counterparts and the total number of (non-)equivalent mutants). Note that the highlighted cells contain the values for the *mutation score* (mut_score or green gamut) and for a derived metric we refer to as *weighted mutation score* (weighted mut_score or blue gamut). We also provide the *positive predictive value* (PPV) as the ratio of true positives over the sum of true and false positives. It corresponds to the conditional probability of a true positive hit upon indicating a mutant and is the weighting factor for calculating the weighted mut_score. The rationale for this is that the weighted mut_score represents a more accurate figure of merit for quality evaluation as it accounts for false positives.

Mutation Scores vs. Strategies. The collected mut_score values suggest that the overall quality of the test suites is quite acceptable, with values ranging from 0.714 to 1.0 for Java and from 0.8 to 1.0 for GraTra, supporting the hypothesis that such generated tests are able to detect real errors. When it comes to comparing the test suites, our measurements show that **AP** and **TMD** based test sets perform similarly, outperforming the other two strategies, **ERO** and

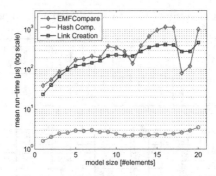

Fig. 4. Mean run time over model size for the 3 oracles

RD, in terms of mut_score values. **AP** and **TMD**, however, lead to much bigger suites (#tests), as explained above, which fits the naïve intuition that more tests probably detect more defects. Closer analysis reveals that the test suites also contain bigger test models (in terms of element count), and some mutations only show themselves in case of bigger models (e.g., altered control variables in the Java case only take effect if loop counts exceed certain limits). Nevertheless, even the two test cases derived from the triple produced by **RD**, or the eight test cases in case of **RO** already achieve acceptable mutation scores. They also require less execution time (**AP**: 15ms, **ERO**: 5ms, **RD**: 1ms, **TMD**: 400ms).

Influence of Oracles. An aspect worth mentioning relates to the differences in false positive counts w.r.t. the transformation directions. In the forward case, no false positives occurred, meaning that all correct output models were recognized as being correct by the oracles. This is not surprising as this direction is a function-like mapping with unique output models. When it comes to the backward direction, EMFCompare still features a relatively high mutation score, but at the cost of misclassifying most of the equivalent mutants (up to *all* seven equivalent mutants for Java). This implies that the oracle misjudges the results because the actual output model cannot be found in the set of pre-calculated outputs. This effect is especially noticeable when using (selective) depth-first search (as in **TMD**), since this greatly reduces the chances of generating equivalent outputs. Consequently, *model-diff seems to be of limited use for non-function-like mappings.* Hash comparison tends to classify more test outputs as being "equal" to expected results than EMFCompare because the underlying algorithm implements a notion of equality that is less sensitive to minor model differences (e.g., differences in the ordering of child elements are ignored). Consequently mutation scores are lower, but the problem of false positives still prevails. Link creation, on the other hand, can obviously cope well with ambiguous results and does not produce any false positives. This finding is backed by the weighted mut_score values which favor link creation over EMFCompare and hash comparison.

Another important aspect relates to run time penalties induced by the oracle options. This issue becomes relevant with increasing model size. Figure 4 shows the mean run time (5% biggest and smallest samples were cropped) of the oracle runs over the size of the output models (measured on a Core2-Duo P8600 2.4GHz with 8.0GB of RAM). Hash comparison obviously outperforms the other options by magnitudes. An increase over model size is not noticeable. EMFCompare reuses the hash function of hash comparison for pre-filtering, which explains the sporadic drops in its run-time (when hashing sorts out several options). Neglecting these, the run time grows considerably with model size and it seems apparent that model diff oracles get impractical for (very) large models and/or large sets of valid outputs. Our measurements also suggest that link creation leads to a verdict faster than EMFCompare; except for cases when hash-based pre-filtering dominates. We infer that there is (probably) no generic oracle that solves all problems at once. Link creation clearly outperforms the other two approaches w.r.t. verdict validity in case of ambiguous transformation results, but needs to be programmed/generated for the specific transformation. On the other hand, it shows better run-time behavior than the diff-based solution for most cases.

Threats to Validity. Although we performed all experiments with utmost care, some underlying parameters potentially threaten the validity of the results:

(i) The case study is obviously limited in size and scope, i.e., only a single transformation is considered, which can be captured with four TGG rules. Although this makes implying general conclusions difficult, our example is chosen to feature complex cases including non-functionality (in the backward direction), attribute constraints, and negative application conditions. With this we are indeed able to demonstrate how to perform quality evaluation in conjunction with TGG-based test case generation. Also, we understand our results as a proof-of-concept rather than a full-blown empirical evaluation. A detailed performance evaluation of different strategies with larger transformation examples is left for future work.

(ii) We could create (*and examine*) only a limited and manageable number of mutants. The statistical accuracy would certainly benefit from larger sample sizes, but generating mutants for Java automatically seems futile considering the high abstraction level of typical model transformations. Finally, our mutant-generator for GraTra-like SUTs is still in its infancy and needs to be improved and extended prior to additional measurements.

6   Related Work

Our work follows an approach first described in [18,17], but incorporates extended TGG-features such as the support for relation-like mappings which, we believe, is important for many real-world transformations. In addition, we provide new contributions as we: (i) present a generic framework including a feature model to clarify design options, (ii) explain how to practically evaluate concrete decisions concerning the framework w.r.t. test suite adequacy, and (iii) present initial evaluation results for several strategies and oracle options.

Comparable approaches to evaluate generated test suites by mutation analysis for model transformation testing exist [23,15] (the latter approach also generates oracles). In these cases, test generation is based on solving derived constraint satisfaction or SMT problems. Compared to the pattern-based approach of [15], TGG rules are constructive in nature, i.e., specifying "negative" rules is not allowed. It is, however, possible to specify global negative constraints in the source and target domains and automatically derive appropriate NACs for a given TGG [2]. Furthermore, a TGG-based approach is generally able to generate (very) large test models *and* expected outputs (or other oracles) without necessarily suffering from intolerable run time – an inherent threat to approaches based on model finders such as Alloy. Finally, choosing between a rule-based or constraint/pattern-based approach is also a matter of style, preference, training, and suitability to a specific problem or application domain.

Other benefits of our approach include: (i) attribute values and constraints are handled in an integrated manner (as in [15]), and (ii) custom strategies offer great control and flexibility w.r.t. model properties, test case size, and number of tests. A drawback of our approach is that we require a TGG specification, which might be hard/impossible to derive for an arbitrary transformation.

In [9] and [28], the respective authors describe approaches to derive instance-generating graph grammars from (restricted) metamodels, whereby the derived grammars generate exactly the same languages as the original metamodels. Another work that also advocates a comparable approach, but does without advanced graph transformation concepts like, e.g., NACs, is [10]. In all cases, the grammar productions can be used for instantiation, and transformation testing is mentioned by all authors explicitly as one prominent use cases. In our approach, the (triple graph) grammar needs to be specified by the transformation developer or test engineer. Other main differences (despite general focus) include that we: (i) derive oracles (and not only input models), (ii) support bidirectionality, and (iii) explicitly consider attributes.

Several model generation tools exist: (a) PRAMANA [23], (b) UML2Alloy [1], (c) UMLtoCSP, EMFtoCSP [6,13], (d) USE [12], or (e) the framework based on PAMOMO and ocl2smt [14,15]. These tools rely on *constraint solving* for finding either (test) models or constraint-violations based on given metamodels and (OCL) constraints. A detailed comparison with our approach is future work.

The idea of evaluating string grammar based testing and related coverage concepts, such as (extended) rule coverage (cf. [25,21]), in terms of mutation adequacy was pursued in [16]. One of the findings was that reduced test suites – being minimal w.r.t. test case count and size – achieved significantly lower mutant scores than non-reduced test suites. Our results point in the same direction but the case study is too small to provide strong evidence in this regard.

7   Conclusion and Future Work

We presented a transformation test framework constructed around an extended TGG-based model and oracle generation approach, which supports NACs, attribute constraints and relation-like mappings. We argued that TGGs are a suitable choice for such a framework as they are declarative and sufficiently high-level so that all required components (test generator, oracle) can be derived from the same specification. Variability in the framework was captured in form of a feature model and several design decisions were given. We also showed how to use the quality evaluation component to compare test generation strategies and oracle options w.r.t. important properties (adequacy, validity, run time).

The results obtained from our small case study suggest that TGG-based testing of model transformations is feasible and that it is possible to achieve high mutation scores. We showed how to tackle several practical issues related to real world transformations. The presented framework can be adapted easily in several ways to, e.g., cope with quality constraints, or with requirements concerning the generated test suites. A central finding of this work is that test generation strategies and oracle functions have a strong influence on test adequacy and verdict validity. Although correspondence link construction (based on the TGG specification) seems to be a suitable oracle, we found it to be slower than, e.g., model differencing approximations, which might suffice in many cases.

As future work, we plan to conduct more experiments and extend the evaluation. We also need to automate the link creation oracle. Another challenge lies in an extension to testing problems involving *incremental model synchronization.*

References

1. Anastasakis, K., Bordbar, B., Georg, G., Ray, I.: On challenges of model transformation from UML to Alloy. SoSyM 9(1), 69–86 (2010)
2. Anjorin, A., Schürr, A., Taentzer, G.: Construction of Integrity Preserving Triple Graph Grammars. In: Ehrig, H., Engels, G., Kreowski, H.-J., Rozenberg, G. (eds.) ICGT 2012. LNCS, vol. 7562, pp. 356–370. Springer, Heidelberg (2012)
3. Anjorin, A., Varró, G., Schürr, A.: Complex Attribute Manipulation in TGGs with Constraint-Based Programming Techniques. In: Proc. Workshop on BX 2012. ECEASST, vol. 49, EASST (2012)
4. Baudry, B., Dinh-Trong, T., Mottu, J.M., Simmonds, D., France, R., Ghosh, S., Fleurey, F., Le Traon, Y.: Model Transformation Testing Challenges. In: Proc. IMDT Workshop 2006, Bilbao, Spain (2006)
5. Benavides, D., Segura, S., Ruiz-Cortés, A.: Automated analysis of feature models 20 years later: A literature review. Information Systems 35(6), 615–636 (2010)
6. Cabot, J., Clarisó, R., Riera, D.: UMLtoCSP: A tool for the formal verification of UML/OCL models using constraint programming. In: Proc. ASE 2007, pp. 547–548. ACM (2007)
7. Czarnecki, K., Helsen, S.: Feature-based survey of model transformation approaches. IBM Syst. J. 45(3), 621–645 (2006)
8. DeMillo, R., Lipton, R., Sayward, F.: Hints on Test Data Selection: Help for the Practicing Programmer. Computer 11(4), 34–41 (1978)
9. Ehrig, K., Küster, J.M., Taentzer, G.: Generating instance models from meta models. SoSyM 8(4), 479–500 (2009)
10. Fürst, L., Mernik, M., Mahnič, V.: Converting metamodels to graph grammars: doing without advanced graph grammar features. SoSyM, 1–21 (2013)
11. Ganov, S., Khurshid, S., Perry, D.E.: Annotations for Alloy: Automated Incremental Analysis Using Domain Specific Solvers. In: Aoki, T., Taguchi, K. (eds.) ICFEM 2012. LNCS, vol. 7635, pp. 414–429. Springer, Heidelberg (2012)

12. Gogolla, M., Bohling, J., Richters, M.: Validating UML and OCL models in USE by automatic snapshot generation. SoSyM 4(4), 386–398 (2005)
13. Gonzalez, C., Buttner, F., Clariso, R., Cabot, J.: EMFtoCSP: A tool for the lightweight verification of EMF models. In: Proc. FormSERA 2012, pp. 44–50 (2012)
14. Guerra, E., Lara, J., Wimmer, M., Kappel, G., Kusel, A., Retschitzegger, W., Schönböck, J., Schwinger, W.: Automated verification of model transformations based on visual contracts. Autom. Softw. Eng. 20(1), 5–46 (2013)
15. Guerra, E., Soeken, M.: Specification-driven model transformation testing. SoSyM, 1–22 (2013)
16. Hennessy, M., Power, J.F.: An analysis of rule coverage as a criterion in generating minimal test suites for grammar-based software. In: Proc. ASE 2005, pp. 104–113. ACM (2005)
17. Hildebrandt, S., Lambers, L., Giese, H.: Complete Specification Coverage in Automatically Generated Conformance Test Cases for TGG Implementations. In: Duddy, K., Kappel, G. (eds.) ICMT 2013. LNCS, vol. 7909, pp. 174–188. Springer, Heidelberg (2013)
18. Hildebrandt, S., Lambers, L., Giese, H., Petrick, D., Richter, I.: Automatic Conformance Testing of Optimized Triple Graph Grammar Implementations. In: Schürr, A., Varró, D., Varró, G. (eds.) AGTIVE 2011. LNCS, vol. 7233, pp. 238–253. Springer, Heidelberg (2012)
19. Hildebrandt, S., Lambers, L., Giese, H., Rieke, J., Greenyer, J., Schäfer, W., Lauder, M., Anjorin, A., Schürr, A.: A Survey of Triple Graph Grammar Tools. In: Proc. Workshop on BX 2013 (2013) accepted for publ. (to appear)
20. Kossatchev, A., Posypkin, M.: Survey of Compiler Testing Methods. Program. and Comp. Softw. 31(1), 10–19 (2005)
21. Lämmel, R.: Grammar Testing. In: Hussmann, H. (ed.) FASE 2001. LNCS, vol. 2029, pp. 201–216. Springer, Heidelberg (2001)
22. Mottu, J.M., Baudry, B., Le Traon, Y.: Model transformation testing: Oracle issue. In: Proc. the ICSTW 2008, pp. 105–112 (2008)
23. Mottu, J.M., Sen, S., Tisi, M., Cabot, J.: Static Analysis of Model Transformations for Effective Test Generation. In: Proc. ISSRE 2012, pp. 291–300 (2012)
24. Mottu, J.-M., Baudry, B., Le Traon, Y.: Mutation Analysis Testing for Model Transformations. In: Rensink, A., Warmer, J. (eds.) ECMDA-FA 2006. LNCS, vol. 4066, pp. 376–390. Springer, Heidelberg (2006)
25. Purdom, P.: A sentence generator for testing parsers. BIT Numerical Mathematics 12(3), 366–375 (1972)
26. Schürr, A.: Specification of Graph Translators with Triple Graph Grammars. In: Mayr, E.W., Schmidt, G., Tinhofer, G. (eds.) Graph-Theoretic Concepts in Computer Science. LNCS, vol. 903, pp. 151–163. Springer, Heidelberg (1995)
27. Stevens, P.: A Landscape of Bidirectional Model Transformations. In: Lämmel, R., Visser, J., Saraiva, J. (eds.) Generative and Transformational Techniques in Software Engineering II. LNCS, vol. 5235, pp. 408–424. Springer, Heidelberg (2008)
28. Taentzer, G.: Instance Generation from Type Graphs with Arbitrary Multiplicities. In: Proc. GT-VMT 2012. ECEASST, vol. 47, EASST (2012)

A Search Based Test Data Generation
Approach for Model Transformations

Atif Aftab Jilani[1], Muhammad Zohaib Iqbal[1,2], and Muhammad Uzair Khan[1]

[1]Software Quality Engineering and Testing Laboratory (QUEST),
National University of Computer & Emerging Sciences, Pakistan
[2]SnT Centre Luxembourg, Luxembourg
{atif.jilani,zohaib.iqbal,uzair.khan}@nu.edu.pk

Abstract. Model transformations are a fundamental part of Model Driven Engineering. Automated testing of model transformation is challenging due to the complexity of generating test models as test data. In the case of model transformations, the test model is an instance of a meta-model. Generating input models manually is a laborious and error prone task. Test cases are typically generated to satisfy a coverage criterion. Test data generation corresponding to various structural testing coverage criteria requires solving a number of predicates. For model transformation, these predicates typically consist of constraints on the source meta-model elements. In this paper, we propose an automated search-based test data generation approach for model transformations. The proposed approach is based on calculating approach level and branch distances to guide the search. For this purpose, we have developed specialized heuristics for calculating branch distances of model transformations. The approach allows test data generation corresponding to various coverage criteria, including statement coverage, branch coverage, and multiple condition/decision coverage. Our approach is generic and can be applied to various model transformation languages. Our developed tool, MOTTER, works with Atlas Transformation Language (ATL) as a proof of concept. We have successfully applied our approach on a well-known case study from ATL Zoo to generate test data.

Keywords: Software Testing, Model Transformation (MT), ATL, Search Based Testing (SBT), Structural Testing.

1   Introduction

Model transformations (MT) are a fundamental part of Model Driven Engineering (MDE). As for any other software, correctness of model transformation is of paramount importance. Automated testing of model transformations faces a number of specific challenges when compared to traditional software testing [1]. The foremost is the complexity of input/output models. The meta-models involved in the transformations typically comprise of a large set of elements. These elements have relationships, sometimes cyclic, that are restricted by the constraints define on the meta-model/model. Generating input models manually is laborious and error prone. On the

D. Di Ruscio and D. Varró (Eds.): ICMT 2014, LNCS 8568, pp. 17–24, 2014.
© Springer International Publishing Switzerland 2014

other hand automated generation of input models requires solving complex constraints on the meta-models.

In this paper, our objective is to enable automated structural testing of model transformations. The idea is to generate test cases that cover various execution paths of the software under test. We present an automated search-based test data generation approach for model transformations. To guide the search, we propose a fitness function specific for model transformation. The fitness function utilizes a so-called approach level and branch distance. The branch distance is calculated based on heuristics defined for various constructs of model transformations.

We selected Alternating Variable Method (AVM) as the search algorithm for this purpose because it has already been successfully applied for software testing [2]. We tailored AVM for our specific problem. To the best of our knowledge, this is the first work to report an automated model transformation structural test data generation approach based on search-based testing. To support the automation of the proposed approach, we also developed a tool called MOTTER (Model Transformation Testing Environment). We apply the test data generation approach on an open source model transformation from the ATL Zoo[1].

The rest of this paper is organized as follows: Section 2 provides the related work and presents the state of the art related to MT testing and its associated challenges. Section 3 discusses the proposed test model generation methodology. Section 4 discusses the tool support, whereas Section 5 discusses the application of the approach on a case study. Finally Section 6 concludes the paper.

2   Related Work

Fleurey *et al.*,[3] discuss category partitioning scheme and introduced the concept of effective meta-model. Wang *et al*, [4] explores verification and validation of source/target meta-models in term of coverage. Sen *et al.*, [5] proposed various model generation strategies including random/unguided and input domain partition based strategies. Vallecillo *et al.*, [6] propose the use of formal specification for test data generation. Gomez *et al.*, [7] use the concept of simulated annealing to generate test models. Cariou *et al.*, [8] proposed a method that use OCL contracts for the verification of model transformations. The work proposed by Guerra *et al.*, [9], generates automated test models, from formal requirement specification and solved pre/post conditions and invariants using OCL. Wang and Kessentini [10] propose black box technique for the testing of meta-model structural information. The technique use search algorithms and provide structural coverage and meta-model coverage.

Kuster *et al.*, [11] reported the challenges associated with White box MT testing. Buttner *et al.*, [12] proposed the use of first order semantics for a declarative subset of ATL. Gonzalez and Cabot [13] discuss dependency graph, examine dependency graph by applying traditional coverage criteria and generate test case as OCL expression for ATL. McQuillan *et al.*, [14] proposed various white box testing criteria for

---

[1] http://www.eclipse.org/m2m/atl

ATL transformations such as, rule coverage, instruction coverage and decision coverage. Mottu *et al.*,[15] proposed a constraint satisfaction problem in Alloy.

The work presented here is significantly different from the above approaches as we adopt a search-based test data generation approach for automated white-box testing of model transformations. We build on the previous work of OCL solver [2, 16, 17] to generate valid meta-model instances and provide search heuristics for various model transformation language constructs.

3   Automated Test Data Generation for MT

This section discusses the automated test data generation approach for structural testing of model transformations.

3.1   Test Case Representation

A test case in our context is a set of input models (i.e., a set of instances of input meta-model) that provide maximum coverage of the model transformation under test. A number of coverage criteria have been developed for structural testing of software programs [18]. To achieve a specified coverage level, the test data needs to solve various predicates in the transformation language. In the case of model transformations, these predicates are typically constraints on the elements of meta-models.

3.2   Problem Representation

In the context of test data generation for model transformations, a problem is equivalent to a transformation language predicate. A language predicate P (problem) is composed of a set of Boolean clauses $\{b_1, b_2 ... b_n\}$ joined by various Boolean operations, such as, *and*, *or* and *not*. Each clause b_i, itself comprises of various variables $\{b_{i1}, b_{i2} ... b_{iz}\}$ used in the clause. To solve a problem (P), the search algorithm first needs to solve all clauses which are (n) in number, and for each clause (b_i), need to generate correct values for the entire variables till (z). To generate test data for transformation predicates, search algorithm needs guidance. We provide heuristics for various clauses of model transformation languages. The heuristics are defined as a branch distance function $d()$, which returns a numerical value representing how close the value was to solving the branch condition. A value zero represents that branch condition is satisfied; otherwise a positive numerical non-zero value is returned that provides an estimate of distance to satisfy the constraint.

3.3   Test Data Generation

The algorithm for search-based test data generation for model transformations is shown in Fig. 1. Following sections discuss the various steps of the strategy.

Generating Instance Models. The first step is to generate a random instance of meta-model. The generated model should be a valid instance of the source meta-model.

Generating a valid instance requires solving the various constraints on the meta-model. The generated instance should also contain links corresponding to the mandatory associations of the meta-model (i.e., having a multiplicity of 1 or above). A number of techniques have been proposed in the literature for generating meta-model instances [19]. A major problem is satisfying the various constraints on the meta-models, typically written in Object Constrain Language (OCL). For generating instances that satisfy the OCL constraints, we extended the approach presented in [2].

Algorithm	*generateTestData(mm, CFG, max)*
Input	*mm*: source meta-model, *CFG*: Control flow graph, *max*; No of maximum iterations
Declare	*C*: Set of conditions={}, n: # of iteration performed T_m. A random test data (instance of a meta-model), b_i: A Condition from C,

1. **begin**
2.   Generate a random instance T_m of *mm* as test data
3.   Traverse T_m on *CFG* and add all branching conditions into *C*.
4.   **for each** $C_i \in C$
5.   Calculate fitness $f(O) = mini=0 \rightarrow C.size(ACi(O) + nor (BCi(O)))$
6.   **if** $f(O) != 0$ AND $n < max$
7.   **then** modify T_m by adding/modifying instances of meta-elements according to search algorithm.
8.   Increment *n*
9.   **end if.**
10.   **end for**
11. **end**

Fig. 1. Algorithm for the proposed test data generation strategy

To generate an instance of source meta-model we first traverse the model transformation under test to identify the set of meta-model elements used in the transformation. This set is referred to as an effective meta-model [3]. The identified set of elements is typically related to other elements not used in the transformations. We keep all elements as part of the effective meta-model that have mandatory relationships. We initially generate instances of all meta-elements used in the transformation predicate and then add links between the instances based on the meta-model.

Fitness Functions for MT Language. Search algorithms are guided by fitness functions that evaluate the quality of a candidate solution. The fitness function, for example, in the case of structural coverage can evaluate how far a particular test case is from solving a predicate. The fitness functions are problem-specific and need to be defined and tuned according to the problem being targeted.

Model transformation languages are similar to programming languages in a way that they are imperative and have control flow and side effects. The model transformation languages are also similar to Object Constraint Language (OCL), because they are written on modeling elements (and their syntax is inspired from OCL). Therefore the fitness function that we developed for testing of model transformations is adapted from the fitness functions of programming languages and OCL [2]. The goal of the search is to minimize the fitness function f, which evaluates how far a particular test case is from solving a predicate. If the predicate is solved, then f(t) = 0.

Since our approach is based on heuristics, the generated solutions of our approach are not necessarily optimal. The heuristics do not guarantee that the optimal solution will be found in a reasonable time. However, various software engineering problems faced by the industry have been successfully solved using search based algorithms.[20]. Our fitness function is a combination of approach level and branch distance and can be represented by the following equation:

$$f(O) = \min_{i=0 \rightarrow TP.size}(A_{TPi}(O) + \text{nor } (B_{TPi}(O)))$$

where O is an instance of input meta-model generated as a candidate test data, TP is a set of target predicates to be solved. $A_{TPi}(O)$ represents the approach level achieved by test data O. The approach level calculates the minimum number of predicates required to be solved to reach the target predicate TPi.

$B_{TPi}(O)$ represents the branch distance of a target predicate *TP*. The branch distance heuristically evaluates how far the input data are, from solving a predicate. The branch distance guides the search to find instances of meta-model that solve the target predicates. For example, to solve a predicate on a class Account: *account→ size () > 10,* the search needs to create eleven Account instances.

We consider a normalized value (nor) for branch distance between the values [0, 1], since branch distance is considered less important than approach level. We apply a widely used normalizing function for this purpose [2]: $\text{nor}(x) = x/x+1$.

To calculate both the approach level and branch distance, we instrumented the transformation language code. Based on the coverage criterion, in some cases, the generated test data not only needs to satisfy the predicates to true, but also needs to satisfy the negation of the predicates (for example, to achieve branch coverage). In all such cases, we simply negate the predicate and for the negated predicate, generate the data that evaluated the negated predicate to true. To calculate the approach level, an important step is to construct a control flow graph (CFG) of the model transformation code. The CFG provides the guidance to the algorithm to achieve the desire coverage.

Branch Distances for MT Constructs. The transformation languages have a number of predefined data types, called primitive types. Typical primitive types include Boolean, Integer, Real, and String. The predicates are defined on attributes of primitive types, collection types or meta-model classes and combine the attributes with various operators resulting in a Boolean output. Branch distance calculations for various important operations of model transformations are adopted from [2].

Applying the Search Algorithm. We selected Alternating Variable Method (AVM) [2] as the search algorithm. For a set of variables $\{v_1, v_2,....v_n\}$, AVM works to maximize the fitness of v_1, by keeping the values of other variable constant, which are generated randomly. It stops, if the solution is found. Otherwise if solution is not found or fitness is lesser than v_1, AVM switch to the second variable v_2. Now all other variables will be kept constant. The search continues until a solution is found or all the variables are explored. If a randomly generated initial model is not able to satisfy the target predicate, a fitness value is generated for the test model. We generate a new model by modifying the previous model. If the fitness of new model is greater than that of previous model, the new model is used for next search iteration.

4   Tool Support

In this section, we present our implementation of model transformation testing environment (MOTTER). Fig. 2 shows the architectural diagram of the MOTTER tool. We have developed MOTTER in java language that enables it to interact with the already existing components of OCL Solver [2]. Currently, MOTTER support ATL only, but it is designed in a way to support several model transformation languages. MOTTER is performing various tasks, it supports ATL compilation, shows compile time error and at same time able to execute a program in way that CFG could be extracted. For a given program in ATL, MOTTER constructs the CFG for the given transformation, its component ATLExecutor executes the transformation for a given source model and calculates the fitness and the branches covered so far.

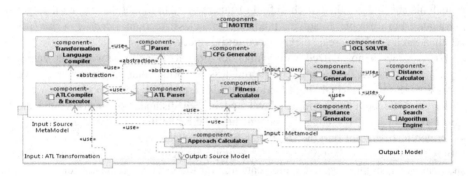

Fig. 2. Architectural diagram of the MOTTER tool

Coverage Analyzer and fitness calculator ensure that coverage criterion, such as branch coverage are achieved. Fitness calculator guides the coverage analyzer regarding the fitness of the instance model and calculates the approach level. The Solver in MOTTER is a refined version of OCL Solver [2]; the original OCL solver is OCL specific and generates data values for OCL queries. For MOTTER, the data values are not simple. The values are classes, instance of meta-model and include the relationships between the classes. Object Generator component generates the object model that serves as a test model to ensure coverage of transformation. Distance Calculator module calculates distances of transformation construct. Search Algorithm Engine component uses AVM to solve the heuristics and test data is generated by the data generator component. The Data Generator component guides the search by generating values that solve the heuristics.

5   Case Study

In this section, we demonstrate how test models are generated by applying our approach on a famous *SimpleClass2SimpleRDBMS* ATL transformation [21]. The case study has six helper methods and one matched rule. The matched rule *Persistent Class2Table* is considered as the main rule. It comprises of nine (9) predicate statements, such as *tuple.type→oclIsKindOf(SimpleClass!Class)*. To exercise various coverage criteria, these predicates have upmost importance. We first generate test data for all branch coverage. All Branch coverage requires exercising of each statement and conditions, and to do so all predicates need to be solved.

We slightly modified some statements in the transformation as some of the code segments of the original transformation could not be executed (part of the dead code). Since, we have nine different branching conditions and for each such condition, our tool has generated data that satisfies the conditions and their negations. Consider a condition, taken from *persistentClass2Table*, *acc→size()=0*. The condition has an approach level value one, because to exercise this we first need to solve the condition, *tuple.type→oclIsKindOf(SimpleClass!Class)*. MOTTER has successfully solved all nine conditions and generates various object models (test models) to satisfy all branch coverage, decision coverage and statement coverage criterion. The case study demonstrates the applicability of the approach on real transformations. The performance and evaluation of the approach is not discussed due to space limitation.

6   Conclusion

We discussed an automated, structural search-based test data generation approach for model transformations testing. Our approach generates test data to satisfy various structural coverage criteria, such as branch coverage. To guide the search, we developed a fitness function that comprises of approach level and branch distance. To calculate branch distance for model transformation constructs, we adopted the existing heuristics for programming languages and Object Constraint Language. We not only generate meta-elements instances of effective meta-model but also handle the mandatory relationships that exist between different meta-elements. Therefore, our instance generation approach is able to generate valid meta-model instances. The output of the approach is a set of instance models of the source meta-model that can be used as test models to attain transformation coverage. The use of search based heuristics for the automated test data (model) generation particularly in the case for model transformation is a major contribution of the work. We applied Alternating Variable Method (AVM) as a search algorithm for test data generation. The applicability of the approach is demonstrated by applying on a widely referred case study from the ATL transformation zoo, the *SimpleClass2SimpleRDBMS* transformation. The case study covers a number of important ATL constructs. The proposed approach successfully generated test models to achieve the desired coverage. We also developed a prototype tool MOTTER to automate the proposed methodology. The tool currently supports transformation written in ATL, but it is extensible to handle other transformation languages.

References

1. Baudry, B., Ghosh, S., Fleurey, F., France, R., Le Traon, Y., Mottu, J.M.: Barriers to systematic model transformation testing. Communications of the ACM 53(6), 139–143 (2010)
2. Ali, S., Iqbal, M., Arcuri, A., Briand, L.: Generating Test Data from OCL Constraints with Search Techniques. IEEE Transactions on Software Engineering 39(10), 26 (2013)

3. Fleurey, F., Baudry, B., Muller, P.A., Traon, Y.L.: Qualifying input test data for model transformations. Software and Systems Modeling 8(2), 185–203 (2009)
4. Wang, J., Kim, S.-K., Carrington, D.: Automatic generation of test models for model transformations. In: 19th Australian Conference on Software Engineering, ASWEC 2008. IEEE (2008)
5. Sen, S., Baudry, B., Mottu, J.-M.: Automatic model generation strategies for model transformation testing. Theory and Practice of Model Transformations, 148–164 (2009)
6. Vallecillo, A., Gogolla, M., Burgueño, L., Wimmer, M., Hamann, L.: Formal specification and testing of model transformations. Formal Methods for Model-Driven Engineering, 399–437 (2012)
7. Gómez, J.J.C., Baudry, B., Sahraoui, H.: Searching the boundaries of a modeling space to test metamodels. In: 2012 IEEE Fifth International Conference on Software Testing, Verification and Validation (ICST). IEEE (2012)
8. Cariou, E., Belloir, N., Barbier, F., Djemam, N.: OCL contracts for the verification of model transformations. In: Proceedings of the Workshop the Pragmatics of OCL and Other Textual Specification Languages at MoDELS (2009)
9. Guerra, E., de Lara, J., Wimmer, M., Kappel, G., Kusel, A., Retschitzegger, W., Schönböck, J., Schwinger, W.: Automated verification of model transformations based on visual contracts. Automated Software Engineering, 1–42 (2012)
10. Wang, W., Kessentini, M., Jiang, W.: Test Cases Generation for Model Transformations from Structural Information. In: 17th European Conference on Software Maintenance and Reengineering, Genova, Italy (2013)
11. Küster, J.M., Abd-El-Razik, M.: Validation of model transformations–first experiences using a white box approach. In: Kühne, T. (ed.) MoDELS 2006. LNCS, vol. 4364, pp. 193–204. Springer, Heidelberg (2007)
12. Büttner, F., Egea, M., Cabot, J.: On verifying ATL transformations using 'off-the-shelf' SMT solvers. In: France, R.B., Kazmeier, J., Breu, R., Atkinson, C. (eds.) MODELS 2012. LNCS, vol. 7590, pp. 432–448. Springer, Heidelberg (2012)
13. González, C.A., Cabot, J.: ATLTest: A White-Box Test Generation Approach for ATL Transformations. In: France, R.B., Kazmeier, J., Breu, R., Atkinson, C. (eds.) MODELS 2012. LNCS, vol. 7590, pp. 449–464. Springer, Heidelberg (2012)
14. McQuillan, J.A., Power, J.F.: White-box coverage criteria for model transformations. In: Model Transformation with ATL, p. 63 (2009)
15. Mottu, J.-M., Sen, S., Tisi, M., Cabot, J.: Static Analysis of Model Transformations for Effective Test Generation. In: ISSRE-23rd IEEE International Symposium on Software Reliability Engineering (2012)
16. Ali, S., Iqbal, M.Z., Arcuri, A., Briand, L.: A Search-based OCL Constraint Solver for Model-based Test Data Generation. In: 2011 IEEE 11th International Conference on Quality Software, pp. 41–50 (2011)
17. Ali, S., Iqbal, M.Z., Arcuri, A.: Improved Heuristics for Solving OCL Constraints using Search Algorithms. In: Proceeding of the Sixteen Annual Conference Companion on Genetic and Evolutionary Computation Conference Companion (GECCO). ACM, Vancouver (2014)
18. Myers, G., Badgett, T., Thomas, T., Sandler, C.: The art of software testing. Wiley (2004)
19. Wu, H., Monahan, R., Power, J.F.: Metamodel Instance Generation: A systematic literature review. arXiv preprint arXiv:1211.6322 (2012)
20. McMinn, P.: Search - based software test data generation: A survey. Software Testing, Verification and Reliability 14(2), 105–156 (2004)
21. Bézivin, J., Schürr, A., Tratt, L.: Model transformations in practice workshop. In: Bruel, J.-M. (ed.) MoDELS 2005. LNCS, vol. 3844, pp. 120–127. Springer, Heidelberg (2006)

Test Data Generation for Model Transformations Combining Partition and Constraint Analysis

Carlos A. González and Jordi Cabot

AtlanMod, École des Mines de Nantes - INRIA, LINA, Nantes, France
{carlos.gonzalez,jordi.cabot}@mines-nantes.fr

Abstract. Model-Driven Engineering (MDE) is a software engineering paradigm where models play a key role. In a MDE-based development process, models are successively transformed into other models and eventually into the final source code by means of a chain of model transformations. Since writing model transformations is an error-prone task, mechanisms to ensure their reliability are greatly needed. One way of achieving this is by means of testing. A challenging aspect when testing model transformations is the generation of adequate input test data. Most existing approaches generate test data following a black-box approach based on some sort of partition analysis that exploits the structural features of the source metamodel of the transformation. However, these analyses pay no attention to the OCL invariants of the metamodel or do it very superficially. In this paper, we propose a mechanism that systematically analyzes OCL constraints in the source metamodel in order to fine-tune this partition analysis and therefore, the generation of input test data. Our mechanism can be used in isolation, or combined with other black-box or white-box test generation approaches.

1 Introduction

Model-Driven Engineering (MDE) is a software engineering paradigm that promotes the utilization of models as primary artifacts in all software engineering activities. When software is developed following a MDE-based approach, models and model transformations are used to (partially) generate the source code for the application to be built.

Writing model transformations is a delicate, cumbersome and error-prone task. In general, MDE-based processes are very sensitive to the introduction of defects. A defect in a model or a model transformation can be easily propagated to the subsequent stages, thus causing the production of faulty software. This is especially true when developing systems of great size and complexity, which usually requires writing large chains of complex model transformations.

In order to alleviate the impact defects can cause, a great deal of effort has been made to find mechanisms and techniques to increase the robustness of MDE-based processes. Thus far, these efforts have been centered on trying to somewhat adapt well-known approaches such as testing or verification to the reality of models and model transformations of MDE (see [1] or [5] for recent

D. Di Ruscio and D. Varró (Eds.): ICMT 2014, LNCS 8568, pp. 25–41, 2014.

surveys). This has resulted in the appearance of a series of testing and verification techniques, specifically designed to target models or model transformations.

In the particular case of testing model transformations, the current picture shares a great deal of similarity with that of traditional testing approaches. Roughly speaking, testing a model transformation consists in first, automatically generating a set of test cases (henceforth test models), second, exercising the model transformation using the generated test models as an input, and finally, checking whether the execution yielded any errors. However, since models are complex structures conforming to a number of constraints defined in a source metamodel, the first and third steps are particularly challenging [4,5].

When addressing test models generation, and along the lines of adapting well-known approaches, expressions such as black-box, white-box or mutation analysis are also of common application. Actually, the black-box paradigm based on the analysis of the model transformation specification is the most exploited one and has given way to a number of techniques (for example [10] or [15]). The objective here is to analyze the model transformation's input metamodel, with the intent of generating a set of test models representative of its instance space, something known as metamodel coverage. The problem though, is that a metamodel's instance space is usually infinite, so what the majority of these methods really do is to use partition analysis to identify non-empty and disjoint regions of the instance space where models share the same features.

The challenge when using partition analysis is building the best partition possible. Since one test model is usually created out of each region identified, partitions should be small enough, so that all the models from the same region are as homogeneous as possible (meaning that the sample model from that region can be used to represent all models from that same region and reduce, this way, the number of test models to use to get a sufficient confidence level on the quality of the transformation). Existing approaches address this by taking advantage of the fact that input metamodels usually come in the form of UML class diagrams complemented with constraints expressed in the OCL (Object Constraint Language). Therefore, partition analysis focuses on elements like association multiplicities, attributes values or OCL constraints to partition the model. However, in this last case, current approaches tend to be very superficial, either focusing only on simple OCL constraints, or deriving just obvious regions that do not require a deep analysis. This limits the representativeness of the generated test models and also the degree of coverage achieved when dealing with non-trivial metamodels.

In this paper, we propose a mechanism for the generation of input test models based on a combination of constraint and partition analysis over the OCL invariants of the model transformation's input metamodel. The method covers a substantial amount of OCL constructs and offers up to three different test model generation modes. Besides, it can be used in isolation, or combined with other black-box or white-box approaches to enhance the testing experience.

The paper is organized as follows: Section 2 outlines our proposal. Section 3 focuses on the analysis of OCL invariants to identify suitable regions of the instance space. Section 4 describes the three test model generation modes. Section 5 is about the implementation of the approach and some scenarios where the tool could be useful. Section 6 reviews the related work and finally, in Section 7, we draw some conclusions and outline the future work.

2   Overview of Our Approach

Category-partition testing [16] consists in partitioning the input domain of the element under test, and then selecting test data from each class in the partition. The rationale here is that, for the purpose of testing, any element of a class is as good as any other when trying to expose errors.

According to this philosophy, our approach is depicted in Fig. 1. The model transformation's input metamodel characterizes a certain domain, and its instance space, possible inputs for the transformation. In the figure, dashed arrows indicate what characterizes certain elements, whereas solid arrows are data flows. When generating test models, the component called "OCL Analyzer" partitions the metamodel's instance space by analyzing its OCL invariants (Sections 3 and 4). As a result, a series of new OCL invariants characterizing the regions of the partition are obtained. This information, along with the input metamodel is then given to the "Test Model Generator" component, for the actual creation of the test models (Section 4).

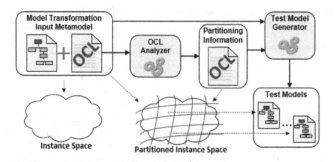

Fig. 1. Overall picture

As mentioned before, the main difference between our approach and other black-box ones based on partition analysis is the way OCL invariants are analyzed. Whereas our approach is capable of analyzing the majority of OCL constructs in a systematic way, approaches like [10] or [15] build partitions by exploiting only simple OCL expressions that explicitly constraint the values a given model element can take. This is because numeric or logical values are an easy target at the time of identifying regions in the instance space. In what follows, we compare this type of analysis with our proposal to show that they are, in many cases, insufficient to derive representative test models.

Fig. 2(a) shows a metamodel describing the relationship between research teams and the papers they submit for publication. A simple partition analysis would try to exploit the presence of a numerical value in the OCL invariant stating that every team must have more than 10 submissions accepted. However, that alone is not enough to generate an interesting partitioning. A more fine-grained analysis of the constraint would reveal that beyond testing the transformation with teams with more than 10 accepted submissions, you should also test the transformation with teams with more than 10 accepted submissions and at least one rejected one. Our method reaches this conclusion by analyzing the "select" condition in the OCL expression (more details on this later on). Fig. 3 shows the difference in the output produced by both analyses. Obviously, the second one exercises more the transformation and therefore may uncover errors not detected when using only the first one.

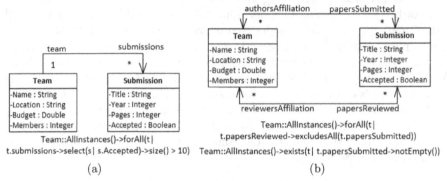

Fig. 2. Metamodels of the examples used throughout the paper

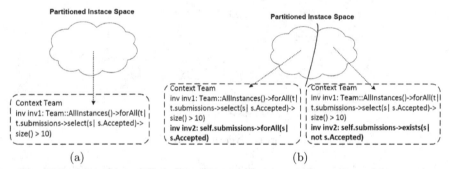

Fig. 3. Results of two different partition analyses over the metamodel example

3   OCL Analysis

In this section, we begin the description of how to identify partitions in the input metamodel's instance space, focusing on the first step: analyzing the OCL invariants in the input metamodel to generate new OCL invariants characterizing suitable regions of the instance space. Next section uses these constraints to create the actual partitions.

Firstly, we talk about the OCL constructs supported by the method. After that, we describe how to systematically analyze complex OCL invariants made up by arbitrary combinations of the supported constructs.

3.1 OCL Constructs Supported

The supported OCL constructs have been classified in five groups and presented here in tabular form. The first group corresponds to expressions involving the presence of boolean operators (Table 1). The second group is about expressions formed by a boolean function operating over the elements of a collection (Table 2). The third group includes those boolean expressions involving the presence of arithmetic operators (Table 3). The fourth group contains other non-boolean expressions, that can be part of more complex boolean expressions (Table 4). Finally, the last group (Table 5) shows equivalent expressions for boolean expressions from Tables 1, 2 and 3 when they are negated.

Tables 1, 2, 3 and 4 share the same structure. For any given row, the second column contains a pattern. Analyzing an OCL invariant implies looking for these patterns, and every time one of them matches, the information in the third column indicates how to derive new OCL expressions characterizing suitable regions in the instance space. A dash (-) indicates that no new OCL expressions are derived. The rationale behind a given pattern and the expressions in the "Regions" column is simple: the pattern represents the invariant that the model must hold, and the information in the "Regions" column are more refined expressions that must also hold when the pattern holds. For example, the entry 1 in Table 1 indicates that the pattern expression holds if the two subexpressions evaluate to the same value. The subexpressions in the "Regions" column indicate that there are two possibilities for this: either both are true, or both are false.

Table 5 is slightly different, though, and that has to do with how the method deals with negated expressions. Each time a negated expression is found, it must be substituted by an equivalent non-negated expression before any new regions can be identified. Second column in the table shows boolean expressions from Tables 1, 2 and 3. The third column contains the equivalents to these expressions when they are negated. In some cases, the substitution process must be applied recursively since, for some expressions, the negated equivalent can also contain negated subexpressions.

3.2 Analyzing OCL expressions

Typically, real-life OCL invariants will be composed by combinations of some of the patterns described above. In the following we give the intuition of how to process some of these combined expressions, in particular, those of type *source* → *operation(argument)*[1]:

---

[1] For the case of more complex expressions, involving boolean (AND, OR, ...) or logical operators ($\leq$, $>$, ...), the process is quite the same. However, this full process cannot be described here due to lack of space.

Table 1. Expressions Involving Boolean Operators

	Pattern	Regions
1	$BExp_1 = BExp_2$	$BExp_1 = FALSE\ AND\ BExp_2 = FALSE$
		$BExp_1 = TRUE\ AND\ BExp_2 = TRUE$
2	$BExp_1\ AND\ BExp_2$	$BExp_1 = TRUE\ AND\ BExp_2 = TRUE$
3	$BExp_1\ OR\ BExp_2$	$BExp_1 = FALSE\ AND\ BExp_2 = TRUE$
		$BExp_1 = TRUE\ AND\ BExp_2 = FALSE$
		$BExp_1 = TRUE\ AND\ BExp_2 = TRUE$
4	$BExp_1\ XOR\ BExp_2$	$BExp_1 = FALSE\ AND\ BExp_2 = TRUE$
		$BExp_1 = TRUE\ AND\ BExp_2 = FALSE$
5	$BExp_1 <> BExp_2$	$BExp_1 = TRUE\ AND\ BExp_2 = FALSE$
		$BExp_1 = FALSE\ AND\ BExp_2 = TRUE$
6	$Class.BAttr = TRUE$	$Class :: AllInstances() \rightarrow forAll(c|\ c.BAttr = TRUE)$
7	$Class.BAttr = FALSE$	$Class :: AllInstances() \rightarrow forAll(c|\ c.BAttr = FALSE)$

Table 2. Expressions Featuring Boolean Functions in the Context of a Collection

	Pattern	Regions
1	$col \rightarrow exists(body)$	$col \rightarrow forAll(body)$
		$col \rightarrow exists(NOT\ body)$
2	$col \rightarrow one(body)$	$col \rightarrow size() = 1$
		$col \rightarrow size() > 1$
3	$col \rightarrow forAll(body)$	$col \rightarrow isEmpty()$
		$col \rightarrow notEmpty()$
4	$col \rightarrow includes(o)$	$col \rightarrow count(o) = 1$
		$col \rightarrow count(o) > 1$
5	$col \rightarrow excludes(o)$	$col \rightarrow isEmpty()$
		$col \rightarrow notEmpty()$
6	$col_1 \rightarrow includesAll(col_2)$	$col_1 \rightarrow size() = col_2 \rightarrow size()$
		$col_1 \rightarrow size() > col_2 \rightarrow size()$
7	$col_1 \rightarrow excludesAll(col_2)$	$col_1 \rightarrow isEmpty()\ AND\ col_2 \rightarrow notEmpty()$
		$col_1 \rightarrow isEmpty()\ AND\ col_2 \rightarrow isEmpty()$
		$col_1 \rightarrow notEmpty()\ AND\ col_2 \rightarrow notEmpty()$
		$col_1 \rightarrow notEmpty()\ AND\ col_2 \rightarrow isEmpty()$
8	$col \rightarrow isEmpty()$	–
9	$col \rightarrow notEmpty()$	–

1. Find a pattern matching the whole invariant. If not found, end here.
2. Generate the new OCL expressions corresponding to the pattern matched.
3. Find a pattern matching the "source" expression.
4. If found, generate the OCL expressions corresponding to the pattern matched.
5. Repeat the process recursively over the subexpressions in the "source" expression, until no more matchings are found.
6. Find a pattern matching the "argument" expression.
7. If found, generate the OCL expressions corresponding to the pattern matched.
8. Repeat the process recursively over the subexpressions in the "argument" expression, until no more matchings are found.

Table 3. Boolean Expressions Involving Arithmetic Operators

	Pattern	Regions
1	$col_1 \rightarrow size() = col_2 \rightarrow size()$	$col_1 \rightarrow isEmpty()\ AND\ col_2 \rightarrow isEmpty()$ $col_1 \rightarrow notEmpty()\ AND\ col_2 \rightarrow notEmpty()$
2	$col_1 \rightarrow size() = NUM$	—
3	$col_1 \rightarrow size() <> col_2 \rightarrow size()$	$col_1 \rightarrow size() > col_2 \rightarrow size()\ AND$ $\quad col_1 \rightarrow notEmpty()\ AND\ col_2 \rightarrow notEmpty()$ $col_1 \rightarrow size() < col_2 \rightarrow size()\ AND$ $\quad col_1 \rightarrow notEmpty()\ AND\ col_2 \rightarrow notEmpty()$ $col_1 \rightarrow isEmpty()\ AND\ col_2 \rightarrow notEmpty()$ $col_1 \rightarrow notEmpty()\ AND\ col_2 \rightarrow isEmpty()$
4	$col \rightarrow size() <> NUM\ AND$ $NUM <> 0$	$col \rightarrow size() > NUM$ $col \rightarrow notEmpty()\ AND\ col \rightarrow size() < NUM$ $col \rightarrow isEmpty()$
5	$col_1 \rightarrow size() >= col_2 \rightarrow size()$	$col_1 \rightarrow isEmpty()\ AND\ col_2 \rightarrow isEmpty()$ $col_1 \rightarrow notEmpty()\ AND\ col_2 \rightarrow isEmpty()$ $col_1 \rightarrow notEmpty()\ AND\ col_2 \rightarrow notEmpty()$
6	$col \rightarrow size() >= NUM$	$col \rightarrow size() > NUM$ $col \rightarrow size() = NUM$
7	$col_1 \rightarrow size() > col_2 \rightarrow size()$	$col_2 \rightarrow isEmpty()$ $col_2 \rightarrow notEmpty()$
8	$col \rightarrow size() > NUM$	—
9	$col_1 \rightarrow size() <= col_2 \rightarrow size()$	$col_1 \rightarrow isEmpty()\ AND\ col_2 \rightarrow isEmpty()$ $col_1 \rightarrow isEmpty()\ AND\ col_2 \rightarrow notEmpty()$ $col_1 \rightarrow notEmpty()\ AND\ col_2 \rightarrow notEmpty()$
10	$col \rightarrow size() <= NUM\ AND$ $NUM <> 0$	$col \rightarrow size() < NUM$ $col \rightarrow size() = NUM$ $col \rightarrow isEmpty()$
11	$col_1 \rightarrow size() < col_2 \rightarrow size()$	$col_1 \rightarrow isEmpty()$ $col_1 \rightarrow notEmpty()$
12	$col \rightarrow size() < NUM$	$col \rightarrow isEmpty()$ $col \rightarrow notEmpty()$
13	$col \rightarrow count(o) > NUM$	$col \rightarrow excluding(o) \rightarrow isEmpty()$ $col \rightarrow excluding(o) \rightarrow notEmpty()$
14	$col \rightarrow count(o) = NUM$	$col \rightarrow excluding(o) \rightarrow isEmpty()$ $col \rightarrow excluding(o) \rightarrow notEmpty()$
15	$col \rightarrow count(o) < NUM$	$col \rightarrow isEmpty()$ $col \rightarrow notEmpty()\ AND$ $\quad col \rightarrow excluding(o) \rightarrow notEmpty()$ $col \rightarrow notEmpty()\ AND$ $\quad col \rightarrow excluding(o) \rightarrow isEmpty()$
16	$Class.NumAttr > NUM$	$Class :: AllInstances() \rightarrow$ $\quad forAll(c|\ c.NumAttr > NUM)$
17	$Class.NumAttr < NUM$	$Class :: AllInstances() \rightarrow$ $\quad forAll(c|\ c.NumAttr < NUM)$
18	$Class.NumAttr = NUM$	$Class :: AllInstances() \rightarrow$ $\quad forAll(c|\ c.NumAttr = NUM)$

Table 4. Other OCL Functions

Pattern	Regions
1 $col \rightarrow select(body)$	$col \rightarrow forAll(body)$
	$col \rightarrow exists(NOT\ body)$
2 $col \rightarrow reject(body)$	$col \rightarrow forAll(NOT\ body)$
	$col \rightarrow exists(body)$
3 $col \rightarrow collect(body)\ AND$	$col \rightarrow forAll(body)$
$body.oclIsTypeOf(boolean)$	$col \rightarrow exists(NOT\ body)$
4 $col_1 \rightarrow union(col_2)$	$col_1 \rightarrow isEmpty()\ AND\ col_2 \rightarrow isEmpty()$
	$col_1 \rightarrow isEmpty()\ AND\ col_2 \rightarrow notEmpty()$
	$col_1 \rightarrow notEmpty()\ AND\ col_2 \rightarrow notEmpty()$
	$col_1 \rightarrow notEmpty()\ AND\ col_2 \rightarrow isEmpty()$
5 $col_1 \rightarrow intersection(col_2)$	$col_1 = col_2$
	$col_1 \rightarrow includesAll(col_2)\ AND$
	$\quad col_1 \rightarrow size() > col_2 \rightarrow size()$
	$col_2 \rightarrow includesAll(col_1)\ AND$
	$\quad col_2 \rightarrow size() > col_1 \rightarrow size()$
	$col_1 <> col_2$
6 $col \rightarrow excluding(o)$	$col \rightarrow isEmpty()$
	$col \rightarrow notEmpty()$
7 $col \rightarrow subsequence(l, u)$	$col \rightarrow size() = u - l$
	$col \rightarrow size() > u - l$
8 $col \rightarrow at(n)$	$col \rightarrow size() = n$
	$col \rightarrow size() > n$
9 $col \rightarrow any(body)$	$col \rightarrow forAll(body)$
	$col \rightarrow exists(NOT\ body)$

9. Once the matching phase finishes, every constraint from each matching group is AND-combined with each one in the rest of the groups. This way, the final list of OCL expressions is obtained. Each of these OCL expressions characterizes a region of the input metamodel's instance space.

As an example, Fig. 2(b) shows another version of the metamodel describing the relationship between research teams and the papers they submit. It includes two OCL invariants. The first one states that the members of a team do not review their own papers, and the second one says that at least one of the teams must have at least one submission.

The analysis starts with the first invariant. It features a "forAll" operation matching entry 3 in Table 2. That entry says that the instance space can be divided in two regions. The region of models with no teams, and the one of models with any number of teams except zero. They can be characterized as:

Team::AllInstances()–>isEmpty()   (A1.1)
Team::AllInstances()–>notEmpty()   (A1.2)

Now, a pattern matching the "argument" of the "forAll" operation is searched. Entry 6 in Table 2 matches. Since the expression is embedded as the argument of a higher level operator, its context must be identified to build the new OCL expressions properly. By doing this, the following OCL constraints are obtained:

Table 5. Boolean Expressions And Their Negated Equivalents

	Pattern	Negated Equivalent
1	$BExp_1 = BExp_2$	$BExp_1 <> BExp_2$
2	$BExp_1\ AND\ BExp_2$	$NOT\ BExp_1\ OR\ NOT\ BExp_2$
3	$BExp_1\ OR\ BExp_2$	$NOT\ BExp_1\ AND\ NOT\ BExp_2$
4	$BExp_1\ XOR\ BExp_2$	$BExp_1 = BExp_2$
5	$col_1 \rightarrow exists(body)$	$col_1 \rightarrow forAll(NOT\ body)$
6	$col_1 \rightarrow one(body)$	$col_1 \rightarrow select(body) \rightarrow size() <> 1$
7	$col_1 \rightarrow forAll(body)$	$col_1 \rightarrow exists(NOT\ body)$
8	$col_1 \rightarrow includes(o)$	$col_1 \rightarrow excludes(o)$
9	$col_1 \rightarrow isEmpty()$	$col_1 \rightarrow notEmpty()$
10	$col_1 \rightarrow size() = col_2 \rightarrow size()$	$col_1 \rightarrow size() <> col_2 \rightarrow size()$
11	$col_1 \rightarrow size() > col_2 \rightarrow size()$	$col_1 \rightarrow size() \leq col_2 \rightarrow size()$
12	$col_1 \rightarrow size() < col_2 \rightarrow size()$	$col_1 \rightarrow size() \geq col_2 \rightarrow size()$
13	$col \rightarrow size() \leq NUM\ AND\ NUM <> 0$	$col \rightarrow size() > NUM$
14	$col \rightarrow size() <> NUM\ AND\ NUM <> 0$	$col \rightarrow size() = NUM$
15	$col \rightarrow size() = NUM$	$(col \rightarrow size() > NUM)\ OR$ $(col \rightarrow size() < NUM)$
16	$col \rightarrow size() > NUM$	$(col \rightarrow size() = NUM)\ OR$ $(col \rightarrow size() < NUM)$
17	$col \rightarrow count(o) > NUM$	$(col \rightarrow count(o) < NUM)\ OR$ $(col \rightarrow count(o) = NUM)$
18	$col \rightarrow count(o) = NUM$	$(col \rightarrow count(o) < NUM)\ OR$ $(col \rightarrow count(o) > NUM)$
19	$col \rightarrow count(o) < NUM$	$(col \rightarrow count(o) = NUM)\ OR$ $(col \rightarrow count(o) > NUM)$
20	$Class.NumAttr > NUM$	$(Class.NumAttr < NUM)\ OR$ $(Class.NumAttr = NUM)$
21	$Class.NumAttr < NUM$	$(Class.NumAttr > NUM)\ OR$ $(Class.NumAttr = NUM)$
22	$Class.NumAttr = NUM$	$(Class.NumAttr < NUM)\ OR$ $(Class.NumAttr > NUM)$

Team::AllInstances()->forAll(t|t.papersReviewed->isEmpty()
   and t.papersSubmitted->NotEmpty())   (A2.1)

Team::AllInstances()->forAll(t|t.papersReviewed->isEmpty()
   and t.papersSubmitted->isEmpty())   (A2.2)

Team::AllInstances()->forAll(t|t.papersReviewed->NotEmpty()
   and t.papersSubmitted->NotEmpty())   (A2.3)

Team::AllInstances()->forAll(t|t.papersReviewed->NotEmpty()
   and t.papersSubmitted->isEmpty())   (A2.4)

With this, the matching phase over the first invariant is over. The rest of elements in the invariant do not match any pattern. Now, the resulting two groups (A1.X and A2.X) must be combined. This produces the following list of expressions:

Team::AllInstances()->isEmpty() and Team::AllInstances()->forAll(t|
    t.papersReviewed->isEmpty() and t.papersSubmitted->NotEmpty())   (A3.1)

Team::AllInstances()->isEmpty() and Team::AllInstances()->forAll(t|
    t.papersReviewed->isEmpty() and t.papersSubmitted->isEmpty())   (A3.2)

Team::AllInstances()->isEmpty() and Team::AllInstances()->forAll(t|
    t.papersReviewed->NotEmpty() and t.papersSubmitted->NotEmpty())   (A3.3)

Team::AllInstances()->isEmpty() and Team::AllInstances()->forAll(t|
    t.papersReviewed->NotEmpty() and t.papersSubmitted->isEmpty())   (A3.4)

Team::AllInstances()->notEmpty() and Team::AllInstances()->forAll(t|
    t.papersReviewed->isEmpty() and t.papersSubmitted->NotEmpty())   (A3.5)

Team::AllInstances()->notEmpty() and Team::AllInstances()->forAll(t|
    t.papersReviewed->isEmpty() and t.papersSubmitted->isEmpty())   (A3.6)

Team::AllInstances()->notEmpty() and Team::AllInstances()->forAll(t|
    t.papersReviewed->NotEmpty() and t.papersSubmitted->NotEmpty())   (A3.7)

Team::AllInstances()->notEmpty() and Team::AllInstances()->forAll(t|
    t.papersReviewed->NotEmpty() and t.papersSubmitted->isEmpty())   (A3.8)

With this, the analysis of the first invariant is finished. The analysis of the second invariant is analogous and yields the constraints in the group B1.X.

Team::AllInstances()->forAll(t|t.papersSubmitted->notEmpty())   (B1.1)

Team::AllInstances()->exists(t|not t.papersSubmitted->notEmpty())   (B1.2)

Putting all together, the analysis of the two invariants in the model of Fig. 2(b) yielded the groups of constraints A3.X and B1.X, respectively. Each constraint in these groups characterizes a region of the instance space. They will be the input for the test model generation phase, described in the next section.

Finally, it is important to mention that the analysis of OCL invariants is not free from inconveniences. From the example, it can be easily seen that some of the generated constraints could be simplified (for example in A.3.1, if there are no "Team" instances, then there is no need to check the subexpression at the right of "and"). More importantly, some of the constraints produced in the combination stage could be inconsistent. These problems can be addressed in two different ways: adding a post-processing stage at this point to "clean" the constraints obtained, or addressing them directly during the test model creation stage (our preferred alternative, as we explain in the next section).

4   Partition Identification and Test Models Generation

This section details the identification of partitions and the generation of test models from the sets of constraints obtained in the previous step. Our approach provides three different alternatives depending on the effort the tester wants to invest to ensure the absence of overlapping test models.

4.1   Simple Mode

As shown before, the analysis of one OCL invariant yields a list of new OCL expressions, each one characterizing a region of the instance space. It cannot

be guaranteed though, that these regions do not overlap (i.e. that they constitute a partition). Looking back at the example, this means that the regions in
A3.X might overlap, and the same goes for the regions in B1.X (we have two
groups here because we had analyzed two invariants). Fig. 4(a) and 4(b) illustrate the best- and worst-case scenarios when three regions are identified from
the analysis of a given invariant. In the worst case, a generated test model to
cover, for example, region 4, could indeed "fall into" this area, or in any of the
adjacent overlapping areas labeled with a question mark (?). In this situation,
when regions overlap, it is likely that generated test models do it as well.

Ensuring that a number of regions do not overlap requires additional effort,
but in "Single Mode", no further effort to identify partitions is made. It simply
runs the test model generator over the regions that were identified in the OCL
analysis, each time passing the input metamodel (and its OCL invariants), and
one of the OCL expressions characterizing these regions. It represents a cheaper
way (compared to the other alternatives) of creating test models without ensuring that they will not overlap. Running "Single Mode" over the example of Fig.
2(b) consists in invoking the model generator for each of the OCL expressions
in A3.X and B1.X.

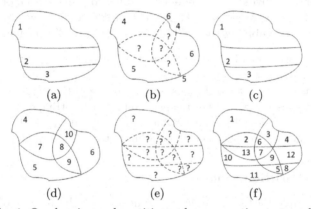

Fig. 4. Overlapping and partitions when generating test models

4.2   Multiple-Partition Mode

Given the set of OCL expressions obtained from the analysis of one OCL invariant, "Multiple-Partition Mode" produces a new set of OCL expressions that
constitute a partition (i.e. do not overlap each other) of the instance space.

In general, if the analysis of one OCL invariant yields "n" regions, a partition
can be derived, with a number of regions somewhere in the interval $[n, 2^n - 1]$.
Although the exact number depends on how the original "n" regions overlap
each other, justifying the lower and upper bounds is rather simple. To show this,
we will focus on the particular case of $n = 3$ and refer to the OCL expressions
characterizing these regions as $B_i, i = 1..3$.

The lower bound corresponds to the best-case scenario (Fig. 4(a)) where the original "n" regions do already constitute a partition. The upper bound corresponds

to the worst-case scenario (Fig. 4(b)) where the "n" regions overlap each other. In this case, it is possible to derive a partition (Fig. 4(d)) with 7 regions, characterized by the following OCL expressions:

- $D_4 = B_4$ AND NOT B_5 AND NOT B_6
- $D_5 = B_5$ AND NOT B_4 AND NOT B_6
- $D_6 = B_6$ AND NOT B_4 AND NOT B_5
- $D_7 = B_4$ AND B_5 AND NOT B_6
- $D_8 = B_4$ AND B_5 AND B_6
- $D_9 = $ NOT B_4 AND B_5 AND B_6
- $D_{10} = B_4$ AND NOT B_5 AND B_6

That is, all the combinations of three elements (the initial number of regions) that can take two different states (to overlap, not to overlap), excepting:

- NOT B_5 AND NOT B_4 AND NOT B_6

which is not representative of any region, since it falls out of the instance space. Generalizing for the case of "n" regions, the upper limit of 2^n - 1 is obtained.

Running "Multiple-Partition Mode" over the example of Fig. 2(b) consists in first, creating all the combinations of the OCL expressions in the groups A3.X and B1.X, and then invoking the model generator to process each of them. The combination of the expressions in A3.X yields a list of 255 new expressions, so only the results of combining the OCL expressions in B1.X are shown.

Team::AllInstances()->forAll(t|t.papersSubmitted->notEmpty()) and
    Team::AllInstances()->exists(t|not t.papersSubmitted->notEmpty())   (B2.1)
not Team::AllInstances()->forAll(t|t.papersSubmitted->notEmpty()) and
    Team::AllInstances()->exists(t|not t.papersSubmitted->notEmpty())   (B2.2)
Team::AllInstances()->forAll(t|t.papersSubmitted->notEmpty()) and not
    Team::AllInstances()->exists(t|not t.papersSubmitted->notEmpty())   (B2.3)

4.3   Unique-Partition Mode

Applying "Multiple-Partition Mode" guarantees that the regions obtained for each OCL invariant do not overlap each other. However, if the input metamodel has more than one invariant, regions in the partition for one invariant might overlap regions in the partitions of the rest of invariants. "Unique-Partition Mode" guarantees that regions do not overlap each other, no matter where they come from. Therefore, in "Unique-Partition Mode" only one partition is characterized, regardless of the number of OCL invariants of the input metamodel. This can be easily seen with an example. If Fig. 4(c) and Fig. 4(d) were the partitions produced by "Multiple-Partition Mode" for two invariants, when putting together, they would overlap as shown in Fig. 4(e). In this scenario "Unique-Partition Mode" would yield the partition of Fig. 4(f).

Applying "Unique-Partition Mode" is a simple three-step process: First, "Multiple-Partition Mode" is applied over each invariant. After that, the lists of OCL expressions characterizing the regions in each partition are merged together to form one big list. Finally "Multiple-Partition Mode" is applied over that list, to generate the final partition. Applying this mode over the example of Fig. 2(b) consists in merging the results of "Multiple-Partition Mode" shown before ($255 + 3 = 258$ OCL expressions) into one big list and run another iteration of "Multiple-Partition Mode" over that list. Clearly, the main problem for the practical utilization of this approach could be the combinatorial explosion in the number of regions conforming the final partition.

4.4   Creating Test Models

After having described how partitions are generated, the last step is the creation of the actual test models. Without regard of the generation mode selected, this is a pretty straightforward process. When fed with the input metamodel (and its OCL invariants) and an OCL invariant characterizing one region of the input space, the "Test Model Generator" component (Fig. 1) tries to build a valid instance of the input metamodel, that also satisfies this additional OCL constraint. The whole set of test models is obtained by repeating this process as many times as regions were found.

In practical terms, we use a separate tool called EMFtoCSP[2] for that. This tool is capable of looking for valid instances of a given metamodel enriched or not with OCL constraints. One of its nicest features is that it transforms the problem of finding a valid instance into a Constraint Satisfaction Problem (CSP). This is especially convenient to address the issues mentioned at the end of Section 3. For example, when presented with an infeasible combination of constraints, EMFtoCSP can dismiss it, yielding no test model.

5   Implementation and Usage Scenarios

We have implemented an Eclipse[3]-based tool that can generate test models following any of the three generation modes exposed before. It can be downloaded from http://code.google.com/a/eclipselabs.org/p/oclbbtesting/ where the user will find all the necessary information for its installation and usage.

When used in isolation, the tool produces models to cover the instance space of the transformation's input metamodel, out of the OCL invariants of that metamodel. Since graphical constraints in a model, like associations, multiplicities, etc can also be expressed in the form of OCL invariants, as detailed in [11], the tool could also be used to derive test models out of these graphical constraints.

There may be occasions though, in which it is convenient to focus only on specific sections of the input metamodel: the model transformation could only "exercise" a part of the input metamodel, or the tester could only be interested on a specific part of the transformation. In the first case, the tool could be combined with approaches capable of identifying what the relevant sections of the input metamodel are, like for example [10]. In the second case, if the preconditions that trigger specific parts of the model transformation are expressed in such a

---

[2] http://code.google.com/a/eclipselabs.org/p/emftocsp/
[3] http://www.eclipse.org

way, that new OCL invariants in the context of the input metamodel can be derived, then these new invariants could be used to limit the generation of test models to those regions of the instance space triggering the sections of the model transformation that are of interest. This could be exploited even further, to allow the generation of test models aimed at satisfying different coverage criteria over the transformation [13].

Finally, the tool could also be useful to complement others that lack the ability to generate test models out of OCL invariants, or do it in a limited way.

6   Related Work

Although not related to model transformation testing, to the best of our knowledge, the first attempt of using partition analysis to derive test models out of UML class diagrams was made by Andrews et al. [3]. In this work, partition analysis is employed to identify representative values of attributes and association ends multiplicities to steer the generation of test models. However, OCL invariants are analyzed only in the context of how they restrict the values an individual attribute can take. This represents only a portion of the analysis of OCL invariants presented in this paper. Andrews et al. served as inspiration for the black-box test model generation approach proposed by Fleurey et al. [10,7] where the partition analysis of [3] is used to identify representative values of the model transformation input metamodel.

The work of Fleurey et al. influenced a number of proposals in this field as well. Lamari [15] proposed a tool for the generation of the effective metamodel out of the specification of a model transformation. Wang et al. [19] proposed a tool for the automatic generation of test cases, by deriving the effective metamodel and representative values out of model transformations rules. Sen et al. [17] presented a tool called "Cartier" for the generation of test cases based on the resolution of a SAT problem by means of Alloy[4]. The SAT problem is built, among other data, out of some model fragments obtained out of a partition analysis of the input metamodel. Since these works are more/less based on the partition analysis technique proposed in [3] the comments made there apply here as well.

Also based on the utilization of constraints solvers are the works of Fiorentini et al. [9] and Guerra [13]. In [9], a logic encoding of metamodels expressed in the MOF[5] language is proposed. The encoding is then exploited by means of a constraint solver, although OCL does not seem to be supported. [13] presents a framework for specification-driven testing, that can be used to generate a complete test suite. It works by transforming invariants and preconditions from the model transformation specification into OCL expressions, that are then fed to a constraint solver.

To finish with black-box approaches, Vallecillo et al. [18] presented a proposal based on the concept of Tract (a generalization of the concept of model transformation contract [4,8]), where test models are generated by means of a language

---

[4] http://alloy.mit.edu/alloy/
[5] http://www.omg.org/spec/MOF/

called ASSL, part of the USE tool[6]. In this approach, the characteristics of the test models to be generated, seem to be explicitly indicated beforehand in the ASSL scripts, whereas in our approach that information is derived automatically from the analysis of the OCL invariants of the input metamodel.

Compared to the number of black-box test model generation proposals, the number of existing white-box approaches is rather small. Fleurey et al. [10] complemented their black-box approach by proposing the utilization of the transformation definition to identify relevant values and the effective metamodel, although not mention of OCL is made. Küster et al. [14] proposed three different test model generation techniques following a white-box approach, although an automatic way of building test models out of OCL constraints is not included. Finally, the approach more similar to our work is [12], where test models are characterized by a series of OCL constraints obtained out of the analysis of the model transformation internals.

Finally, test case generation through partition analysis, has also been object of study in the area of model-based testing. Examples of this are [20,6,2].

7   Conclusions

The generation of test models by means of black-box approaches based on partition analysis has largely ignored the valuable information in the OCL constraints. This limits the test generation process and consequently, the degree of coverage achieved over the input metamodel. In this paper, we have presented a black-box test model generation approach for model transformation testing, based on a deep analysis of the OCL invariants in the input metamodel of the transformation. Our method can be configured to be used at three different levels of exhaustiveness, depending on the user's needs. A tool supporting the process has been implemented, and it can be used in isolation or combined with other test model generation approaches. It can also be useful to generate test models at different degrees of coverage.

In the future, we want to expand our method so that it could be used not only for model transformation testing (where all input models are always assumed to be valid metamodel instances) but also for faulty testing (i.e. to test software implementations that should be able to deal appropriately with wrong models). Additionally, we would also like to improve the way OCL expressions characterizing regions of the instance space are generated, to reduce the number of spurious or infeasible combinations produced.

References

1. Ab Rahim, L., Whittle, J.: A survey of approaches for verifying model transformations. Software and System Modeling (June 2013) (Published online)
2. Ali, S., Iqbal, M.Z.Z., Arcuri, A., Briand, L.C.: Generating test data from OCL constraints with search techniques. IEEE Transactions on Software Engineering 39(10), 1376–1402 (2013)

---

[6] http://sourceforge.net/projects/useocl/

3. Andrews, A.A., France, R.B., Ghosh, S., Craig, G.: Test adequacy criteria for UML design models. Software Testing, Verification and Reliability 13(2), 95–127 (2003)
4. Baudry, B., Dinh-Trong, T., Mottu, J.M., Simmonds, D., France, R., Ghosh, S., Fleurey, F., Traon, Y.L.: Model transformation testing challenges. In: ECMDA Workshop on Integration of Model Driven Development and Model Driven Testing (2006)
5. Baudry, B., Ghosh, S., Fleurey, F., France, R.B., Traon, Y.L., Mottu, J.M.: Barriers to systematic model transformation testing. Comm. of the ACM 53(6), 139–143 (2010)
6. Bernard, E., Bouquet, F., Charbonnier, A., Legeard, B., Peureux, F., Utting, M., Torreborre, E.: Model-based testing from UML models. In: Informatik 2006. LNI, vol. 94, pp. 223–230. GI (2006)
7. Brottier, E., Fleurey, F., Steel, J., Baudry, B., Traon, Y.L.: Metamodel-based test generation for model transformations: An algorithm and a tool. In: 17th Int. Symposium on Software Reliability Engineering, ISSRE 2006, pp. 85–94. IEEE (2006)
8. Cariou, E., Marvie, R., Seinturier, L., Duchien, L.: OCL for the specification of model transformation contracts. In: OCL and Model Driven Engineering Workshop (2004)
9. Fiorentini, C., Momigliano, A., Ornaghi, M., Poernomo, I.: A constructive approach to testing model transformations. In: Tratt, L., Gogolla, M. (eds.) ICMT 2010. LNCS, vol. 6142, pp. 77–92. Springer, Heidelberg (2010)
10. Fleurey, F., Steel, J., Baudry, B.: Validation in model-driven engineering: Testing model transformations. In: 1st Int. Workshop on Model, Design and Validation, pp. 29–40 (2004)
11. Gogolla, M., Richters, M.: Expressing UML class diagrams properties with OCL. In: Clark, A., Warmer, J. (eds.) Object Modeling with the OCL. LNCS, vol. 2263, pp. 85–114. Springer, Heidelberg (2002)
12. González, C.A., Cabot, J.: ATLTest: A white-box test generation approach for atl transformations. In: France, R.B., Kazmeier, J., Breu, R., Atkinson, C. (eds.) MODELS 2012. LNCS, vol. 7590, pp. 449–464. Springer, Heidelberg (2012)
13. Guerra, E.: Specification-driven test generation for model transformations. In: Hu, Z., de Lara, J. (eds.) ICMT 2012. LNCS, vol. 7307, pp. 40–55. Springer, Heidelberg (2012)
14. Küster, J.M., Abd-El-Razik, M.: Validation of model transformations - first experiences using a white box approach. In: Kühne, T. (ed.) MoDELS 2006. LNCS, vol. 4364, pp. 193–204. Springer, Heidelberg (2007)
15. Lamari, M.: Towards an automated test generation for the verification of model transformations. In: ACM Symposium on Applied Computing (SAC), pp. 998–1005. ACM (2007)
16. Ostrand, T.J., Balcer, M.J.: The category-partition method for specifying and generating functional tests. Comm. of the ACM 31(6), 676–686 (1988)
17. Sen, S., Baudry, B., Mottu, J.M.: On combining multi-formalism knowledge to select models for model transformation testing. In: 1st Int. Conf. on Software Testing, Verification and Validation (ICST), pp. 328–337. IEEE (2008)
18. Vallecillo, A., Gogolla, M., Burgueño, L., Wimmer, M., Hamann, L.: Formal specification and testing of model transformations. In: Bernardo, M., Cortellessa, V., Pierantonio, A. (eds.) SFM 2012. LNCS, vol. 7320, pp. 399–437. Springer, Heidelberg (2012)

19. Wang, J., Kim, S.K., Carrington, D.: Automatic generation of test models for model transformations. In: 19th Australian Conf. on Software Engineering (ASWEC), pp. 432–440. IEEE (2008)
20. Weißleder, S., Sokenou, D.: Automatic test case generation from UML models and OCL expressions. In: Software Engineering 2008 - Workshopband, Fachtagung des GI-Fachbereichs Softwaretechnik. LNI, vol. 122, pp. 423–426. GI (2008)

Testing MOFScript Transformations
with HandyMOF

Jokin García, Maider Azanza, Arantza Irastorza, and Oscar Díaz

Onekin Research Group, University of the Basque Country (UPV/EHU)
San Sebastian, Spain
{jokin.garcia,maider.azanza,arantza.irastorza,oscar.diaz}@ehu.es

Abstract. Model transformation development is a complex task. Therefore, having mechanisms for transformation testing and understanding
becomes a matter of utmost importance. Understanding, among others, implies being able to trace back bugs to their causes. In model
transformations, causes can be related with either the input model or
the transformation code. This work describes *HandyMOF*, a tool that
first eases the transition between the effect (i.e. generated code file) and
the causes (i.e. input model and transformations) and then provides the
means to check the transformation coverage obtained by a test suite.
The challenges are twofold. First, the obtainment of input model suites
which yield to a quantifiable transformation coverage. Second, providing fine-grained traces that permit to trace back code not just to the
transformation rule but to the inner 'print' statements. A transformation
that generates *Google Web Toolkit (GWT)* code is used as the running
example.

1   Introduction

Transformations rest at the core of *Model Driven Engineering (MDE)*. As any
other piece of software, transformations need to be designed, programmed and
tested. This last step becomes even more important if we consider that each
transformation can potentially generate multiple applications, to which its errors
would be propagated [15].

Nevertheless, testing model transformation has proved to be a tough challenge
[1]. Compared to program testing, model transformation testing encounters additional challenges which include the complex nature of model transformation
inputs and outputs, or the heterogeneity of model transformation languages
[17]. To face this situation, both black-box techniques [3,5,16] and white-box
techniques [6,8,10] have been proposed. These two approaches are complementary and should be carried out in concert. In black-box techniques the challenge
rests on coming up with an adequate set of input models. On the other hand,
white-box techniques capture the mechanics of the transformation by covering
every individual step that makes it up [1]. We concentrate on the latter, particularly focusing on *Model-to-Text (M2T)* transformations, which have received
little attention. Specifically, *MOFScript* language [1] is used along the paper.

---

[1] http://modelbased.net/mofscript/

D. Di Ruscio and D. Varró (Eds.): ICMT 2014, LNCS 8568, pp. 42–56, 2014.

The drawback of white-box testing approaches is that they are tightly coupled to the transformation language and would need to be adapted or completely redefined for another transformation language [1]. While standards [14] or well established languages [9] exist in *Model-to-Model (M2M)* transformation languages, the situation is more blurred in M2T transformations. This is the reason why, while aiming at the same goals as white-box testing (i.e., covering every step of the transformation), we opted to realize it using a mixed approach. The model test suite is generated using black-box techniques and then both input models and the generated code are traced to the transformation. The purpose is twofold: (1) if a bug is detected in the generated code, it can be traced back to the transformation line that generated it, and (2) the transformation coverage obtained by the model test suite can be calculated based on transformation lines being transited.

Consequently our approach heavily rests on trace models. Broadly, trace models need to capture a ternary relationship between the source model elements, the transformation model elements, and the generated code. We chose MOF-Script as the M2T transformation language as it already supports traceability between source model elements and locations in generated text files [12]. That is, it is possible to trace back the generated code from the source elements. Unfortunately, the third aspect (i.e. the transformation model elements) is captured at a coarse-grained granularity: the transformation rule. This permits coverage analysis to be conducted at the rule level (i.e., have all transformation rules been enacted?) but it fails to provide a deeper look inside rules' code. It would be similar to programming language testing stopping at the function calls without peering within the function body. Transformation rules might in themselves be complex functions where conditional statements and loops abound. Rule-based coverage might then fail to consider the diversity of paths which are hidden in the rule's body.

On these grounds, we complement MOFScript's native trace model with a second model that enables traceability between fine-grained transformation elements (e.g., 'print' and 'println' statements) and locations in generated text files. An algorithm is introduced to aggregate trace models to ascertain which 'print' statements have not yet been visited during testing so that designers can improve their testing model suites to obtain full coverage. These ideas are realized in *HandyMOF*, a debugger for MOFScript transformations. A video of MOFScript at work is available[2]. We start by setting the requirements.

2   Setting the Requirements

A common methodology for code testing generally comprises a number of well known steps: the creation of input test cases (i.e., the test suite), running the software with the test cases, and finally, analyzing the goodness of the results. Next paragraphs describe some of the challenges brought by transformation testing.

---

[2] http://onekin.org/downloads/public/screencasts/handyMOF

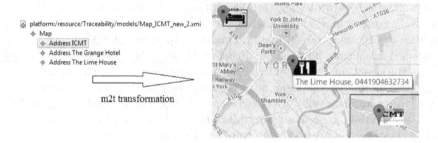

Fig. 1. Input map model and desired output

Creation of Test Suites. Obtaining the appropriate *test suites* becomes critical to ensure that all the transformation variations are covered, and hence, representative code samples are obtained. So far, different proposals have been made for black-box testing of transformations, based on metamodel coverage [4,16]. Specifically, *Pramana* is a tool that implements black-box testing by automatically generating 'model suites' for metamodel coverage [16].

```
1   var index:Integer = 1;
2   ec.Map::main() {
3     [...]
4     f.println("public void onModuleLoad() {");
5     f.println("MapWidget map = new MapWidget();");
6     f.println("map.setSize(\"1000\", \"500\");");
7     f.println("map.setZoomLevel(14);");
8     ec.objectsOfType(ec.Address)->forEach(ecc:ec.Address) {
9       ecc.address();
10    }
11    f.println("RootPanel.get(\"mapContainer\").add(map);");
12    f.println(" }");
13  }
14  ec.Address::address(){
15    f.println("LatLng point"+ index +"= LatLng.newInstance(" + self.latitude + "," + self.longitude + ");");
16    f.println("MarkerOptions markeroptions" + index + " = MarkerOptions.newInstance();");
17    f.print("markeroptions" + index + ".setTitle(\"" + self.name + ", " + self.description);
18    if(self.description = "restaurant"){
19      f.print(", " + self.telephone);
20    }
21    f.println("\");");
22    f.println("Marker marker" + index + " = new Marker(point" + index + ", markeroptions" + index + ");");
23    f.println("LatLng sw" + index + " = LatLng.create("+self.latitude +","+self.longitude+");");
24    f.println("LatLng ne" + index + " = LatLng.create("+ self.latitude +","+self.longitude +");");
25    self.pictures->forEach(pic){
26      f.println("LatLngBounds bounds"+index+" = LatLngBounds.create(sw"+index+", ne"+index+");");
27      f.println("GroundOverlay go"+index+" = new GroundOverlay(\""+ pic +"\", bounds"+index+");");
28      f.println("map.addOverlay(go" + index + ");");
29    }
30    f.println("map.addOverlay(marker" + index + ");");
31  index += 1; }}
```

Fig. 2. Map2GWT transformation

However, black-box testing approaches do not guarantee that the generated samples cover all the branches of the transformation. This calls for tools like *Pramana* to be complemented with white-box testing approaches where the unveiling of the transformation code provides additional input to obtain the test suite.

As an example, consider a model that is transformed to markers in Google maps (see Figure 1). Markers represent *Points of Interest (POI)*. A conference page contains the locations of the venue and the main hotels or restaurants available in the area. Those markers are captured through a *Map* metamodel (Figure 3). Transformation rules are defined to handle the two elements of the *Map* metamodel, namely, *Map* and *Address*. The output is a Google map where markers are depicted together with their pictures, if available. Besides, if the marker stands for a restaurant, the phone is shown as part of the marker's content. This last rule illustrates the need for white-box testing. The significance of 'restaurant' as a key value for changing the transformation flow cannot be ascertained from the string-typed property 'place'. Therefore, the use of metamodel-based test suite generators like *Pramana* does not preclude the need to check that all paths of the transformation have been traversed.

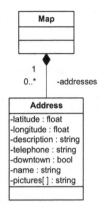

Fig. 3.   Map metamodel

Analyzing the Goodness of the Results. In the testing literature, an oracle is a program, process or body of data that specifies the expected outcome for a set of test cases as applied to a tested object [2]. Oracles can be as simple as a manual inspection or as complex as a separate piece of software. We focus on assisting manual inspection. This requires means for linking code back to generators (i.e., MOFScript rules), and vice versa. MOFScript's native trace model provides such links at the rule level. However, a rule-based granularity might not be enough. The *address* rule (see Figure 2 - lines 14-31) illustrates how transformation complexity is tied to the complexity of the metamodel element to be handled or the logic of the transformation itself. This results in 'print' statements being intertwined along control structures such as iterators and conditionals. A rule-based granularity encloses the whole output within a single trace, failing to indicate the rule's paths being transited. A print-based granularity will account for a finer inspection of the transformation code. This in turn, can redound to the benefit of coverage analysis and code understanding. This sets the requirement for fine-grained traces.

3   The HandyMOF Tool

The previous section identifies two main requirements: semi-automatic construction of test suites, and fine-grained linkage between transformations and generated code. These requirements guide the development of *HandyMOF*, a debugger for MOFScript included as part of Eclipse (see Figure 4). The canvas of *Handy-MOF* is basically divided in two areas:

– *Configuration area,* where the testing scenario is defined. This includes: (1) the project folder, (2) the transformation to be debugged (obtained from the *transformation* folder in the project), and (3), the input model to be tested (obtained from the trace models that link to the chosen transformation).

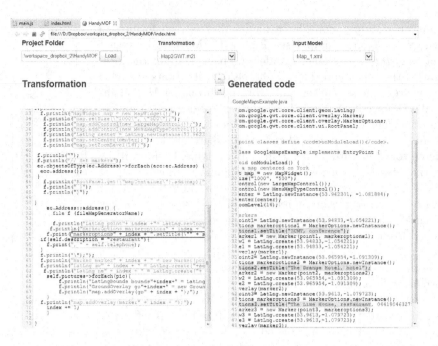

Fig. 4. *HandyMOF* as a debugger assistant: from transformation to code

– *Inspection area.* Previous configuration accounts for a transformation enactment that can output one or more code files. The inspection area permits to peer at both the transformation and the code files. The output reflects a single transformation enactment (the one with the input model at hand). Figure 5 shows the case for the input model *Map_1.xmi*. In this case, only one code file is generated (i.e. *GoogleMapsExample.java*). Additional code files would have been rendered through additional tabs.

The added value of *HandyMOF* basically rests on two utilities. First, it permits to selectively peer at the generated code. To this end, both the transformation and the generated files are turned into hypertexts. Code is fragmented in terms of 'traceable segment' (i.e. set of characters outputted by the enactment of the same 'print', see later). Finally, both MOFScript print statements and 'traceable segments' are turned into hyperlinks. In this way, debugging answers are just a click away. Answers to questions such as 'which code does this print statement generate?' or ' which print statement caused this traceable segment?' are highlighted by just clicking on the respective hyperlink. Figures 4 and 5 illustrate two debugging scenarios:

1. Inspecting the output of a given 'print': which code snippet results from the enactment of this 'print'? Click on the print statement ('Transformation' textarea, line 56) and the answer is highlighted.

Fig. 5. *HandyMOF* as a debugger assistant: from code to transformation

Fig. 6. *HandyMOF* as a testing assistant

2. Tracing back a code snippet to its generator (i.e. 'print' statement), respectively. Which 'print' statement causes this code snippet? Click on the code snippet ('Generated code' textarea, line 44) and the answer is highlighted ('Transformation' textarea, line 58).

The second utility is the role of *HandyMOF* as a coverage analysis assistant. First, by identifying 'holes' in the *Pramana* generated model suite in terms of 'print' statements not yet visited by any input model. Second, by identifying the smaller set of model inputs that provides the larger coverage (see later), hence coming up with a *minimal model suite* which can speed up future testing. The process starts by selecting 'all' as for the input model configuration parameter (see Figure 6). This triggers the algorithm for the obtainment of the minimal model suite. The output is reflected in two ways. First, it renders the model identifiers of such suite. Second, it aggregates the resulting trace models, collects the visited 'print' statements, and in the inspection area highlights those 'print' statements not yet transited. This helps developers to elaborate additional input models to increase transformation coverage. As can be seen in Figure 6, when <all> input models are selected, *HandyMOF* returns the minimal model suite (right) and highlights those 'print' statements not yet covered by any input model sample (left).

4   The HandyMOF Architecture

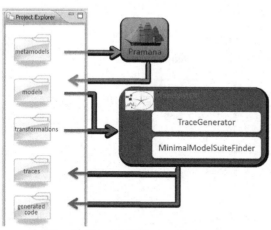

Fig. 7. *HandyMOF*'s Architecture

Figure 7 depicts the main components and flows of *HandyMOF*. The Project Explorer handles the folder structure. *Pramana* provides input models from the corresponding metamodel. Finally, *HandyMOF* consumes input models and transformations to obtain its own trace models, that complement MOFScript's native ones, and the generated code files.

An important question is whether this approach can be generalized to other M2T transformation languages. Basically, *HandyMOF* rests on two main premises. First, the existence of a trace model that links the input model with the generated code. Second, the existence of a transformation metamodel (and the corresponding injector) that permits to move from the transformation text to its corresponding transformation model, and vice versa. Provided these characteristics are supported, *HandyMOF* could be extended to languages other than MOFScript. Next subsections delve into the main components of *HandyMOF*, namely the *Trace Generator* and the *Minimal Model Suite Finder*.

4.1 Trace Generator

The goal of this component is to trace the input model, the generated code and the M2T transformation. It leverages on the trace natively provided by MOFScript that links the input model with the generated code. The metamodel for *Handy-MOF*'s traces is first described, followed by how these traces are generated.

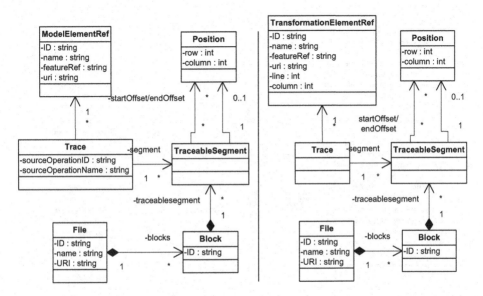

Fig. 8. MOFScript's Traceability Metamodel (left, obtained from [16]) and *Handy-MOF*'s trace metamodel (right)

HandyMOF's Trace Metamodel

MOFScript's trace metamodel defines a set of concepts that enable traceability between source model elements and locations in generated text files (see Figure 8 left) [12]. A trace contains a reference to the operation (transformation rule) that generated the trace and references the originating model element and the target traceable segment. The model element reference contains the 'id' and 'name' for the originating element. It also contains a feature reference, which points out a named feature within the model element (such as 'name' for a property class). On the other hand, the generated code file is captured in terms of 'blocks'. Blocks are identifiable units within a file. A block contains a set of segments which are relatively located within the block in terms of a starting and ending offset.

```
f.println("LatLng point"+ index +"= LatLng.newInstance("
    + self.latitude + "," + self.longitude + ");");
```

⇩

```
LatLng point1= LatLng.newInstance(53.94833,-1.054221);
```

✦ Model Element Ref Address:ICMT:->latitude	_ _ _	✦ Trace ec.Address _ _ _	✦ Traceable Segment
✦ Model Element Ref Address:ICMT:->longitude		✦ Trace ec.Address	✦ Traceable Segment
✦ Model Element Ref Address:The Grange Hotel:->latitude	_ _ _	✦ Trace ec.Address _ _ _	✦ Traceable Segment
✦ Model Element Ref Address:The Grange Hotel:->longitude		✦ Trace ec.Address	✦ Traceable Segment
✦ Model Element Ref Address:The Lime House:->latitude	_ _ _	✦ Trace ec.Address _ _ _	✦ Traceable Segment
✦ Model Element Ref Address:The Lime House:->longitude		✦ Trace ec.Address	✦ Traceable Segment

	Property	Value		
✦ Transformation Model Element Ref ⟍	Column	29	✦ Trace	✦ Traceable Segment
✦ Transformation Model Element Ref	Line	54	✦ Trace	✦ Traceable Segment
✦ Transformation Model Element Ref			✦ Trace	✦ Traceable Segment
✦ Transformation Model Element Ref	_ _ _ _ _		✦ Trace _ _ _ _ _	✦ Traceable Segment
✦ Transformation Model Element Ref			✦ Trace	✦ Traceable Segment
✦ Transformation Model Element Ref			✦ Trace	✦ Traceable Segment
✦ Transformation Model Element Ref	Property	Value	✦ Trace	✦ Traceable Segment
	Column	29		
✦ Transformation Model Element Ref ⟍	Line	54	✦ Trace	✦ Traceable Segment
✦ Transformation Model Element Ref			✦ Trace	✦ Traceable Segment
✦ Transformation Model Element Ref	_ _ _ _ _		✦ Trace _ _ _ _ _	✦ Traceable Segment
✦ Transformation Model Element Ref			✦ Trace	✦ Traceable Segment
✦ Transformation Model Element Ref			✦ Trace	✦ Traceable Segment
✦ Transformation Model Element Ref			✦ Trace	✦ Traceable Segment
	Property	Value		
	Column	29		
✦ Transformation Model Element Ref ⟍	Line	54	✦ Trace	✦ Traceable Segment
✦ Transformation Model Element Ref			✦ Trace	✦ Traceable Segment
✦ Transformation Model Element Ref			✦ Trace	✦ Traceable Segment
✦ Transformation Model Element Ref	_ _ _ _ _		✦ Trace _ _ _ _ _	✦ Traceable Segment
✦ Transformation Model Element Ref			✦ Trace	✦ Traceable Segment
✦ Transformation Model Element Ref			✦ Trace	✦ Traceable Segment
✦ Transformation Model Element Ref			✦ Trace	✦ Traceable Segment

Fig. 9. Complementary trace model: between model and code (above) and between transformation and code (below)

This metamodel nicely captures traces from source model elements to the generated code file through traceable segments. Unfortunately, traceable segments are related to their transformation rule counterparts rather than to the inner 'print' statements. We claim that a finer granularity might help a more accurate debugging in the presence of large transformation rules. On these grounds, we complement the natively provided MOFScript trace model with our own trace model where 'traceable segments' are linked back not just to transformation rules but to the transformation's 'print' statements. Figure 8 right depicts *HandyMOF*'s trace model. Differences stem from the granularity of traceable segments. MOFScript traceable segments account for rule enactments. In *HandyMOF*, these segments are now partitioned into fine-grained segments: one for each enacted 'print' statement. Figure 9 illustrates the two complementary traces for a simple case: between model and code (above) and between transformation and code (below). In this case, as the 'println' is composed of seven parts, seven traces will be given, one for each. As the 'print' is executed three times (one to create a location for a conference, one for an hotel and the other for a restaurant), we can see that those traces are tripled. The position of the 'print' in the transformation to be the same, as captured in *TransformationModelElement*.

Obtaining Trace Models in *HandyMOF*

The process starts by generating the test model suite, in our case this is achieved using *Pramana*. Once the model suite is obtained the next step is to link the M2T transformation with the code that is generated from these models. The first obstacle rests on the generated code being plain text, so that the trace model links the transformation elements with the position where the related code fragment starts (see Figure 8 right). This position can be different depending on the input model and depends on the execution flow. As a case in point, imagine an *if-then-else* statement in the transformation. Each branch may have a different number of 'print' statements. As a consequence, the position where the first statement after the 'if' starts may vary depending on the executed branch. The same holds for loops, depending on the input model they may be executed a different number of times thus changing the position where the rest of the statements start.

So additional information is required for a particular model, e.g. whether a conditional instruction is true or false, or the number of iterations, to know which specific statements have been executed and how many times. This data is collected in a tracing file.

Transformations are also models and can thus be analyzed or be the input of another transformation. Therefore, in this proposal, the original M2T transformation will be used to get internal information of its execution, and save it in the execution trace model. More specifically, taking the original M2T transformation as input, a *Higher Order Transformation (HOT)* transformation will modify it, e.g. inserting counter variables in each iterator and flags to mark conditional instructions. As a result, this leveraged transformation not only outputs the code but also the *execution tracing model*.

That execution tracing model, and the trace between the input model and the generated code, along with the original M2T transformation, are used to get the trace model between the M2T transformation and the code corresponding to each input model. An ATL M2M transformation is in charge of this trace generation, calculating the length of each 'print' from the transformation to set the offset values in the 'Segment' elements; and having into account how many times each 'print' is executed.

4.2   The Minimal Model Suite Finder

In order to analyze the M2T transformation and to see to what extent its statements have participated in the code generation, the use of input models is unavoidable.

The goal is to get the input models that obtain a 100% coverage of the transformation code. However, to the best of our knowledge no tool exists that, given an input domain metamodel and a M2T transformation, generates the models that provide full coverage of the transformation. As a result, we opted for using *Pramana* (formerly known as *Cartier*) [16], a tool that implements black-box testing for metamodels [16].

Are models generated by *Pramana* enough to obtain our goal? *Pramana* serves engineers by generating *model suites* for *metamodel coverage* but its purpose is not *transformation coverage*. However, transformations have embedded semantics that need to be considered if the goal is the latter. Different conditions present in if statements or loops require specific test cases that may not be generated if the criteria is merely metamodel coverage. As a case in point, the if statement in Figure 2 (line 18) checks whether the *Address* corresponds to a restaurant. Among the many test cases that can be generated from the metamodel, this statement requires one with precisely that value in the *description* attribute to obtain *transformation coverage,* which is not guaranteed if the generation of the test cases does not take the transformation into account. Hence, as in program testing where black-box testing and white-box testing approaches are used in concert, we need to cater for both metamodel and transformation coverage.

The proposal of this work is the use of trace models for the analysis of *transformation coverage.* What is needed is to link the code samples with the transformation, via the tracing models obtained by the trace generator module. We need to see how much coverage has been reached using the input models generated by *Pramana.*

Hence, the task of the *MinimalModelSuiteFinder* module (see Figure 7) is to quantify the transformation coverage, and to rule out those input models whose transformation only enacts transformation statements that have already been traversed by previous models. The goal of the module is then to minimize set of input models and obtain the higher coverage percentage of the transformation code (specifically, the 'print' instructions that generate the target code). We name this set the *minimal model suite.* While not optimal, the presented greedy algorithm permits to reduce the test suite size.

```
1 helper def : getModels (availableModels : Sequence(Trace!TraceModel),
2   minimalModelSuite : Sequence(Trace!TraceModel),
3   coveredPrints : Sequence(String)) : Sequence(Trace!TraceModel) =
4   minimalModelSuite->append(availableModels->select(e|self.bestModel(e, availableModels, coveredPrints))->first()),
5   coveredPrints->append(availableModels->select(e|self.bestModel(e, availableModels, coveredPrints))
6     ->first().trace ->collect(e|e.line)->flatten())
7   if coveredPrints.size() = self.numberOfLines or availableModels.size()=0 then
8     minimalModelSuite
9   else
10    self.getModels(availableModels->excluding(availableModels->select(e|self.bestModel(e, availableModels,
11    coveredPrints))->first())
12  endif ;
```

Fig. 10. Minimal model suite algorithm (main rule)

Figure 10 shows one of the functions of the algorithm used in obtaining this suite. It is a recursive function that finishes when all lines are covered or there are not more input models to use (line 7). The algorithm can be summarized as follows:

1. The best model is added to the list of selected models (*minimalModelSuite*) (line 4).
2. The prints covered by the best model are added to the list of covered prints (*coveredPrints*) (lines 5-6).
3. The best model (i.e., the one that covers most prints) is excluded from the available models (*availableModels*) (lines 10-11).

Using these two modules the interface of *HandyMOF* can be used to check the correspondence between the M2T transformation and the generated code, be it on a single instance (see Figure 5) or for the complete model suite to check the obtained coverage (see Figure 6).

5   Related Work

This work sits inbetween testing and traceability for M2T transformations. Testing wise, no standard or well established proposal exists for M2T transformation testing [17]. Wimmer et al. present an extension of *tracts* [7] to deal with model-to-text transformations [18]. Their approach is complementary to ours as it focuses on black-box testing (i.e., it considers the specification of the transformation, not its implementation). Our work highlights the complementariness of black-box and white-box testing techniques. Black-box testing approaches do not capture the mechanics of the transformation [1], which is precisely where we intend to aid. McQuillan et al. propose white-box coverage criteria for transformations [11]. Although their work centers in ATL [9] (i.e., a model-to-model transformation), their coverage criteria could be applicable to our case as well. We focus on instruction coverage (more precisely on coverage of instructions that produce an output in the generated code). Gonzalez et al. present a white-box testing approach for ATL transformations [8]. It follows a traditional white-box testing strategy where input models are created based on the inner structure of the transformation. This involves a coupling between the approach and the transformation language. This might not be problem for M2M transformation languages (where ATL has become *de facto* standard) but rises portability issues for M2T transformations where no predominant language exists. This is why we opt for a mixed approach where input models are generated using black-box testing on the search for transformation-language independence. This approach, albeit less precise, can be applied to any language provided adequate traces can be obtained. This moves us to traceability.

The table in Figure 11 compares main M2T tools and their traceability support. Values are obtained from the literature or grasped from videos or forums. Comparison is set in terms of trace availability for model-to-code, transformation-to-code and transformation-to-model. The underlying mechanisms and the pursued aim is also included. Within the model-to-code and transformation-to-code

	ModelTo Code	TransfTo Code	TransfTo Model	Mechanism	Aim
Acceleo	element to block	rule to code	rule to element	---	transf./code sync. & model/code sync.
Epsilon (EGL)	---	rule to block	---	API	transf. auditing & model/code sync.
Mof2Text	element to block	---	---	---	---
MOFScript	element to block	rule to block	---	Trace mm	model/code sync.
xTend	element to code	---	---	---	---

Fig. 11. Traceability comparison.

options, a *'block'* is nothing more than a piece of code, i.e. an identifiable unit within a file. In these proposals, code blocks to generate and to be traced must be delimited by special keywords in the transformation. When *'code'* is indicated in the table, there is a traceability but no information about the underlying details.

Mof2Text specification (i.e. the OMG standard for MOF M2T Transformation Language) [13] provides support for tracing model elements to text parts. Specifically, a trace block relates text that is produced in a block to a set of model elements. Some text parts may be marked as *protected* in order to be preserved and not overwritten by subsequent M2T transformations. *MOFScript* implements that proposal and handles the traceability between generated text and the original model, aiming to be able to synchronize the text in response to model changes and vice versa. *MOFScript* does not specify any language-specific mechanisms to support traceability, but a metamodel manages the traces from a source model to target generated text files. Central in this trace model is the logical segmentation of a file into blocks; thus, a trace contains a reference to the transformation rule that generated the trace and references to the originating model element and to the target traceable segment.

Another implementation of OMG's M2T specification is the *Acceleo* code generator. Acceleo Pro Traceability [3], a tool complementary to the generator, enables round trip-support: updates in the model or the code are reflected in the connected artefacts. Since this is a commercial tool, restricted information describing the solution is available.

Epsilon[4] is a platform for model management where several task-specific languages are integrated, among them one is *Epsilon Generation Language (EGL)*, which is a template-based code generator, i.e. their proposal for M2T transformations. EGL provides a traceability API that facilitates exploration of the executed templates, affected files and protected regions that are processed during a transformation. Like previous work, this tool does not have support for transformation coverage either.

---

[3] http://www.obeo.fr/pages/obeo-traceability/en

[4] https://www.eclipse.org/epsilon/

As far as we know, the Xtend language does not create traces automatically. And last but not least, JET [5], Velocity [6], and StringTemplate [7] are other M2T languages, that with JSP-like or Java-based templates render source code including java, HTML, XML, SQL, and so on. No information has been found about traceability in these platforms.

6 Conclusions

This work presented a proposal for white-box testing of M2T transformations. Due to the heterogeneity of M2T transformation languages, the test suite is generated using black-box testing and then, the generated code is traced back to the transformation and the input model. Main outcomes include: (1) if a bug is detected in the generated code, it can be traced back to the generating 'print' statement, (2) each generator statement (i.e., 'print') can be traced to the generated code line, and (3) the transformation coverage obtained by the test model suite can be calculated in terms of visited 'prints'. If the obtained coverage is not complete, the developer can create input models that cover the missing transformation lines. This is realized in *HandyMOF*, a tool for debugging MOFScript transformations.

This proposal could be generalized for any transformation language fulfilling our both premises, namely, the existence of a transformation metamodel (and its injector) and a trace model linking the input model with the generated code. The part of the tool that would need to be reimplemented in case of exporting the idea to other languages is the *trace generation* module, that would have to be adapted to language structures of the new transformation language. Both the interface and the coverage analysis are reusable.

Future work includes guiding transformation developers in creating the missing input models from the unvisited 'prints'. We also contemplate integrating *HandyMOF* with other testing approaches to provide an integrated solution.

Acknowledgments. This work is co-supported by the Spanish Ministry of Education, and the European Social Fund under contract TIN2011-23839. Jokin enjoyed a grant from the Basque Government under the "Researchers Training Program". We thank Cristóbal Arellano for his help developing *HandyMOF*, and the reviewers for their comments.

References

1. Baudry, B., Ghosh, S., Fleurey, F., France, R.B., Le Traon, Y., Mottu, J.-M.: Barriers to Systematic Model Transformation Testing. Communications of the ACM 53(6), 139–143 (2010)

---

[5] https://www.eclipse.org/modeling/m2t/?project=jet

[6] http://veloedit.sourceforge.net/

[7] http://sourceforge.net/projects/hastee/

2. Bezier, B.: Software Testing Techniques. Van Nostrand Reinhold, New York (1990)
3. Brottier, E., Fleurey, F., Steel, J., Baudry, B., Le Traon, Y.: Metamodel-based Test Generation for Model Transformations: An Algorithm and a Tool. In: 17th International Symposium on Software Reliability Engineering (ISSRE 2006), Raleigh, USA (2006)
4. Cadavid, J.J., Baudry, B., Sahraoui, H.A.: Searching the Boundaries of a Modeling Space to Test Metamodels. In: 5th International Conference on Software Testing, Verification and Validation (ICST 2012), Montreal, Canada (2012)
5. Fleurey, F., Baudry, B., Muller, P.-A., Le Traon, Y.: Qualifying Input Test Data for Model Transformations. Software and System Modeling (SoSyM) 8(2), 185–203 (2009)
6. Fleurey, F., Steel, J., Baudry, B.: Validation in Model-driven Engineering: Testing Model Transformations. In: 1st International Workshop on Model, Design and Validation (SIVOES-MoDeVa 2004), Rennes, France (2004)
7. Gogolla, M., Vallecillo, A.: Tractable Model Transformation Testing. In: France, R.B., Kuester, J.M., Bordbar, B., Paige, R.F. (eds.) ECMFA 2011. LNCS, vol. 6698, pp. 221–235. Springer, Heidelberg (2011)
8. González, C.A., Cabot, J.: ATLTest: A White-Box Test Generation Approach for ATL Transformations. In: France, R.B., Kazmeier, J., Breu, R., Atkinson, C. (eds.) MODELS 2012. LNCS, vol. 7590, pp. 449–464. Springer, Heidelberg (2012)
9. Jouault, F., Allilaire, F., Bézivin, J., Kurtev, I.: ATL: A Model Transformation Tool. Science of Computer Programming (SCP) 72(1-2), 31–39 (2008)
10. Kuster, J.M., Abd-El-Razik, M.: Validation of Model Transformations - First Experiences using a White Box Approach. In: 3rd International Workshop on Model Development, Validation and Verification (MoDeVa 2006), Genova, Italy (2006)
11. McQuillan, J.A., Power, J.F.: White-Box Coverage Criteria for Model Transformations. In: 1st International Workshop on Model Transformation with ATL (MtATL 2009), Nantes, France (2009)
12. Olsen, G.K., Oldevik, J.: Scenarios of Traceability in Model to Text Transformations. In: Akehurst, D.H., Vogel, R., Paige, R.F. (eds.) ECMDA-FA. LNCS, vol. 4530, pp. 144–156. Springer, Heidelberg (2007)
13. OMG. MOF Model to Text Transformation Language, v1.0. Formal Specification (January 2008), http://www.omg.org/spec/MOFM2T/1.0/PDF
14. OMG. Query/View/Transformation, v1.1. Formal Specification (January 2011), http://www.omg.org/spec/QVT/1.1/PDF/
15. Selim, G.M.K., Cordy, J.R., Dingel, J.: Model Transformation Testing: The State of the Art. In: 1st Workshop on the Analysis of Model Transformations, AMT 2012, Innsbruck, Austria (2012)
16. Sen, S., Baudry, B., Mottu, J.-M.: On Combining Multi-formalism Knowledge to Select Models for Model Transformation Testing. In: 1st International Conference on Software Testing, Verification, and Validation (ICST 2008), Lillehammer, Norway (2008)
17. Tiso, A., Reggio, G., Leotta, M.: Early Experiences on Model Transformation Testing. In: 1st Workshop on the Analysis of Model Transformations, AMT 2012, Innsbruck, Austria (2012)
18. Wimmer, M., Burgueño, L.: Testing M2T/T2M Transformations. In: Moreira, A., Schätz, B., Gray, J., Vallecillo, A., Clarke, P. (eds.) MODELS 2013. LNCS, vol. 8107, pp. 203–219. Springer, Heidelberg (2013)

Towards a Rational Taxonomy for Increasingly Symmetric Model Synchronization

Zinovy Diskin[1,2], Arif Wider[3,4], Hamid Gholizadeh[2], and Krzysztof Czarnecki[1]

[1] University of Waterloo, Canada
{zdiskin,kczarnec}@gsd.uwaterloo.ca
[2] McMaster University, Canada
{diskinz,mohammh}@mcmaster.ca
[3] Humboldt-Universität zu Berlin, Germany
wider@informatik.hu-berlin.de
[4] Beuth Hochschule für Technik Berlin, Germany
awider@beuth-hochschule.de

Abstract. A pipeline of unidirectional model transformations is a well-understood architecture for model driven engineering tasks such as model compilation or view extraction. However, modern applications require a shift towards *networks* of models related in various ways, whose synchronization often needs to be incremental and bidirectional. This new situation demands new features from transformation tools and a solid semantic foundation. We address the latter by presenting a taxonomy of model synchronization types, organized into a 3D-space. Each point in the space refers to its set of synchronization requirements and a corresponding algebraic structure modeling the intended semantics. The space aims to help with identifying and communicating the right tool and theory for the synchronization problem at hand. It also intends to guide future theoretical and tool research.

1 Introduction

Early model-driven engineering (MDE) was based on a simple generic scenario promoted by the *Model Driven Architecture* (MDA) vision [13]: platform-independent models describing a software system at a high-level of abstraction are transformed stepwise to platform-dependent models, from which executable source code is automatically generated. The generated code can be discarded anytime, whereas models are the primary artifacts to be maintained. Software development in the MDA perspective appears as a collection of model-transformation chains or streams "flowing through the MDE-pipe", as shown in Fig. 1.

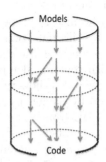

Fig. 1. MDE-pipe in MDA

However, this nice pipeline architecture fails to capture two important aspects of practical MDE. First, it turns out that some changes are easier to make in lower-level models (including code) rather than high-level models. This requirement

D. Di Ruscio and D. Varró (Eds.): ICMT 2014, LNCS 8568, pp. 57–73, 2014.

leads to round-trip engineering in which transformation-streams in the MDE-pipe flow back and forth. Second, models (on the same or different abstraction levels) are typically overlapping rather than disjoint, which in our pipe analogy means that transformation-streams interweave rather than flow smoothly. Round-tripping and overlapping thus change the flow from "laminar" to "turbulent", as illustrated by the inset figure below on the right. Instead of separated and weakly interacting transformation-streams, we have a network of intensively in-teracting models with bidirectional horizontal (the same abstraction level) and vertical (round-tripping) arrows as shown in Fig. 2.

"Turbulency" of modern model transformation brings several theoretical and practical challenges. Semantics of turbulent model transformation is not well understood, whereas clear semantics is crucial for synchronization tools because otherwise users have no trust in automatic syn-chronization. Moreover, tool users and tool developers need a common language to communicate required and provided features because not every synchronization problem requires the same set of features, and implementation of unnecessary features can be costly and increases chances of unwanted interaction. Having a taxonomy of synchronization behaviors, with a clear semantics for each taxo-nomic unit, would help to manage these problems.

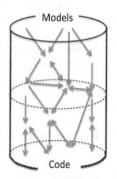

We will analyse the basic unit of a model network – a pair of interrelated models to be kept in sync – and build a taxonomy of relationships between two models from the viewpoint of their synchronization, assuming that concurrent updates are not allowed. It is a strong sim-plifying assumption; however, this setting already covers many cases of practical interest and the presented con-cepts provide a basis for investigating the more complex concurrent change scenarios. We identify three orthogo-nal dimensions in the space of such relationships, and 16 synchronization types —points in the space. The space equips this multitude of types with a clear structure: ev-ery type is characterized by a triple of its coordinates, which together determine its synchronization behavior.

Fig. 2. Modern MDE pipe

We will also show that synchronization types can be or-dered by having more or less symmetry in their behavior. Then the evolution of MDE from its early pipeline setting to its current state can be seen as a trend through the space from asymmetric to symmetric synchronization types. Therefore, we call this trend *symmetrization* (an impatient reader may look at Fig. 5 on p.65 that visualizes the idea). In the journal version of this paper [2], we build an algebraic framework in which all our synchronization types can be formally defined. Algebraic laws related to a synchronization type give rise to re-quirements to synchronization procedures realizing the type. Hence, classifying a concrete synchronization case by its type helps to identify and communicate the right specification and the right tool for the synchronization problem at hand.

The paper is structured as follows. Section 2 introduces two basic features of model synchronization and shows their orthogonality. Section 3 adds a third orthogonal feature and presents the 3D space. Section 4 describes symmetrization and discusses its challenges. Section 5 presents related work. Section 6 concludes the paper. Appendix A provides examples for each synchronization type. Appendix B presents a sketch of the formal semantic foundation for the space.

2   Organizational and Informational Perspectives on Model Synchronization

In this section, we consider two basic features of binary synchronization scenarios: *organizational symmetry* (org-symmetry) and *informational symmetry* (info-symmetry), and then discuss the 2D-plane formed by their combination. Org-symmetry is fundamental for model synchronization but, to our knowledge, has not been discussed in the literature in technical (and formal) terms. It captures the idea of two models being equally authoritative in terms of permitted updates and their propagation. Info-symmetry characterizes "equality" of informational contents of models. This feature, and its phrasing in terms of symmetry, is well known in the literature on algebraic models of bidirectional transformations [3,4,10].

2.1   Organizational Symmetry

Suppose that two models to be synchronized, A and B, are given together with a consistency relation between them. Assume that A_1 and B_1 are two inconsistent states of the models, and one of the models is to be changed to restore consistency (recall that concurrent updates are not considered). There may be different policies for such changes. A simple one is when one of the models (say, A), is considered entirely dominating the other model B, so that consistency restoration always goes via changing B_1 to B_2 consistent with A_1. This situation is common when a low-level model B (e.g., bytecode) is generated from a high-level (more abstract) model A (Java program). Generating Java code (this time model B) from a UML model A is similar, if round-tripping is not assumed. The low-level model B is not supposed to be modified manually. When the high-level model A is changed, the original low-level model is discarded and a new model is regenerated from scratch. In all such cases, we say that model A *organizationally dominates* B, and write $A >_{org} B$. Equivalently, we say that B is dominated by A and write $B <_{org} A$. We will also refer to the case as *org-asymmetry*.

We have an entirely different synchronization type for code generation with round-tripping. Suppose that a UML model A_0, and a Java program B_0 generated from A_0, were initially consistent, but later model A was changed to state A_1 inconsistent with B_0. Then program B_0 must be changed to B_1 that is consistent with A_1. We say that update $A_0 \to A_1$ on the A-side is propagated to the

B-side. Conversely, if model B_0 (code) was changed to B_1 inconsistent with A_0, then model A must be changed to restore consistency, and we say that update $B_0 \to B_1$ was propagated to A. Thus, in contrast to the org-dominance, now change propagation can go in either direction based on the history: the freshly updated model dominates irrespectively to whether this freshly updated model is either A or B. We say that *neither* model *organizationally dominates* the other, write $A \times_{\mathsf{org}} B$, and call this situation *org-symmetry*. Thus, the basic question that characterizes the organizational dimension is the following: *in what direction are updates propagated? Are they propagated only from A to B, only from B to A, or in either direction?*

There are also important synchronization cases in-between strict asymmetry and strict symmetry considered above. A model can be *partially dominated* in the sense that *some* (but not all) updates on this model are allowed to propagate to the other side depending on the type of the update. Consider, for example, the *outline view* of the Java Development Tools (JDT) of the Eclipse IDE. The outline view is regenerated every time the Java code changes. Thus, there seems to be an org-dominance of the Java code over the outline view. However, the JDT allows the user to make some selected operations in the outline view, e.g., renaming elements, or moving elements within the hierarchy. These updates are then propagated to the code. So, whereas all updates from the code (model B) are propagated to the outline abstract view A, only a few operations are allowed, and their results then propagated, from the outline A to the code B. We call this situation *org-semi-symmetry* and write $A \geq\!\!<_{\mathsf{org}} B$. Note the difference between the left and the right halves of the symbol, which refer to, respectively, *weak* (some updates are propagated) and strong (all updates are propagated) dominance of the direction. A similar semi-symmetric variant of code generation from UML models could be also constructed. In contrast to the strict asymmetry version discussed above, some code updates, e.g., changes in method heads, are allowed to be propagated to the model. Therefore we will sometimes refer to org-semi-symmetry as *partial round-tripping*.

Org-symmetry also includes a setting, in which both models are partially dominated, i.e., both update propagation directions are sensitive for the update type. Consider, for example, a system model consisting of a UML class diagram (CD) and a UML sequence diagram (SD) with the following synchronization policy. If a class name is changed in the CD, this change has to be reflected in the SD, but class name changes are not allowed in the SD. Dually, if a method signature is changed in the SD, this change has to be reflected in the CD, but the latter are not allowed to change method signatures. We call such a case *poorly* org-symmetric, and write $A \gtrless_{\mathsf{org}} B$, to distinguish it from *rich* org-symmetry $A \times_{\mathsf{org}} B$ considered above.

Thus, to completely characterize the org-dimension, one has to ask: *Which updates (if any) are propagated in what direction?*

2.2 Informational Symmetry

The notion of *informational symmetry* (info-symmetry) is based on intermodel consistency. The latter can be modeled as a binary relation $K \subset M{\times}N$ over model spaces M and N, in which models A and, resp., B reside (these spaces are determined by the respective metamodels, or grammars for textual models, e.g., code). In general, the consistency relation is of type many-to-many. For example, if M is a space of UML models, and N is a space of Java programs, a given UML model $A{\in}M$ can be correctly implemented by many Java programs $B{\in}N$; differences between these Bs are usually termed as "implementation details". On the other hand, A normally contains some information not relevant for code generation, e.g., layout of boxes and arrows, timestamps, etc. Furthermore, there may be structural differences between two UML models, e.g., in their inheritance hierarchies, which also result in the same code if the generator flattens the inheritance hierarchy. Hence, the same Java program can be a correct implementation of, generally speaking, different UML models. Thus, each of the models (code and UML) has some *private* information not needed for the other model, and they both share some *public* information important for the other model, but represent it differently. We then write $A \times_{inf} B$ and term the case as *info-symmetry*.

We have an essentially different synchronization situation between code and its outline view in a typical IDE, e.g., JDT mentioned above. The outline only shows parts of the information that is presented in the code, or, more generally, an abstract view of the code so that only one outline model A is consistent with a given piece of code B. Of course, the same outline A may be consistent with many versions of B, so that the consistency relation is of the one-to-many type. We then write $A <_{inf} B$ and term the case as *info-asymmetry*.

Note that info-asymmetry appears in the case of code generation, if we consider UML models up to their code-relevant context. That is, we consider two UML models equivalent if their differences do not result in different generated code. Then consistency becomes a one-to-many relationship, and we have $A <_{inf} B$. This view on code generation is a useful model of the situation.

An important characteristic of info-asymmetry is that the computational nature of update propagation essentially depends on the direction. Propagating updates from the source B to the view A is a relatively simple computational procedure. In contrast, propagating updates from the view to the source is very non-trivial because some missing information on the source side is to be restored (see [5,3]). For the info-symmetric case, both update propagation directions need restoration of missing information, and both are non-trivial.

A special case of info-symmetry is when the consistency relation is of the one-to-one type and determines a bijection between two model spaces: now neither of the two models has private data, i.e., both models are just different representations of the same information. An example is synchronization of a wiki article described in a lightweight markup language like MediaWiki with the equivalent HTML description of the article. Each of the two models can be uniquely extracted from the other and update propagation is simple in both directions.

We call the case *poor* info-symmetry and write $A \approx_{inf} B$, to distinguish it from *rich* info-symmetry considered above.

2.3   Organizational and Informational Symmetries Together

Recall two cases of info-asymmetry, $A <_{inf} B$, considered above. The first is when A is the outline abstract view of code B. The second is when A is a UML model whose private data is ignored for synchronization, and B is the code generated from A. Despite the same info-asymmetry relationship between the models, their synchronization situations (we also say synchronization types) are different. Indeed, in the former case, the view is mostly a passive receiver of the source updates, and we have $A <_{org} B$ (or $A \gtrless_{org} B$, if some updates can be propagated from the view to the source). In the latter case, the view is active and generates the source that appears as a passive receiver of the view updates, $A >_{org} B$. What determines the synchronization type of the case is a combination of two parameters indexing the org- and the info-symmetry, resp. As these two parameters are independent, they can be considered as two orthogonal coordinates forming the plane shown in Fig. 3.

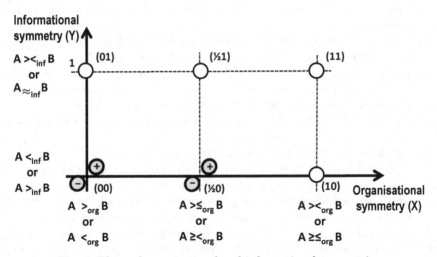

Fig. 3. Plane of organizational and informational symmetries

The vertical axis has two points corresponding to the two possibilities of the info-(a)symmetry: Y=0, which corresponds to info-asymmetry $A <_{inf} B$, and Y=1, which combines two symmetric cases, $A \approx_{inf} B$ and $A \times_{inf} B$. The horizontal axis has three basic points corresponding to the three possibilities of org-(a)symmetry considered in Section 2.1: X=0 ($A <_{org} B$), X=$\frac{1}{2}$ ($A \gtrless_{org} B$), and X=1 ($A \gtrless_{org} B$ and $A \times_{org} B$). The latter again combines poor and rich org-symmetry.

2D-types are formed by combining info- and org-symmetries, and, strictly speaking, type (11) contains four subtypes corresponding to different combinations of poor and rich symmetries. An accurate indexing of such subtypes can be found in [2], but in this paper we use a simpler version of the space, and do not additionally index subtypes inside a type when subtyping is caused by the existence of poor and rich symmetries. However, there is yet another subtyping mechanism caused by the interaction of two asymmetric relations: Each of the types (00) and $(\frac{1}{2}0)$ splits into two subtypes depending on whether two dominant models coincide or not. For example, a non-editable outline view is dominated both organizationally and informationally, whereas with code generated from a UML model without private data, the model dominates organizationally but the code dominates informationally. Both scenarios are examples of type (00). In contrast to subtyping caused by rich and poor symmetries, we want to index these subtypes explicitly. We denote them by $(XY)^-$ (even less symmetry, since the same model is dominated in both relations), or $(XY)^+$ (more symmetry as one model dominates in one relation, while the other model in the other relation). Thus, the plane comprises eight synchronization types, and each synchronization scenario considered above obtains its unique synchronization type (which can be further specialized by distinguishing poor and rich symmetries).

3   Incrementality: From the Plane of Symmetries to a 3D-Space of Synchronization Types

The third dimension for our taxonomy is *incrementality*, a well-recognized feature of model transformations. In Sect. 3.1, we discuss semantic aspects of incrementality and its connections with the informational dimension. In Sect. 3.2, we show how the entire 3D-space of synchronization types is built.

3.1   Incrementality and Delta Propagation

A *non-incremental* unidirectional model transformation $t \colon M \to N$ from a model space M to a model space N creates a new target model $B = t(A)$ from scratch every time the source model A changes, no matter how big the change is. An *incremental* model transformation is supposed to be more intelligent: a small change a in model A is transformed into a respective small change b in model B.

In some synchronization scenarios, incrementality is optional and just improves efficiency. For example, incremental building of the outline view of code in an IDE may improve efficiency when dealing with very large code files. There are, however, situations in which incrementality is crucial and the required synchronization cannot be realized without incrementality. An example is partial code generation. Suppose a UML tool that generates code stubs from class diagrams, but does not support round-tripping: Code for class declarations and method heads is generated, but code in method bodies is to be added at code level. Now, when method signatures are changed in the class diagram, method heads must be regenerated while preserving method bodies, otherwise method implementations would be lost. Thus, while non-private parts of code (method heads, class names, etc.) are updated to reflect changes in the UML model, the private data of the code —the method bodies— must be preserved.

Such a situation is typical when updates are propagated to a side with private data, if the latter is to be preserved. In more detail, an incremental transformation takes an update (delta) on one side, say, $a\colon A_0 \to A_1$, and the original model B_0 on the other side, and produces an update (delta) on the other side, $t(a, B_0) = b\colon B_0 \to B_1$, which restores consistency between A_1 and B_1, and keeps the private part of B_0 unchanged in B_1. Deltas are ideally implemented as *traces* of what happened (or should happen) to individual model elements. If correspondences between models A and B are also precisely traced, an update propagation satisfying the requirements above can be assured [3,4,8]. In case not all necessary traces can be provided (e.g., updates to code are often not tracked individually), updates can be provided as pairs of states (e.g., $a = (A_0, A_1)$) from which individual traces can be inferred (e.g., using heuristics-based model-matching tools). We call so implemented update propagation *state-based*.

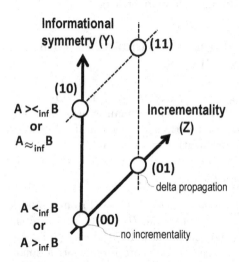

Fig. 4. Plane of incr. synchronization

By considering our examples of code generation, and an IDE's outline view of the code, it is easy to see that non-incremental transformation can be implemented in either direction irrespective to the info-symmetry relation between models. Moreover, correspondences between models can be established and then used for incremental synchronization also irrespective to the info-symmetry relation. Hence, the absence or presence of incrementality can be seen as a new dimension orthogonal to info-symmetry, and together they form a taxonomic plane in Fig. 4.

Importantly, although incrementality can be added to any type of the info-symmetry between two models, the way incrementality is implemented does depend on this type. Indeed, the very semantics of incremental synchronization depends on the info-symmetry relation as the latter determines partitioning of model's data into shared and private, which is crucial for a proper incremental synchronization. The same is true for non-incrementality as well: non-incremental code generation and external view computation are as different semantically as their incremental versions are. Thus, each of the points on the plane in Fig. 4 determines a specific semantic framework for model synchronization. Such frameworks (we will refer to them as *computational*) can be formalized with a family of algebraic structures called *(delta) lenses* [3,4,8,2] (see also Appendix B).

3.2   A 3D-Space of Model Synchronization Types

Clearly, org-symmetry and incrementality are orthogonal: dominance of one or another direction of update propagation, and the way the latter is implemented, can be freely combined. For example, all cases of org-symmetry discussed in Sect. 2.1 can be implemented incrementally or non-incrementally. We have also seen in Sect. 2.3 that org-symmetry is orthogonal to info-symmetry. Hence, the org-symmetry axis X is orthogonal to the plane YZ of computational frameworks in Fig. 4, so that together they form a 3D-space as shown in Fig. 5. Each point in the space, i.e., a triple of coordinates, characterizes a certain synchronization behavior or *synchronization type*.

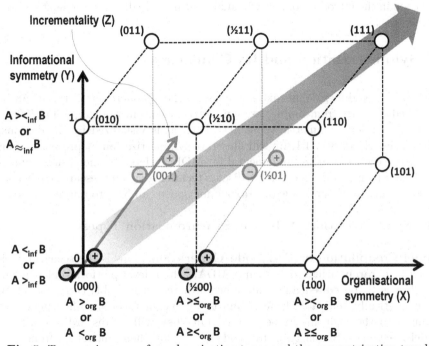

Fig. 5. Taxonomic space of synchronization types and the symmetrization trend

Recall that axis X is for indexing org-symmetry: asymmetry is indexed by 0, symmetry by 1, and semi-symmetry or partial round-tripping has index $\frac{1}{2}$. Axis Y is for info-symmetry: asymmetry and symmetry are indexed by 0 and 1 resp. Axis Z only denotes whether incrementality is present or not (incr.=1 or 0), i.e., whether transformations take previous versions of models into account or execute always from scratch. In the journal version we also index which direction is incremental and distinguish between poor (state-based, no traces) and rich (delta-based) incrementality. Because of the split points on the bottom plane (Sec. 2.3, Fig. 3), the space comprises $10 + 6 = 16$ distinct synchronization types.

Every example we discussed obtains its unique type: e.g., a non-incremental passive outline view is located at type $(000)^-$, and a symmetric multi-model specification of a system, using incrementally synchronized high-level models is at type (111). Correspondingly, a synchronization tool or approach can be selected (or developed) that supports a given synchronization type. For instance, unidirectional ATL (in its standard non-incremental version) supports synchronization type (010); GRoundTram [9] is a tool for (informationally) asymmetric, state-based bidirectional transformations that supports type (101).

The space also allows us to classify several important database concepts. Database views that are not updatable but incrementally computed have the type $(001)^-$. If some of the view updates can be propagated to the source, the type is $(\frac{1}{2}01)^-$. Appendix A provides a table of examples for each synchronization type (without distinguishing between poor and rich symmetries).

The diagonal arrow in Fig. 5 is a visualization of the symmetrization trend discussed in the introduction; we will analyse it in more detail in the next section.

4   Symmetrization and Its Challenges

With the three-dimensional taxonomic space, the *symmetrization* trend can be described as a path from simple, less symmetric synchronization types like $(000)^+$ to more complex, symmetric types like (111), as is visualized by the diagonal arrow in Fig. 5. In Sec. 4.1, we will illustrate symmetrization by presenting four synchronization scenarios fundamental for MDE, ordered by increasing symmetry of their behavior. In Sec. 4.2, we discuss technological and research challenges posed by this trend, and how our taxonomic space can help to approach them.

4.1   Symmetrization: A Tour of Synchronization Types

Model Compilation or Full Code Generation. This is the scenario envisioned (but rarely achieved) by early MDA: a high-level platform-independent model A is to be edited and maintained, whereas executable code, model B, is automatically generated from A and is not meant to be modified manually. Changes to the code might be allowed but they will be discarded whenever model A changes. Similarly, in bytecode generation (here, model B) from Java code (model A), it is possible to do some optimization on the generated bytecode but they will be discarded with every compilation. We have $A >_{\text{org}} B$ (X=0) because updates can only be propagated from A to B, and $A \times_{\text{inf}} B$ (Y=1 with rich info-symmetry) because both A and B have private data (A has layout data etc., and B has implementation-specific details). Incrementality is not assumed (Z=0), and the scenario thus has synchronization type (010). A conceptually useful, and often used model of the scenario is to ignore private data of model A and consider it as an abstract view of code B, which results in informational asymmetry $A <_{\text{inf}} B$ and type $(000)^+$. In fact, this simplification can also be applied to the subsequently presented scenarios, so that there are multiple paths through the space which follow the symmetrization trend. Note that (irrespectively of info-symmetry) lack of incrementality combined with organisational asymmetry results in a lack of autonomy for model B. *Models are the only assets of software development* has been the motto of the early MDA.

Implementation as an Asset or Partial Code Generation. This scenario occurred more often in early MDA in practice and is still common in current MDE. High-level modeling languages are often not expressive enough to allow completely automatic code generation. Then code B generated from high-level model A is supposed to be manually augmented with implementation details, for example, method bodies. There is no round-tripping, but in order to preserve manual modifications of B, incremental model transformation is required. In practice, this incrementality has often been achieved by marking parts of generated code as protected against manual modifications. Wrt. our taxonomy, we have $A >_{\mathrm{org}} B$ (updates are still to be propagated only from A to B) and $A \times_{\mathrm{inf}} B$, which combined with incrementality results in type (011). Note that although B is still dominated organizationally, incrementality gives B some autonomy.

Partial Round-Tripping. This scenario is sometimes achieved by more sophisticated MDE technologies. In comparison with partial code generation, we now allow some changes in code B to be backward propagated to the high-level model A. However, full round-tripping is not supported yet: only some modifications in the generated code are allowed, e.g., method signatures can be modified but class names can not. Thus, we have organizational semi-symmetry $A \gtrless_{\mathrm{org}} B$, informational symmetry $A \times_{\mathrm{inf}} B$, and incrementality, which results in type ($\frac{1}{2}$11). Model B gains even more autonomy but is still organizationally dominated by A.

Full Round-Tripping. All updates can be propagated in both directions. This is the (rarely achieved) goal of UML tools which promise full round-tripping with the generated code. We have $A \times_{\mathrm{org}} B$, $A \times_{\mathrm{inf}} B$, and incrementality, resulting in type (111). Now A does not dominate B in any way, and we have a completely symmetric situation (with both rich org-symmetry and rich info-symmetry). There is still a distinction between A as a high-level model and B as a low-level model, but this distinction is not captured by our taxonomy: both models have equal organizational and informational rights. *Models are the only assets of software development*, but code is a first-class model as well.

4.2   Challenges of Symmetrization: Discussion

Symmetrization of model synchronization demands tools that support bidirectionality, incrementality, informational symmetry, and ultimately concurrent updates. Some of the challenges posed by these requirements are discussed below in terms of our taxonomic space.

Orthogonality in Tool Architectures. Developing synchronization tools that meet all the requirements above is challenging. However, as we explained in the paper, several of these requirements are independent of each other (we will discuss concurrent updates below), and their orthogonality can be effectively used by tool developers. For example, it is commonly agreed that asymmetric lenses implement a solution to the view update problem [5]. With our taxonomic space, this view of lenses can be refined: lenses implement a computational framework (a point on the YZ-plane), which can be augmented with required organizational facilities (along axis X) to provide different synchronization policies — an entirely or partially dominating view, or an entirely dominated view. Moreover, a semi-symmetric situation with both the view and the source being partially dominating (and partially dominated) is also implementable on top of the computational framework provided by asymmetric lenses. Such an extension of an existing approach is more efficient, both conceptually and implementation-wise, than developing separate tools which can only be applied to one synchronization type. In general, tool architectures that reflect feature orthogonality would allow for flexible combination of required features, and facilitate the trade-off between synchronization capabilities and development costs.

Semantics of Bidirectional Transformations. When updates can be propagated in both directions, two procedures of update propagation, from A to B and from B to A, must be consistent and satisfy some invertibility property (see [3,4] for details). When implementing those procedures separately, proving and maintaining invertibility for complex synchronization becomes a major maintenance issue. The goal of bidirectional transformations (BX) is to specify a consistency relation and let the update propagation procedures be inferred from this specification, so that they are always consistent by construction. As usually there are many different possibilities to restore consistency, the implemented behaviour of the inferred procedures must be clear and predictable for the user. The situation with QVT-R shows how unclear semantics of a BX tool hinders its acceptance by the user [14]. When released, QVT-R did not clearly specify the info-symmetry type of scenarios it was intended for. Particularly, it allowed for non-bijective synchronization but did not provide clear semantics for such tasks. We think that many problems could have been avoided if first releases of QVT-R would have targeted the bijective synchronization case, and clearly communicated this to the user. Info-symmetric synchronization could have been added later, with a clear semantics corresponding to this type (e.g., provided by symmetric lenses). An important use of our taxonomic space is that if a synchronization scenario targeted by the tool is identified by its type in the space, the scenario is provided with formal semantics for the benefits of both tool developers and tool users.

Concurrent Updates: Towards the Fourth Dimension. The possibility to update both sides in parallel can be seen as an independent feature of model synchronization. Indeed, concurrency can be added to each of the org-symmetry types on axis X (including the multitude of types hidden in semi-symmetry). Of course, adding concurrency for the strictly org-asymmetric type (when one side is entirely dominated) does not make sense practically as any changes on the suppressed side will be discarded anyway, but we see it as a logically possible (although practically not usable) case. Thus, each of the org-symmetry types is split into two: with concurrency allowed or not allowed, all are supplied with a computational framework. For the non-concurrent cases, computational frameworks we considered above (see also Appendix B) work without any changes, but concurrent updates need an essential development of their computational support. They need special procedures and policies for conflict reconciliation, and subsequent update merging [11]. Formal algebraic models of concurrent updates is an active research area, especially the info-symmetric case is challenging.

Therefore we leave adding the fourth dimension of concurrent updates for future work but kept a reminder about it in Fig. 5: the symmetrization arrow goes beyond the space towards even more symmetric scenarios with concurrent updates.

5   Related Work

Existing works on synchronization – practical and theoretical – usually focus on only one specific type, i.e., one point in our space. For instance, original lenses as presented by Foster et al. [5] formalize info-asymmetric state-based BX. Info-symmetric state-based lenses were proposed in [14]. Delta-based lenses were introduced for informational asymmetry [3] and symmetry [4]. Triple Graph Grammars (TGG) [12,7] provide a more operational approach to BX; for example, delta-lenses can be implemented by TGG [8]. Incrementality in TGG has been also studied [6,8]. The org-symmetry dimension has been discussed in the literature as unidirectional vs. bidirectional transformations [1,12]. We present a more fine-grained taxonomy by introducing organizational semi-symmetry.

There is little related work that describes the combination of several dimensions of model synchronization and provides a formal foundation. Antkiewicz and Czarnecki's [1] is closest to ours in its intention to classify different synchronization scenarios, but deltas are not considered there, and orthogonality of the dimensions is not elaborated. We consider our work as a continuation of [1] and we are not aware of other classification work in-between.

6   Conclusion

Symmetrization of MDE, i.e., the shift from model transformation pipelines to networks of interacting models, poses several challenges for model synchronization tools: support of bidirectionality, incrementality, informational symmetry, and ultimately concurrent updates create a package of non-trivial technological and theoretical issues to resolve. Having a taxonomy of synchronization behaviors, with a clear semantics for each taxonomic unit, can help to manage these problems. In the taxonomic space that we presented, two dimensions are computational and form a plane classifying pairs of mutually inverse update propagation operations realizing BX. The third dimension is orthogonal to the plane and classifies relationships of organizational dominance between the models to be kept in sync. As far as we know, the notion of organizational (a)symmetry and its orthogonality to incrementality and informational symmetry is novel.

The space can be used to locate the type of the synchronization problem at hand. From this type, we can infer the requirements for model synchronization tools, and theories to be applied to the problem. We think of the space as a communication medium for tool users and tool developers, in which they can specify tool capabilities and behavior. We hope that our space can also guide future research about bidirectional transformations by identifying synchronization types that are currently not covered, particularly, organizational semi-symmetry. Of course, concurrent updates are an important dimension, and we plan to integrate it into our framework in a future work.

Acknowledgements. Thanks go to the anonymous reviewers for comments on a preliminary version of the paper. Arif Wider was supported by the German Academic Exchange Service (DAAD) and by the Federal Ministry of Education and Research (BMBF), FHprofUnt grant 17075A10 (MOSES). The Canadian part of the author team was financially supported by Automotive Partnership Canada within the NECSIS project.

References

1. Antkiewicz, M., Czarnecki, K.: Design Space of Heterogeneous Synchronization. In: Lämmel, R., Visser, J., Saraiva, J. (eds.) Generative and Transformational Techniques in Software Engineering II. LNCS, vol. 5235, pp. 3–46. Springer, Heidelberg (2008)
2. Diskin, Z., Gholizadeh, H., Wider, A., Czarnecki, K.: A Three-Dimensional Taxonomy for Bidirectional Transformation and Synchronization. Journal of Systems and Software – Special Issue on Models and Evolution (submitted, 2014)
3. Diskin, Z., Xiong, Y., Czarnecki, K.: From State- to Delta-Based Bidirectional Model Transformations: The Asymmetric Case. Journal of Object Technology 10(6), 1–25 (2011)
4. Diskin, Z., Xiong, Y., Czarnecki, K., Ehrig, H., Hermann, F., Orejas, F.: From State- to Delta-Based Bidirectional Model Transformations: The Symmetric Case. In: Whittle, J., Clark, T., Kühne, T. (eds.) MODELS 2011. LNCS, vol. 6981, pp. 304–318. Springer, Heidelberg (2011)
5. Foster, J.N., Greenwald, M., Moore, J., Pierce, B., Schmitt, A.: Combinators for Bidirectional Tree Transformations: A Linguistic Approach to the View-Update Problem. ACM Trans. Program. Lang. Syst. 29(3) (2007)
6. Giese, H., Wagner, R.: From Model Transformation to Incremental Bidirectional Model Synchronization. Software and Systems Modeling 8, 21–43 (2009)
7. Golas, U., Lambers, L., Ehrig, H., Giese, H.: Toward bridging the gap between formal foundations and current practice for triple graph grammars: Flexible relations between source and target elements. In: Ehrig, H., Engels, G., Kreowski, H.-J., Rozenberg, G. (eds.) ICGT 2012. LNCS, vol. 7562, pp. 141–155. Springer, Heidelberg (2012)
8. Hermann, F., Ehrig, H., Orejas, F., Czarnecki, K., Diskin, Z., Xiong, Y.: Correctness of model synchronization based on triple graph grammars. In: Whittle, J., Clark, T., Kühne, T. (eds.) MODELS 2011. LNCS, vol. 6981, pp. 668–682. Springer, Heidelberg (2011)
9. Hidaka, S., Hu, Z., Inaba, K., Kato, H., Nakano, K.: GRoundTram: An Integrated Framework for Developing Well-behaved Bidirectional Model Transformations. In: ASE 2011, pp. 480–483. IEEE (2011)
10. Hofmann, M., Pierce, B., Wagner, D.: Symmetric Lenses. In: POPL (2011)
11. Orejas, F., Boronat, A., Ehrig, H., Hermann, F., Schölzel, H.: On Propagation-Based Concurrent Model Synchronization. In: Proc. of the 2nd Int'l Workshop on Bidirectional Transformations (BX 2013). EC-EASST, vol. 57, EASST (2013)
12. Schürr, A., Klar, F.: 15 Years of Triple Graph Grammars. In: ICGT, pp. 411–425 (2008)
13. Soley, R., et al.: Model Driven Architecture. OMG White Paper (2000)
14. Stevens, P.: Bidirectional model transformations in QVT: Semantic Issues and Open Questions. Software and System Modeling 9(1), 7–20 (2010)

A   Synchronization Types And Example Scenarios

$(000)^-$	Typical non-editable outline view of an IDE
$(000)^+$	Simplified code generation, i.e., ignoring private data
$(\frac{1}{5}00)^-$	Partially editable view w/o incr.; impractical b/c source info is not preserved
$(\frac{1}{5}00)^+$	Simplified code generation with partial non-incremental round-tripping
(100)	Simplified code generation with full round-tripping but w/o incr.; impractical
(010)	Non-simplified code generation, i.e., the model hass private data, too
$(\frac{1}{2}10)$	Bijective synchronization, e.g., WikiMedia/HTML, w/ partial round-tripping
(110)	Bijective synchronization, e.g., WikiMedia/HTML, with full round-tripping
$(001)^-$	Incrementally updated, non-editable outline view
$(001)^+$	Simplified partial code generation
$(\frac{1}{5}01)^-$	Partially editable outline view (like the one of Eclipse JDT)
$(\frac{1}{5}01)^+$	Simplified partial code generation with partial round-tripping
(101)	Simplified partial code generation with full round-tripping
(011)	Partial code generation
$(\frac{1}{2}11)$	Partial code generation with partial round-tripping
(111)	Full model round-tripping

B   A Sketch of Formal Semantics

The semantics is algebraic and based on operations over models, updates, and intermodel correspondence mappings—all considered as abstract nodes and arrows. We define a family of algebraic structures given by their carrier sets and operations over them, which must satisfy a set of equational laws. The presentation below is a dry sequence of briefed definitions (with omitted laws) due to space limitations. Details, explanations, and discussions can be found in [2].

Formalizing Info-symmetry: Consistency frameworks. A *model space* is a directed graph $M = (M_\bullet, M_\Delta)$ with a set $M_\bullet$ of nodes called *models*, and a set M_Δ of arrows called *deltas* or *updates*. Deltas can be sequentially composed, and each model A is assigned with an identity-loop delta id_A denoting the idle update on A. Taken together, these data mean that M is a *category*.

Let (M, N) be a pair of model spaces. An *consistency framework* $K \colon M \leftrightsquigarrow N$ from M to N is given by the following components. **(i)** Any pair of model $A \in M$ and $B \in N$ is assigned with a set $R(A, B)$ of *correspondence mappings* or just *corrs*, together with a subset $K \subset R$ of *consistent* corrs. We do not exclude the cases when $K(A, B)$ has more than one corr, or is empty. We write $r \colon A \leftrightarrow B$ for a corr $r \in R(A, B)$. **(ii)** *(Re)alignment* operations are defined: given a corr $r \colon A \leftrightarrow B$ and updates $a \colon A \to A'$, $b \colon B \to B'$, two new corrs, $(a * r) \colon A' \to B$ and $(r * b) \colon A \leftrightarrow B'$, are uniquely defined. **(iii)** For any two models $A, A' \in M_\bullet$, there is a set (perhaps, empty) of updates $a \colon A \to A'$ called *private*, composition of two private updates is private, and idle updates are private. Similarly for the N side. Non-private updates are called *public*. It is required that private updates do not affect consistency: for any corr $r \colon A \leftrightarrow B$ and any private updates $a \colon A \to A'$, $b \colon B \to B'$, we have $a * r \in K$ iff $r \in K$ iff $r * b \in K$.

We say that a consistency framework $K\colon M \leftrightarrow N$ determines (informationally) *poor symmetry, asymmetry,* or *rich symmetry* relation between spaces if, resp., neither, only one, or both sides have private updates. Similar relations between two models are actually the respective relations between the spaces where the models live. The consistency framework may be implicit, but it is always assumed to be given.

Formalizing Incrementality: Delta Lenses. A *(delta) lens* over a consistency framework $K\colon M \leftrightarrow N$ is a pair of operations over corrs and updates, fPpg and bPpg, called *forward* and *backward update propagation*. The arities of the operations are specified in the inset figure below right with output arrows dashed, and output nodes non-framed. We denote a delta lens by a double arrow $\lambda\colon M \leftrightarrows N$ to recall two operations. A lens λ is called *well-behaved (wb)* if it satisfies several laws described in [2]. In particular, if $r \in K(A, B)$ (see the inset figure), then $r' \in K(A', B')$; if, in addition, a is private, then $B' = B$ and b is identity. Dual laws hold for bPpg.

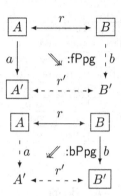

Info-symmetry of the underlying framework K influences update propagation. It can be proved that if K is info-asymmetric, then a lens defined above gives rise to an asymmetric delta lens defined in [3]. In this way, delta lenses provide computational frameworks for types (01) and (11) in Fig. 4.

Non-incremental propagation can be defined as a special case of the incremental one, if model spaces contain *minimal* models; see [2] for details. Thus, a delta lens relating two spaces can provide non-incremental update propagation as well (types (00) and (10) in Fig. 4).

Organizational dimension: Models as Trajectories. Organizational symmetry is about the dominance of change propagation, and we will consider a changing model as a *trajectory* in the respective space. Let $M = (M_\bullet, M_\Delta)$ be a model space. We define a model to be a mapping $A\colon I \to M_\bullet$, whose domain I is a linearly ordered set of *version numbers* or *indexes*. That is, A appears as model's immutable identity, whereas its state $A_i = A(i)$ changes as index i runs over I. Moreover, if we convert the index set I into a graph whose arrows are pairs $(i_1 i_2)$ with $i_1 \le i_2$, then A can be seen as a graph mapping that send an arrow $(i_1 i_2)$ to update delta $A_{12}\colon A_1 \to A_2$, where $A_1 = A(i_1)$ and $A_2 = A(i_2)$.

Synchronization of two models is about maintaining certain correspondences between two trajectories, say, $A\colon I \to M$ and $B\colon J \to N$, in two model spaces related by a lens $\lambda\colon M \leftrightarrows N$. Given these data, a *(consistent) synchronization case* is a pair of trajectories, $A\colon I \to M$ and $B\colon J \to N$ with the following additional structure. Sets I^{pub} and J^{pub} are partitioned, $I^{\mathrm{pub}} = I^{\mathrm{act}} \uplus I^{\mathrm{pas}}$ and $J^{\mathrm{pub}} = J^{\mathrm{act}} \uplus J^{\mathrm{pas}}$, with the following intuitive meaning of components. If $i \in I^{\mathrm{act}}$, model A_i is to be thought of as independently built on the M-side and propagated to the N-side. To simplify presentation, assume that propagation is non-incremental. Then there must be an index $i\triangleright\in J$ such that $B_{i\triangleright} = \mathsf{fPpg}(A_i)$. If $i\in I^{\mathrm{pas}}$, then model A_i is to be thought of as propagated from the N-side, so that $A_i = \mathsf{bPpg}(B_{i\triangleright})$ for some $i\triangleright\in J$. We require that mappings $i \to i\triangleright$ establish isomorphisms $I^{\mathrm{act}} \cong J^{\mathrm{pas}}$ and $I^{\mathrm{pas}} \cong J^{\mathrm{act}}$. Interpretation of B_j with $j\in J^{\mathrm{act}}$ and $j\in J^{\mathrm{pas}}$ is similar, and we require that mapping $\triangleleft j \leftarrow j$ be the inverse of $i \to i\triangleright$. A synchronization case is denoted by $\sigma\colon A \rightleftarrows B$; and the class of all synchronization cases over a given lens λ is $\boldsymbol{SC}[\lambda]$.

The notion of a synchronization case accurately formalizes a general intuition of two synchronized trajectories, but does not impose any *specific* conditions on this synchronization. However, if special *organizational* relations between the models are assumed, some synchronization cases can be a priori prohibited. For example, we can make model A an entirely passive receiver of changes from B by requiring $I^{\mathrm{act}} = \varnothing = J^{\mathrm{pas}}$. Thinking extensionally (i.e., in terms of sets), an organizational relation *is* a set $T \subset \boldsymbol{SC}[\lambda]$ of synchronization cases, considered legal wrt. this relation. We call such sets *synchronization types*. Different synchronization types we considered in the paper can be defined formally by imposing special conditions on index sets like above. We again refer to [2] for details.

Correctness of Incremental Model Synchronization with Triple Graph Grammars

Fernando Orejas* and Elvira Pino

Universitat Politècnica de Catalunya, Spain
{orejas,pino}@lsi.upc.edu

Abstract. In model-driven software development, we may have several models describing the same system or artifact, by providing different views on it. In this case, we say that these models are consistently integrated.

Triple Graph Grammars (TGGs), defined by Schürr, are a general and powerful tool to describe (bidirectional) model transformations. In this context, model synchronization is the operation that, given two consistent models and an update or modification of one of them, finds the corresponding update on the other model, so that consistency is restored. There are different approaches to describe this operation in terms of TGGs, but most of them have a computational cost that depends on the size of the given models. In general this may be very costly since these models may be quite large. To avoid this problem, Giese and Wagner have advocated for the need of *incremental* synchronization procedures, meaning that their cost should depend only on the size of the given update. In particular they proposed one such procedure. Unfortunately, the correctness of their approach is not studied and, anyhow, it could only be ensured under severe restrictions on the kind of TGGs considered.

In the work presented, we study the problem from a different point of view. First, we discuss what it means for a procedure to be incremental, defining a correctness notion that we call *incremental consistency*. Moreover, we present a general incremental synchronization procedure and we show its correctness, completeness and incrementality.

Keywords: Model Transformation, Model Synchronization, Triple Graph Grammars, Incremental Model Synchronization.

1 Introduction

In model-driven development, we may have several models describing the same system or artifact, by providing different views on it. Then, we say that these models are consistently integrated. Similarly, we say that two models are consistent if they are complementary descriptions of some system. In this context, given two integrated models, model synchronization is the problem of restoring consistency when one of these models has been updated by propagating that update to the other model. The same problem is also studied in other areas like databases or programming languages [1,14,9].

---

* This work has been partially supported by the CICYT project (ref. TIN2007-66523) and by the AGAUR grant to the research group ALBCOM (ref. 00516).

D. Di Ruscio and D. Varró (Eds.): ICMT 2014, LNCS 8568, pp. 74–90, 2014.
© Springer International Publishing Switzerland 2014

Triple Graph Grammars (TGGs) [11,12] are a general and powerful tool to describe (bidirectional) model transformations. On the one hand, a TGG allows us to describe classes of consistently integrated models and, on the other hand, given some source model M_1, using the so-called derived operational rules associated to the TGG, we can find a corresponding consistent target model M_2. There are different approaches to describe model synchronization in terms of TGGs, but most of them have a computational cost that depends on the size of the given models. This may be rather inefficient since the given models may be large. To avoid this problem, Giese and Wagner [4] have advocated for the need of *incremental* synchronization procedures, meaning that their cost should depend only on the size of the given update. In particular they proposed one such procedure. Unfortunately, the correctness of this approach is not studied and, anyhow, it could only be ensured under severe restrictions on the kind of TGGs considered, since the approach only works for the case when source and target models are bijective.

In this paper we address the problem from a different point of view. First, we discuss what it means for a procedure to be incremental. Specifically, given a derivation used to create a model and an update on it, we establish what does it means incrementality with respect to a consistent submodel not affected by the update. Essentially, it means that there exists a derivation that builds the new model preserving that consistent submodel. Then, this idea is formulated as a correctness notion, that we call *incremental consistency*. This may be considered a first contribution of the paper.

Our second and main contribution is the introduction of a new general incremental synchronization procedure. In principle, the input for this procedure would be given by an integrated model $\overline{G}$, a derivation of $\overline{G}$ representing its structure, and an update on the source model of $\overline{G}$. However, since storing a derivation may be expensive in terms of the amount of storage needed, we replace the derivation by dependence relations on the elements of $\overline{G}$ that are shown to be equivalent, in an adequate sense, to the derivation. Specifically, we prove a theorem (Th.1 in Sec.4) that guarantees that the largest consistent submodel not affected by the update can be obtained from that dependencies without cost depending on the model. Then, the procedure consists of five steps. In the first one, based on the above result, we identify the part of the model that needs to be reconstructed and we mark all the elements that may need to be deleted. In the second step, if needed, we enlarge the part of the model that needs to be reconstructed. As we will discuss, this second step is only needed in some cases when the update does not allow incremental consistency with respect to the largest consistent submodel not affected by the update, but with respect to a smaller one. In the third step, following the same idea presented informally in [5], we build a model that is already consistent, by applying a variation of forward translation rules [8,6] allowing us to reuse most relevant information from the target model. For this reason, we call these rules *forward translation rules with reuse*. However, the resulting model may not include elements from the target model that do not have a correspondence in the source model. To avoid this, in the fourth step we recover these elements by just using our dependence relations. Finally, in the fifth step we effectively delete target elements that are still marked to be deleted. We prove that the results of this procedure are always incrementally correct and complete in the sense that, if there is an incrementally correct solution, the procedure will find it.

When describing our procedure, sometimes we refer to *user interaction* to take some decisions that may be not obvious. We want to point out that, from a theoretical point of view, this is equivalent to considering that our procedure is nondeterministic. On the other hand, it is important to notice that we do not assume any restriction on the kind of grammars or graphs considered in this paper. This is not the case of most other approaches that impose reasonable restrictions to ensure efficiency. As a consequence, the implementation of our procedure may be computationally costly since, at some points some exhaustive search may be needed. However, our ideas could also be used in the context of the restrictions considered by other authors. In that case, our procedure would be as efficient (or more efficient) than these other approaches. Anyhow, it must be understood that our contribution is related to the study of when and how we can proceed incrementally in the synchronization process in the most general case, rather than restricting its application to the cases where a certain degree of efficiency is ensured.

The paper is organized as follows. In Section 2 we introduce some basic material needed in the paper and we present a running example that we use to illustrate our approach and results. In the third section we study the notion of incremental consistency and in Section 4 we present the dependency relations that are used to represent derivations. In Section 5 we present our incremental synchronization procedure. Finally, in Section 6 we discuss related work and we draw some conclusions.

2   Preliminaries

In this section, we describe some basic notions and terminology concerning, model transformation and model synchronization with Triple Graph Grammars (TGGs). Moreover, we introduce the examples that we will use in the paper.

2.1   Model Synchronization with Triple Graph Grammars

Model synchronization is the operation that, given two consistent models and an update or modification of one of them, finds the corresponding update on the other model, so that consistency is restored. Let us be more precise. First, we consider that models are some kind of typed graphs with attributes (see, e.g., [2]). This means that our models consist of nodes, edges and attributes[1], which are values associated to nodes and edges. Moreover, a type graph, which is similar to a metamodel, describes the kind of elements (nodes, edges and attributes) that are part of the given class of models. For example, in Fig. 1 we can see the type graph of the example considered in this paper. Second, we consider that integrated models are not just pairs of graphs but *triple graphs* that, in addition, provide a correspondence between elements of the given models. Formally, a triple graph $\overline{G} = (G^S \xleftarrow{s_G} G^C \xrightarrow{t_G} G^T)$ consists of a *source graph* G^S and a *target graph* G^T, which are related via a *correspondence graph* G^C and two mappings (graph morphisms) $s_G : G^C \rightarrow G^S$ and $t_G : G^C \rightarrow G^T$ specifying how source elements correspond to target elements. For example in figure 2 we can see a triple graph typed by the graph in figure 1. For simplicity, we use double arrows, $\langle G^S \leftrightarrow G^T \rangle$, as an equivalent shorter notation for triple graphs, whenever the explicit correspondence graph can be omitted.

---

[1] For simplicity, our example includes no attributes.

A simple but powerful way of describing a class of consistently integrated models is by using a *Triple Graph Grammar* [11,12], consisting of a start triple graph, $\overline{SG}^2$, and a set of production rules of the form $p : \overline{L} \to \overline{R}$, where $\overline{L}$ and $\overline{R}$ are triple graphs and $\overline{L} \subseteq$ 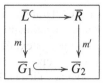 $\overline{R}$. That is, $\mathcal{L}(\mathcal{G}) = \{\overline{G} \mid \overline{SG} \overset{*}{\Longrightarrow} \overline{G}\}$ is the language defined by a triple grammar $\mathcal{G}$, where $\overset{*}{\Longrightarrow}$ is the reflexive and transitive closure of the one step transformation relation $\Longrightarrow$ defined by the grammar as follows. $\overline{G}_1 \Longrightarrow \overline{G}_2$ if there is a production rule $p : \overline{L} \to \overline{R}$ in $\mathcal{G}$ and a matching monomorphism $m : \overline{L} \to \overline{G}_1$ such that $\overline{G}_2$ can be obtained by replacing (the image of) $\overline{L}$ in $\overline{G}_1$ by (a corresponding image of) $\overline{R}$. Formally, this means that the diagram above on the right is a pushout in the category of triple graphs. In this case, we write $\overline{G}_1 \overset{p,m}{\Longrightarrow} \overline{G}_2$, or just $\overline{G}_1 \Longrightarrow \overline{G}_2$ if p and m are implicit.

Hence, we say that a triple graph $\overline{G}$ is consistent if $\overline{G} \in \mathcal{L}(\mathcal{G})$. Similarly, we say that a source graph G^S (respectively, a target graph G^T) is consistent if there exists a triple graph $\langle G^S \leftrightarrow G^T \rangle \in \mathcal{L}(\mathcal{G})$.

Finally, we consider that an *update* or *modification* of a graph G, denoted $u : G \Rightarrow G'$ is a span of inclusions (or, in general, injective morphisms) $G \leftarrow G_0 \to G'$ for some graph G_0. Intuitively, the elements in G that are not in G_0 are the elements deleted by u, and the elements in G' that are not in G_0 are the elements added by u.

Now we can express formally the synchronization problem in terms of the diagram on the right [7]. Given a triple graph $\overline{G}$ and an update $u^S : G^S \Rightarrow G'^S$ on the source graph[3], the synchroniza- 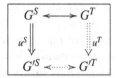 tion problem is to find an update $u^T : G^T \Rightarrow G'^T$ and a triple graph $\overline{G}'$ such that $\overline{G}'$ is consistent. These results, u^T and $\overline{G}'$, are called the forward propagation of u^S over $\overline{G}$. Notice that finding the triple graph $\overline{G}'$ means computing the new correspondences of that graph. Notice also that, in general, there may be no solution to the synchronization problem. In particular, this is the case if G'^S is not consistent, i.e. when there is no consistent triple graph $\langle G'^S \leftrightarrow G'^T \rangle$.

For example, below we will consider the synchronization problems when deleting the subclass edge between classes C_3 and C_2 in the triple graph in Fig. 3.

2.2   Model Transformation with Triple Graph Grammars

Model transformation is the problem of finding a consistent triple graph $\langle G^S \leftrightarrow G^T \rangle$, when given a TGG $\mathcal{G}$ and a source model G^S. This problem is very related to the problem of model synchronization. Each of these problems can be seen as a special case of the other one. In particular, the model transformation problem can be seen as a special case of model synchronization since it can be solved by computing the propagation of the update $u^S : \emptyset \Rightarrow G^S$ over the empty triple graph $\langle \emptyset \leftrightarrow \emptyset \rangle$. Similarly, model synchronization can be reduced to model transformation, since given $\langle G^S \leftrightarrow G^T \rangle$ and a source update $u^S : G^S \Rightarrow G'^S$ we can solve the synchronization problem just computing

---

[2] In general, without loss of generality, we will consider that $\overline{SG}$ is always the empty triple graph.

[3] Note that the synchronization problem after a target update can be seen as a special case of the problem considered in this paper, since triple graphs are symmetric structures.

the model transformation of G'^S. However, this would not be an efficient solution of the synchronization problem[4].

In the context of TGGs, the model transformation problem can be solved using the so-called operational rules (forward, backward, source, and target rules) associated to $\mathcal{G}$. The key idea is that forward rules, generated from the rules in $\mathcal{G}$, preserve the given source model but add the missing target and correspondence elements. Solving this problem is equivalent to finding a source consistent derivation [3].

$$\langle G^S \leftrightarrow \emptyset \rangle \Longrightarrow_{p_1} \langle G^S \leftrightarrow G_1^T \rangle \Longrightarrow_{p_2} \ldots \Longrightarrow_{p_n} \langle G^S \leftrightarrow G_n^T \rangle$$

where $p_1, p_2, \ldots, p_n$ are forward rules associated to $\mathcal{G}$.

Finding source consistent derivations or checking if a derivation with forward rules is source consistent is, in general, quite costly. For this reason, [6] introduces a new technique based on the use of Boolean-valued *translation attributes*. These attributes are associated to all elements in the graph (i.e. nodes, edges, and also other attributes) to denote if that element has been *created* or not by a rule. The idea is quite simple. Let us first consider a slightly different problem. Suppose that we want to know if a given triple graph is consistent, i.e. if $\overline{G} \in \mathcal{L}(\mathcal{G})$. Obviously, we may try to see if we can derive $\overline{G}$ using the rules in $\mathcal{G}$. However, we can use a different approach: we modify slightly the TGG rules so that, instead of creating new elements, we just mark the existing ones, so that to check if $\overline{G}$ is consistent, we check if we can mark all its elements with the modified rules. These marks are the translation attributes, that is, the attribute of an element states if the element has been marked or not. Then, to check if $\overline{G}$ is consistent we just have to add all the translation attributes set to false, and try to see if applying the modified rules we can arrive to a graph with all its translation attributes set to true.

The above idea can be generalized. Suppose that we have a grammar $\mathcal{G}$ and a (not necessarily consistent) triple graph $\overline{G}$, and we want to extend it until we arrive to a consistent graph. A straightforward approach would be to use the rules in $\mathcal{G}$ to find a graph $\overline{G}'$ that extends $\overline{G}$. But we can also modify the rules in $\mathcal{G}$, so that, if an old rule would have created an element already in $\overline{G}$, the new rule would just mark it; but if the old rule would create a new element not in $\overline{G}$, the new rule would also create it. We can say that these new rules *reuse* the elements in $\overline{G}$. A similar idea was informally introduced in [5]. For example, *forward translation rules* [6] follow this idea to solve the model transformation problem. The part that is reused is the given source graph G^S, and the extension that we are looking for consists of the target and correspondence parts of the result. That is, $\langle G^S \leftrightarrow \emptyset \rangle$ is the given triple graph that we want to complete. So, to solve the model transformation problem, we would first add false translation attributes to all the elements in G^S and then apply the new rules until we arrive to a triple model $\overline{G}$ whose source part is like G^S, but with all its translation attributes set to true .

2.3 Example

In this subsection we introduce the example that is used to illustrate our techniques. It is a simplified, and slightly modified, version of the well-known transformation between

---

[4] Actually it would neither be an adequate solution [13].

class diagrams and relational schemas. The type graphs of source, target and correspondence models are depicted in Fig. 1. Source models, whose type graph is depicted on the left, consist of two kinds of nodes, classes and attributes, and two kinds of edges. On the one hand, an edge between two classes represents a subclass relationship between them. On the other hand, attributes are bound to their associated classes by the second kind of edges. Similarly, the type graph of target models is depicted on the right of the figure, consisting of tables, columns and foo nodes[5], together with edges between columns and tables, and between foo nodes and columns. Finally, in the center of Fig. 1, we depict the type graph of the correspondence models, consisting of two kinds of nodes: square nodes to bind classes with their associated tables, and round nodes to bind attributes with their associated columns.

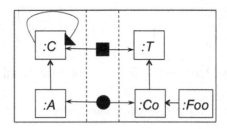

Fig. 1. Type graph

The rules of the TGG defining the transformation between class diagrams and relational schemas are depicted in Fig. 2 in short notation, i.e. left and right hand sides of a rule are depicted in a single triple graph. Elements which are created by the rule are labelled with $++$ and additionally marked by purple line colouring. Rule 1, Class2Table creates a new class and its corresponding table. and it also creates the correspondence element that relates the class and the table. Rule 2, Attribute2Column, given a class C_1 and a corresponding table T_1, creates an attribute A_1 of C_1 and a related column c_1 of T_1, together with the associated correspondence element. Rule 3, Subclass2Table, given a class C_1 and a corresponding table T_1, creates a new class C_2 that is a subclass of C_1. In this case, C_2 is related to T_1 through a new correspondence element. Finally, Rule 4, FooCreation creates a new foo node associated to an existing column. Notice that, in this rule, the source and correspondence parts of the triple rule are empty.

In the left of Fig. 3 we depict a triple graph generated by this TGG. That triple graph could have been generated by a derivation d_1 consisting of, first, applying twice the rule Class2Table, to create classes C_1, C_2 and tables T_1, T_2; then, applying the rule Subclass2Table, to create C_3, and applying three times the rule Attribute2Column to create attributes A_1, A_2, A_3 and columns c_1, c_2, c_3; finally applying the rule FooCreation to create the foo node associated to column c_3. But it could have also been created by other derivations that are *permutation equivalent* to d_1 [2], like derivation d_2, consisting of applying twice the rules Class2Table and Attribute2Column, to create classes C_1, C_2, tables T_1, T_2, attributes A_1, A_2, and columns c_1, c_2.; then, applying rule Subclass2Table, to

---

[5] These foo nodes have no special meaning. They are just introduced for our convenience.

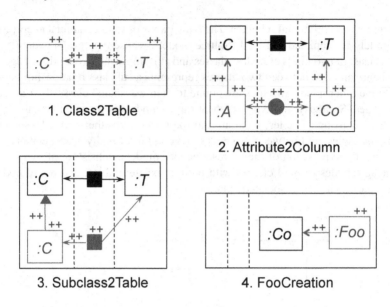

Fig. 2. Transformations Rules

create C_3, rule Attribute2Column to create attribute A_3 and column c_3, and rule FooCreation to create the foo node.

Finally, in the rest of the paper, we will use green colour[6] to depict the elements affected by an update, in contrast to the black coloured elements that are not affected by the update.

3   Incremental Model Synchronization and Incremental Consistency

In the literature on model synchronization, the term "incremental" has two possible meanings. On the one hand, in most papers, a synchronization procedure is called incremental if the propagation of a source update reuses the information included in the given target model. Actually, according to this meaning of incrementality, rather than saying if a procedure is incremental or not, we should say how much incremental it is, depending on the amount of target information reused. For instance, an extreme case would be a procedure that, given an integrated model $\overline{G}$ and a source update $u^S : G^S \rightarrow G'^S$, would compute the propagation of u by computing the model transformation of G'^S, without taking into account the information in G'^T. Obviously, this would be the most non-incremental (or the least incremental) procedure.

On the other hand, in [4], Giese and Wagner advocate that synchronization should be *incremental*, meaning that its computational cost should depend mainly on the size of the modification and not on the size of the given models. This is not the case in most

---

[6] For readers of black and white prints, green elements appear as lighter grey.

existing approaches. Even if they build the solution by modifying the given target model and reusing its information, their cost still depends on the size of the given models, because they have to analyze the models to ensure correctness. Our aim is to develop a procedure that is incremental in both senses.

Our approach is based on assuming that if $\overline{G}$ is the given integrated model, we know which derivation $d = \overline{SG} \Longrightarrow \ldots \Longrightarrow \overline{G_i} \Longrightarrow \ldots \Longrightarrow \overline{G}$ generated it. In this context, if we know that the given update $u^S : G^S \Rightarrow G'^S$ does not affect any element in G_i^S, i.e. $G_i^S \subseteq G'^S$ and the result of the synchronization, $\overline{G'}$, also includes $\overline{G_i}$, then we say that $\overline{G'}$ is *incrementally consistent* with respect to $\overline{G_i}$. Then, the idea underlying our procedure is to find the largest $\overline{G_i} \subseteq \overline{G}$ so that we can build over it the solution $\overline{G_i} \subseteq \overline{G'}$. Moreover, since we want our procedure to be incremental in the sense of [4], the cost of finding $\overline{G_i}$ should not depend on its size.

However, there are many derivations that can be considered equivalent, because the order in which we apply some productions is irrelevant. These transformations are called *sequentially independent* and the derivations are *permutation equivalent* (for the concrete definitions see, e.g., [2]). For instance, in the example, derivations d_1 and d_2 mentioned in subsection 2.3, are permutation equivalent. This means that it is not relevant if we first create classes C_1, C_2, C_3 and tables T_1, T_2 and then we add the attributes and columns $A_1, A_2, A_3, c_1, c_2, c_3$, or if we first create C_1, T_1, A_1, c_1, then C_2, T_2, A_2, c_2 and finally C_3, A_3, c_3, or if we create the classes, attributes, tables and columns in a different order. The only limitations are that we cannot create C_3 before C_2 and T_2, because the rule to create C_3 needs that C_2, T_2 are already there, neither we can create an attribute/column before their associated class/table, nor we can create a foo node before its corresponding column. As a consequence, when looking for the submodel $\overline{G_i}$ to build the synchronization, we must consider, not only the given derivation d that generated $\overline{G}$, but also all derivations that are permutation equivalent to d.

For example, let us suppose that, in the graph on the left of Fig. 3, we delete the subclass relation between C_3 and C_2. The result of the (expected) synchronization is depicted on the right of that figure. We may see that this result is incrementally consistent with respect to the subgraph depicted in black on the left. So, in this case, our procedure would first need to find that subgraph and, then, it would construct the result on the right.

Definition 1 (Incremental consistency). *Given a TGG $\mathcal{G}$, a derivation $d = \overline{SG} \overset{*}{\Longrightarrow} \overline{G}$ and an update $u : G^S \Rightarrow G'^S$. Let $\overline{H} \subseteq \overline{G}$ be such that no element in H^S is deleted by u and there is a derivation d_0, permutation equivalent to d with $d_0 = \overline{SG} \overset{*}{\Longrightarrow} \overline{H} \overset{*}{\Longrightarrow} \overline{G}$. We say that an integrated model $\overline{G'} = \langle G'^S \leftrightarrow G'^T \rangle \in \mathcal{L}(\mathcal{G})$ is incrementally consistent with respect to d, u and $\overline{H}$ if there exists a derivation $d' = \overline{SG} \overset{*}{\Longrightarrow} \overline{G'}$ sastifying that, $d' = \overline{SG} \overset{*}{\Longrightarrow} \overline{H} \overset{*}{\Longrightarrow} \overline{G'}$.*

In most cases, we may consider that the submodel $\overline{G_i} \subseteq \overline{G}$ that we look for in our procedure should always be the largest submodel of $\overline{G}$ generated by a derivation permutation equivalent to d that is not affected by the given update. This works fine in many cases, like in the example that we have just described. However, there are cases where this largest model cannot be completed to an incrementally consistent model. For instance, let us suppose that the given integrated model $\overline{G}$ is the triple graph on the right

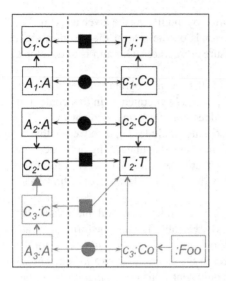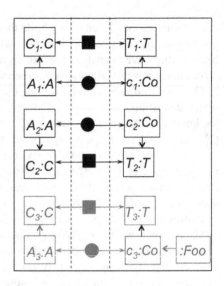

Fig. 3. Model Synchronization

of Fig. 3 and let us suppose that the given updates consists just of the addition of a subclass relation between C_3 and C_2. In this case, the largest submodel of $\overline{G}$ not affected by that update is the whole model $\overline{G}$, since the update includes no deletion. However, there is no way to extend G^T so that the final result is consistent. In this case, the submodel of $\overline{G}$ that we can use to build an incrementally consistent result is the part of $\overline{G}$ depicted in black in the triple graph on the left of Fig. 3.

Nevertheless, the following proposition shows that, given a derivation d of an integrated model $\overline{G}$ and given a subset of elements $D \subseteq \overline{G}$ that must be deleted when applying a given update, there is a largest consistent graph $\overline{G}_{d \setminus D} \subseteq \overline{G}$ that consists of all the elements of $\overline{G}$ that can be generated by d without the use of elements from D in any derivation d' that is permutation equivalent to d. Moreover, some of these derivations d' include the derivation of $\overline{G}_{d \setminus D}$, i.e. $d' : \overline{SG} \overset{*}{\Longrightarrow} \overline{G}_{d \setminus D} \overset{*}{\Longrightarrow} \overline{G}$, then we say that d' is *maximally preserving* with respect to D.

The idea is that the result of the synchronization will be built from $\overline{G}_{d \setminus D}$. As a consequence, in most cases, D will be the set of elements deleted by the given update and, as a consequence, $\overline{G}_{d \setminus D}$ would be be the largest submodel of $\overline{G}$ generated by a derivation permutation equivalent to d that is not affected by the given update. However, as explained above, we will need to include in D some additional elements from G^S to ensure that we can extend $\overline{G}_{d \setminus D}$ to a consistent graph.

Proposition 1 (Maximal preserving derivations). *Given a derivation* $d = \overline{SG} \overset{*}{\Longrightarrow} \overline{G}$ *and a subset of elements* $D \subseteq \overline{G}$ *, there is a consistent graph* $\overline{G}_{d \setminus D} \subseteq \overline{G}$ *such that, for every derivation* d' *permutation equivalent to* d*, if* $d' = \overline{SG} \overset{*}{\Longrightarrow} \overline{G}_i \overset{*}{\Longrightarrow} \overline{G}$ *and* $\overline{G}_i$ *does not include any element from* D *then* $\overline{G}_i \subseteq \overline{G}_{d \setminus D}$*. Moreover, there are derivations* $d' = \overline{SG} \overset{*}{\Longrightarrow} \overline{G}_{d \setminus D} \overset{*}{\Longrightarrow} \overline{G}$ *which are* maximally preserving *and permutation equivalent to* d*.*

The idea of the proof is quite simple. The consistent submodel $\overline{G}_{d\backslash D}$ is built by including in $d_0 = \overline{SG} \stackrel{*}{\Longrightarrow} \overline{G}_{d\backslash D}$ all transformations in d that are sequentially independent with respect to the productions in d that need from elements in D. Then, d' is built by extending d_0 with the remaining transformations in d.

4   Derivation Dependencies

To build incrementally consistent solutions we need information about the derivation that generated the given integrated model, since we need to know what part of the model must remain unchanged after update propagation. However, saving derivations and working with them may be costly and cumbersome. In this section, we show that just saving some dependence information associated to the given derivation is enough for our purposes. The basic idea is to define some dependency relations between the elements (nodes, edges and attributes) of the given integrated model $\langle G^S \leftrightarrow G^T \rangle$ that describe if an element e_1 was needed for the creation of e_2 in a given derivation d. The first relation, called *strict dependency* and denoted $e_1 \lhd_d e_2$, holds if e_1 was matched by the left-hand side of the rule that created e_2. For instance, in Example 2, $C_2 \lhd_{d_1} C_3$ and $T_2 \lhd_{d_1} C_3$, since the application of rule Subclass2Table that created C_3 in derivation d_1 had to match its lefthand side to C_2 and T_2 (and also to their correspondence element). The second relation, called *interdependency* and denoted $e_1 \bowtie_d e_2$, holds if e_1 and e_2 are created by the same rule. For instance, in Example 2, $C_2 \bowtie_{d_1} T_2$, since they are both created by the same application of the Class2Table rule in d_1. Obviously, C_2 and T_2 are also interdependent with their correspondence node.

Definition 2 (Dependency relations). *Given $\mathcal{G}$ and a derivation $d : \overline{SG} \stackrel{*}{\Longrightarrow} \overline{G}$, we define the following relations on elements of $\overline{G}$:*

1. *Strict dependency: $\lhd_d$ is the smallest relation satisfying that if d includes the transformation step depicted below:*

$$
\begin{array}{ccc}
\overline{L} & \lhook\joinrel\longrightarrow & \overline{R} \\
m \downarrow & & \downarrow m' \\
\overline{G}_{i-1} & \lhook\joinrel\longrightarrow & \overline{G}_i
\end{array}
$$

   then for every e in $\overline{L}$ and e' in $\overline{R} \backslash \overline{L}$, $m(e) \lhd_d m'(e')$.
2. *Strict interdependency: $\bowtie_d$ is the smallest relation satisfying that if d includes the transformation step depicted above, then for every e, e' in $\overline{R} \backslash \overline{L}$, $m'(e) \bowtie_d m'(e')$.*

The key result for our synchronization procedure is the following theorem that shows that if in the given integrated model we delete the set of elements D that are dependent on a given update, the resulting triple graph is $\overline{G}_{d\backslash D}$. Moreover, it also shows that if we are interested in any submodel of $\overline{G}_{d\backslash D}$ that is also generated by the given derivation (or some permutation equivalent derivation), it is enough to remove from $\overline{G}_{d\backslash D}$ some additional elements together with all the elements that depend on them.

Theorem 1 (Dependency Relations and Incrementality). *Let* $d = \overline{SG} \overset{*}{\Longrightarrow} \overline{G}$ *be a derivation,* D *be a the subset of elements of* $\overline{G}$, *and* $Clos_d(D)$ *be the least set satisfying that:*

- $D \subseteq Clos_d(D)$,
- *If* $e' \in Clos_d(D)$ *and* $e' \prec_d e$ *or* $e' \bowtie_d e$ *then* $e \in Clos_d(D)$,

then:

1. *$\overline{G}_{d \backslash D} = \overline{G} \backslash Clos_d(D)$.*
2. *Given a subset D_0 of elements of $\overline{G}_{d \backslash D}$, there is a derivation $d_0 = \overline{SG} \overset{*}{\Longrightarrow} (\overline{G} \backslash Clos_d(D)) \backslash Clos_d(D_0) \overset{*}{\Longrightarrow} \overline{G}$ permutation equivalent to d.*
3. *Conversely, if $\overline{H}$ is a submodel of $\overline{G}_{d \backslash D}$ such that there is a derivation $d_0 = \overline{SG} \overset{*}{\Longrightarrow} \overline{H} \overset{*}{\Longrightarrow} \overline{G}$ permutation equivalent to d, then there is a subset D_0 of elements of $\overline{G}_{d \backslash D}$ such that $\overline{H} = (\overline{G} \backslash Clos_d(D)) \backslash Clos_d(D_0)$.*

The proof of this theorem is not difficult. The key issue is to show that the elements in $Clos_d(D)$ or of $Clos_d(D \cup D_0)$ are exactly the elements generated by the last transformations in a maximally preserving derivation as constructed in Prop.1.

5   A Procedure for Incremental Model Synchronization

In this section we present our procedure for incremental synchronization and we show its correctness. The input for this procedure is, not only the given integrated model and source update, but also the dependency relations. Moreover, we assume that there is a translation attribute set to `true` for every element in the model. This allows us to use our techniques needed to ensure the incrementality of solutions. Then, the output is, not only the resulting integrated model (and the resulting update), but also the updated dependence relations, so that they can be used to deal with further updates. Notice that handling explicitly the dependence relations and the translation attributes is not costly, neither in space nor in time, since all this information is boolean.

According to Theorem 1, we could consider a quite simple incremental synchronization procedure. For instance, if we know that we can build an incremental solution from $\overline{G}_{d \backslash D}$, where D is the set of elements deleted by the given source update u, we could proceed as follows. In a first step, the procedure would delete from G^T and G^C all the elements depending on the elements deleted by u and would mark as non-created all source elements added by u and all source elements depending on the elements deleted by u (except the deleted elements themselves). Then we would apply forward translation rules to the resulting model until arriving to a consistent $\overline{G'}$. The dependency relations would be updated accordingly. Unfortunately, this procedure would not work as we would like as the following example shows.

Let us consider again the deletion of the subclass relation between C_3 and C_2 in the triple graph depicted on the left of Fig. 3. The result of the first step is depicted on the left of Fig. 4, where the source elements marked as non-created are depicted in green. The reason is that all the deleted target and correspondence elements depend on the creation of C_3 as a subclass of C_2. Finally, the result after applying forward translation rules is depicted on the right of Fig. 4. As we may see, the foo element related to column c_3 is now not present. Moreover, since c_3 has been deleted and created again, if it included some additional information (e.g. some data attributes), this information may have been lost.

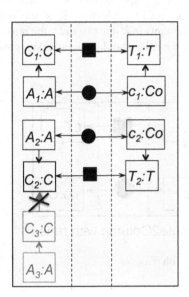 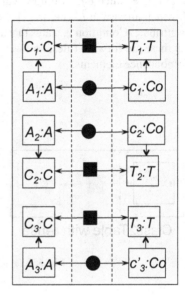

Fig. 4. Model Synchronization

To avoid these problems, we apply three ideas. The first one, quite obvious, is that the elements in the target (and correspondence) graphs should not be deleted but marked, in order not to lose information. Only at the end of the process we should delete some of these elements. The second idea is that, when building the resulting model, we should reuse the information included in the model, using a general form of forward translation rules, that use the idea presented in [5]. For this purpose, the following notion of *forward transformation rule with reuse* plays a main role, where $RemAttr(\overline{G})$ denotes the graph resulting from removing from $\overline{G}$ all its translation attributes:

Definition 3. *Given a rule $p : \overline{L} \to \overline{R}$, we say that $p' : \overline{L'} \to \overline{R'}$ is a* forward transformation rule with reuse *over p if:*

1. *$RemAttr(\overline{R'}) = \overline{R}, \overline{L} \subseteq RemAttr(\overline{L'}) \subseteq \overline{R}$.*
2. *$R^S \subseteq RemAttr(L'^S)$.*
3. *The translation attributes in $\overline{L'}$ are* true *for all the elements in $\overline{L}$, otherwise they are* false.
4. *All translation attributes in $\overline{R'}$ are* true.

The intuition of these new rules is based on the idea that the given graph $\overline{G}$ includes some elements with translation attribute true, which are elements considered really in the graph, and some other elements with false attribute, meaning that they have not yet been created, i.e. they are not *real* elements of $\overline{G}$. So, in a rule with reuse, $\overline{L'}$ includes all elements in $\overline{L}$ with attribute true since, to apply the rule, all these elements must really be in $\overline{G}$. But $\overline{L'}$ may also include some elements from $\overline{R} \setminus \overline{L}$, with false attribute, that are reused. Then, after applying p', all the reused elements have now a true attribute, since they are now real elements of the graph, and all the elements in $\overline{R} \setminus \overline{L}$ which are not in $\overline{L'}$ (i.e. they have not been reused) are added to the graph with true attribute. Condition 2. states that all source elements in $\overline{R}$ must be in $\overline{L'}$, the reason is that these are forward rules, i.e., we assume that the rules should only add target and correspondence elements.

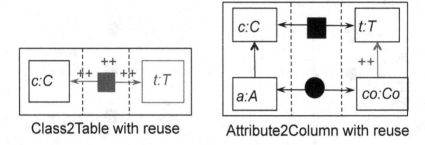

Class2Table with reuse   Attribute2Column with reuse

Fig. 5. Examples of rules with reuse

We may notice that, for each original rule, we may have quite a big amount of associated rules with reuse. This means that creating a priori all of them can make the model transformation and synchronization processes quite costly. Instead, we believe that, for implementation, the right approach is to work directly with the original triple graph rules, $\overline{L} \rightarrow \overline{R}$, as proposed in [5]. The idea would be that after finding a match between $\overline{L}$ and the given graph $\overline{G}$, we check how much of $\overline{R}$ we can reuse, and we proceed accordingly. However, we must warn that, in some situations, if we reuse as much as possible, some of this reuse could be inadequate. For instance, suppose that in our example the given triple graph includes also a class C_0 and a related table T_0 and suppose also that the given update not only deletes the subclass relation between C_3 and C_2, but it also includes the deletion of the class C_0. Then, with maximal reuse, instead of creating a new table T_3 and associating it to C_3, we would reuse T_0, associating it to C_3. This is probably wrong according to what the user expects, even if the result is technically correct. Anyhow, we believe that, in the worst case, it is better to produce an inadequate result that the user can easily amend, that producing some result, which is also inadequate, but where some information has been lost and can be difficult to recover. In any case, we also believe that, in general, the decision on how much to reuse should not be automatic, but it should be taken by the user.

The third idea is related to rules like FooCreation on figure 2, that includes no source elements. The model transformation process, to construct the synchronization, is driven by the source elements of the given graph. This means that, while there are source elements with false translation attributes, we look for a rule that would transform some of these `false` source attributes into `true`. So, a rule like FooCreation will never be applied in this process. The problem is to know when to apply this kind of rules. The solution is given by our dependence relations. If there is a target element e with `false` translation attribute (i.e. the element was in the original model, but the previous process has not created it); if all elements e' such that $e' \lhd e$ have `true` attribute (i.e. the elements that were used to create e have already been created); and if all elements e'', such that $e \bowtie e''$, have `false` attribute (i.e. the other elements created together with e have not been created either); then we can turn the translation attributes of e and all the elements e'' to `true`, because this is like applying the same rule that created e. We call this operation the *recreation of e and all its interdependent elements*.

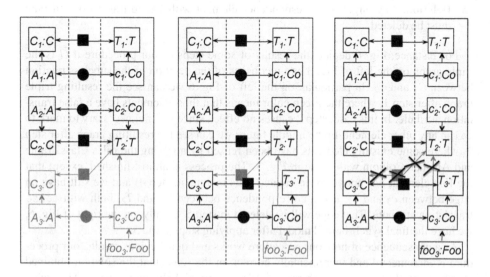

Fig. 6. Synchronization: Some intermediate steps and final model

Following the above ideas, our procedure for incremental synchronization has five steps. As said above, we assume given the original integrated model, $\overline{G} = \langle G^S \leftrightarrow G^T \rangle$, including translation attributes set to `true` for all its elements, an update $u : G^S \Rightarrow G'^S$, and the dependency relations associated to the derivation that created $\langle G^S \leftrightarrow G^T \rangle$.

1. **Updating and Marking.** All elements deleted by u are deleted from G^S. All elements added by u are added to G^S with `false` translation attribute. All elements in $\overline{G}$ that are dependent on the elements deleted are marked as false. Finally, any correspondence element whose associated source element has been deleted, is deleted. As a consequence of Theorem 1, all the elements with true translation attribute form the submodel $\overline{G}_{d \setminus D}$, where D is the set of elements deleted by u.

2. **Selection of a submodel of $\overline{G}_{d \setminus D}$.** If needed, the translation attributes of some other elements of $\overline{G}_{d \setminus D}$ and the elements depending on them are set to false. This step is needed in the case where we cannot build an incrementally consistent derivation

out of $\overline{G}_{d\backslash D}$. For instance, in the case where $\overline{G}$ is the triple graph on the right of Fig. 3 and u consists of the addition of a subclass relation between C_3 and C_2, we would need to set to false the attributes of C_3 and all the elements depending on it. The decision of which translation attributes have to be set to false may be either taken by the user or by some search procedure based on some heuristics or just on backtracking.

3. **Forward Model Transformation.** While there are elements in G^S with false translation attribute, select a rule that can match at least one of these elements. Select the amount of the rule to be reused and apply it. [7]

4. **Recreation of Target Elements.** For each element in G^T with false translation attribute, try to recreate it together with all its interdependent elements.

5. **Deletion.** Any target or correspondence element with false translation attribute must be deleted.

For instance, Fig. 6 depicts the results of some steps of our procedure if $\overline{G}$ is the triple graph on the left of Fig. 3 and u consists of the deletion of the subclass relation between C_3 and C_2. In particular, on the left of Fig. 6 we can see the resulting triple graph after step 1, where the green color means that those elements have a false translation attribute. In this case, step 2 causes no effect, since it is not necessary to mark to false any other element. In the middle figure we can see the resulting graph after step 3, where some existing elements have been reused by applying the rules Class2Table and AttributeColumn with reuse in Fig. 5. The process is almost finished, except that the Foo element has not yet been created (this is done in step 4) and we still have an edge between c_3 and T_2, and a correspondence between C_3 and T_2, both with false translation attribute. That edge will be deleted in step 5. Finally, on the right of Fig. 6, we have the final synchronized model after applying steps 4 and 5.

As a consequence of how our procedure works and our previous results, our procedure is incremental and incrementally correct, in the sense that the solution obtained is incrementally consistent with respect to the submodel chosen in step 2. Moreover, the procedure is complete, in the sense that if there is an incrementally consistent solution with respect to some submodel, the procedure will find it. Finally, the cost of the procedure is independent of the size of the submodel chosen in step 2.

Theorem 2. *The procedure is incremental, incrementally correct and complete.*

6   Related Work and Conclusion

As said in the introduction, model synchronization[8] is a problem studied in different areas in Computer Science. In particular, in databases (e.g., [1]), programming languages (e.g., [9]) and in model-driven software development (MDD). In the former two areas the kind of models considered are very specific, however in the latter area the kind of

---

[7] In general, some choices may not lead to a result where all elements in the source part have true translation attribute. In that case, this step may need backtracking.

[8] In some cases model synchronization is called incremental model transformation, or just model transformation. Obviously, this is quite confusing.

models considered may be very different. For this reason, in MDD we need general approaches, as TGGs [11,12], that can be used for dealing with most kinds of models.

There are several approaches based on TGGs that propose a solution to the model synchronization problem (that we know [4,7,5,10] and some variations on them) but all of them are, in our opinion, not completely satisfactory. In particular, even if the construction of the solution does not start from scratch but from the given integrated model $\overline{G}$, the approach in [7] has to analyze the complete graph $\overline{G}$ to know what parts must be modified, so its cost depends on the size of the given model. In addition, in [7] not all elements of the original graph that could be reused are indeed reused. In particular, in our example, column c_3 would have been deleted and created again. This means that, if that column would have included some additional information, this information would have been lost. Moreover, the foo element associated to c_3 would not be present in the final result. On the other hand, the only restriction considered in [7] is that the given TGG should be deterministic, to ensure that their procedure is deterministic.

The approach in [4] does not need to analyze the complete graph $\overline{G}$ to check which parts must be modified, so its cost only depends on the size of the modification. However, their approach only works for the case when source and target models are bijective, which excludes the case where source models are views of target models (or vice versa). Moreover, rules like FooCreation, with empty source graph, are forbidden. In addition, this approach shares with [7] the information loss problem. Finally, that approach has not been fully formalized.

The approach in [5] proposes a technique to avoid the loss of information in [4] that is essentially similar to our forward rules with reuse. Unfortunately, even if it is based on [4], it needs to analyze the complete graph $\overline{G}$ to check which parts must be modified, so its cost depends on the size of $\overline{G}$. Moreover, the approach imposes the same restrictions as [4] and lacks formality.

Finally, in [10], like us, the authors use precedence relations to avoid having to analyze the complete graph $\overline{G}$ to find which parts must be modified. However, their relation is coarser than ours. The reason is that our relations are directly based on a given derivation while in [10], their relation is based on the dependences established by the rules of the TGG. In particular, this means that two given elements of a model may be independent, but their relation may say that one depends on the other. This has some important consequences. In particular, their synchronization procedure only works if the given triple graph is *forward precedence preserving* and if, when adding new elements, the resulting precedence graph includes no cycles. In addition, to ensure correctness, the approach also requires that the given TGG is *source-local complete*. On the other hand, the procedure needs to use a data structure that encodes how the given graph $\overline{G}$ has been derived with the given TGG. No details are given about this structure, but we suppose that it is more complex than our dependency relations. Finally, this approach also shares with [7] the information loss problem.

To conclude, in this paper we have presented a new approach for incremental model synchronization based on TGGs that has been shown to be incremental, correct and complete. Moreover, our approach is general, in the sense that we do not restrict the class of TGGs considered. As pointed out in the introduction, we do not assume any restriction on the kind of grammars or graphs, as other approaches does. On the contrary, we have focussed on the study of when and how we can proceed incrementally in the synchronization process in the most general case, rather than on finding out specific conditions and limitations on graphs and grammars that could make some techniques more efficient. As a consequence, it is difficult to provide an accurate evaluation of its performance: for some TGGs our procedure may exhibit an exponential (on the size of the updated part) behavior. But for the kind of more restricted TGGs, as the ones considered in other approaches, the behavior could be close to linear. Anyhow, what obviously remains to be done is to implement the approach and evaluate it in practice.

Acknowledgements. The authors would like to thank the reviewers of this paper, whose comments have contributed to improve it.

References

1. Dayal, U., Bernstein, P.A.: On the Correct Translation of Update Operations on Relational Views. ACM Trans. Database Syst. 7(3), 381–416 (1982)
2. Ehrig, H., Ehrig, K., Prange, U., Taentzer, G.: Fundamentals of Algebraic Graph Transformation. EATCS Monographs of Theoretical Comp. Sc., Springer (2006)
3. Ehrig, H., Ehrig, K., Hermann, F.: From model transformation to model integration based on the algebraic approach to triple graph grammars. ECEASST 10 (2008)
4. Giese, H., Wagner, R.: From model transformation to incremental bidirectional model synchronization. Software and System Modeling 8(1), 21–43 (2009)
5. Greenyer, J., Pook, S., Rieke, J.: Preventing information loss in incremental model synchronization by reusing elements. In: France, R.B., Kuester, J.M., Bordbar, B., Paige, R.F. (eds.) ECMFA 2011. LNCS, vol. 6698, pp. 144–159. Springer, Heidelberg (2011)
6. Hermann, F., Ehrig, H., Golas, U., Orejas, F.: Formal analysis of model transformations based on triple graph grammars. Software and System Modeling (2012) (to appear)
7. Hermann, F., Ehrig, H., Orejas, F., Czarnecki, K., Diskin, Z., Xiong, Y.: Correctness of Model Synchronization Based on Triple Graph Grammars. In: Whittle, J., Clark, T., Kühne, T. (eds.) MODELS 2011. LNCS, vol. 6981, pp. 668–682. Springer, Heidelberg (2011)
8. Hermann, F., Ehrig, H., Orejas, F., Golas, U.: Formal analysis of functional behaviour for model transformations based on triple graph grammars. In: Ehrig, H., Rensink, A., Rozenberg, G., Schürr, A. (eds.) ICGT 2010. LNCS, vol. 6372, pp. 155–170. Springer, Heidelberg (2010)
9. Hofmann, M., Pierce, B.C., Wagner, D.: Symmetric lenses. In: POPL 2011, pp. 371–384. ACM (2011)
10. Lauder, M., Anjorin, A., Varró, G., Schürr, A.: Efficient model synchronization with precedence triple graph grammars. In: Ehrig, H., Engels, G., Kreowski, H.-J., Rozenberg, G. (eds.) ICGT 2012. LNCS, vol. 7562, pp. 401–415. Springer, Heidelberg (2012)
11. Schürr, A.: Specification of graph translators with triple graph grammars. In: Mayr, E.W., Schmidt, G., Tinhofer, G. (eds.) Graph-Theoretic Concepts in Computer Science. LNCS, vol. 903, pp. 151–163. Springer, Heidelberg (1995)
12. Schürr, A., Klar, F.: 15 years of triple graph grammars. In: Ehrig, H., Heckel, R., Rozenberg, G., Taentzer, G. (eds.) ICGT 2008. LNCS, vol. 5214, pp. 411–425. Springer, Heidelberg (2008)
13. Stevens, P.: Towards an Algebraic Theory of Bidirectional Transformations. In: Ehrig, H., Heckel, R., Rozenberg, G., Taentzer, G. (eds.) ICGT 2008. LNCS, vol. 5214, pp. 1–17. Springer, Heidelberg (2008)
14. Terwilliger, J.F., Cleve, A., Curino, C.A.: How Clean Is Your Sandbox? - Towards a Unified Theoretical Framework for Incremental Bidirectional Transformations. In: Hu, Z., de Lara, J. (eds.) ICMT 2012. LNCS, vol. 7307, pp. 1–23. Springer, Heidelberg (2012)

Towards a Language for Graph-Based Model Transformation Design Patterns

Hüseyin Ergin and Eugene Syriani

University of Alabama, USA
hergin@crimson.ua.edu, esyriani@cs.ua.edu

Abstract. In model-driven engineering, most problems are solved using model transformation. However, the development of a model transformation for a specific problem is still a hard task. The main reason for that is the lack of a development process where transformations must be designed before implemented. As in object-oriented design, we believe that "good design" of model transformation can benefit tremendously from model transformation design patterns. Hence, in this paper, we present DelTa, a language for expressing design patterns for model transformations. DelTa is more abstract than and independent from any existing model transformation language, yet it is expressive enough to define design patterns as guidelines transformation developers can follow. To validate the language, we have redefined four known model transformation design patterns in DelTa and demonstrated how such abstract transformation guidelines can be implemented in five different model transformation languages.

1 Introduction

Model-driven engineering heavily relies on model transformation. However, although expressed at a level of abstraction closer to the problem domain than code, the development of a model transformation for a specific problem is still a hard, tedious and error-prone task. As witnessed in [1], one reason for these difficulties is the lack of a development process where the transformation must first be designed and then implemented, as practiced in software engineering. One of the most essential contribution to software design was the GoF catalog of object-oriented design patterns [2]. Similarly, we believe that the design of model transformations can tremendously benefit from model transformation design patterns. Although very few design patterns have been proposed in the past ([3,4,5,6,7]), they were each expressed in a specific model transformation language (MTL) and hence hardly re-usable in any other.

As stated in [8], a design pattern language must be independent from any MTL in which patterns are implemented. Furthermore, it must be fit to define *patterns* rather than *transformations*. For example, GoF design patterns are described in UML class diagram which is independent from the object-oriented programming language used for the implementation of software. A design pattern language must also be understandable and implementable by a transformation developer. Additionally, it must allow one to verify if a transformation correctly implements a pattern. To satisfy the language independence and implementability requirements, this paper proposes DelTa, a domain-specific language to describe design patterns for model transformations. Furthermore,

D. Di Ruscio and D. Varró (Eds.): ICMT 2014, LNCS 8568, pp. 91–105, 2014.
© Springer International Publishing Switzerland 2014

DelTa is expressive enough to define design patterns as guidelines transformation developers can follow. Note that DelTa currently focuses on graph-based model transformation only.

In Section 2, we present the syntax and informal semantics of DelTa. To validate the language in Section 3, we redefine four known model transformation design patterns using DelTa and demonstrate how design patterns expressed in DelTa can be implemented in existing graph-based MTLs. In Section 4, we discuss related work. We finally discuss limitations of our approach and conclude in Section 5.

2   Design Pattern Language for Graph-Based Model Transformation

DelTa is a neutral language, independent from any MTL. It is designed to define design patterns for model transformations, hence it is not a language to define model transformations. We could have used an existing MTL as a notation for DelTa, however our need is a notation that expresses how elements within a rule are related and how rules are related with each other. In this respect, DelTa offers some concepts borrowed from any MTL, abstracts away concepts specific to a particular MTL, and adds concepts to more easily describe design *patterns*. This is analogous to how Gamma *et al.* [2] used UML class, sequence and state diagrams to define design patterns for object-oriented languages. In the following, we describe the abstract syntax, concrete syntax, and informal semantics of DelTa.

2.1   Abstract Syntax

As depicted in Fig. 1, a model transformation design pattern (MTDP) consists of three kinds of components: transformation units (TU), pattern elements and transformation unit relations (TUR). This is consistent with the structure of common MTLs [9]. TUs represent the concept of rule in graph-based model transformations [10]. A MTDP rule consists of a constraint, an action, and optional negative constraints. These correspond to the usual left-hand side (LHS), right-hand side (RHS) and negative application conditions (NACs) in graph transformation. A constraint defines the pattern that must be present, a negative constraint defines the pattern that shall not be present, and the action defines the changes to be performed on the constraint (creation, deletion, or update). All these expressions operate on strongly typed variables.

There are three types for variables: a pattern metamodel, a metamodel element, or a trace. The pattern metamodel is a label to distinguish between elements from different metamodels, since a MTDP is independent from the source and target metamodels used by an actual model transformation. When implementing a MTPD, the pattern metamodel shall not be confused with the original metamodel of the source and/or target models of a transformation, but ideally be implemented by their ramified version [11]. The metamodel labels also indicate the number of metamodels involved in the transformation to be implemented. Metamodel elements are typically either entity-like and relation-like elements, this is why it is sufficient to only consider entities or relations in DelTa. An element may be assigned boolean flags to refer to the same variables across

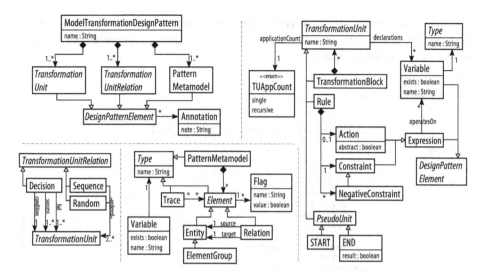

Fig. 1. DelTa Metamodel

rules. Undeclared flags are defaulted to `false`. This is similar to pivot passing in Mo-Tif [12] and GReAT [13], and parameter passing in Viatra2 [14]. When implementing a MTDP, flags may require to extend the original or ramified metamodels with additional attributes. An element group is an entity that represents a collection of entities and relations implicitly, when fixing the number of elements is too restrictive. Traceability links are crucial in MTLs but, depending on the language, they are either created implicitly or explicitly by a rule. In DelTa, we opted for the latter, which is more general, in order to require the developer to take into account traceability links in the implementation.

As surveyed in [15], different MTLs have different flavors of TUs. For example, in MoTif, an ARule applies a rule once, an FRule applies a rule on all matches found, and an SRule applies a rule recursively as long as there are matches. Another example is in Henshin [16] where rules with multi-node elements are applied on all matches found. Nevertheless, all MTLs offer at least a TU to apply a rule once or recursively as long as possible which are two TU application counts in DelTa. All other flavors of TUs can be expressed in TURs as demonstrated in [15]. For reuse purposes, rules in DelTa can be grouped into transformation blocks, similarly to a Block in GReAT.

As surveyed in [12,17], in any MTL, rules are subject to a scheduling policy, whether it is implicit or explicit. For example, AGG [18] uses layers, MoTif and VMTS [19] use a control flow language, and GReAT defines causality relations between rules. As shown in [20], it is sufficient to have mechanisms for sequencing, branching, and looping in order to support any scheduling offered by a MTL. This is covered by the three TURs of DelTa: Sequence, Random, and Decision that are explained in Section 2.3. The former two act on at least two TUs and the latter has three parts; condition, success and fail TUs. PseudoUnits mark the beginning and the end of the scheduling part of a design pattern.

Finally, annotations can be placed on any design pattern element in order to give more insight on the particular design pattern element. This is especially used for element groups and abstract actions.

2.2 Concrete Syntax

Listing 1.1. EBNF Grammar of DelTa in XText

```
 1  MTDP:       'mtdp' NAME
 2              'metamodels:' NAME (',' NAME)* ANNOTATION?
 3              (('tblock' NAME '*'? ANNOTATION?)?
 4                  'rule' NAME '*'? ANNOTATION?
 5                      ElementGroup?
 6                      Entity?
 7                      Relation?
 8                      Trace?
 9                      Constraint
10                      NegativeConstraint*
11                      Action)+
12                  TURelation+ ;
13
14  ElementGroup: 'ElementGroup' ELEMENTNAME (',' ELEMENTNAME)* ;
15  Entity: 'Entity' ELEMENTNAME (',' ELEMENTNAME)* ;
16  Relation: 'Relation' NAME '(' ELEMENTNAME ',' ELEMENTNAME ')'
17              (',' NAME '(' ELEMENTNAME ',' ELEMENTNAME ')')* ;
18  Trace: 'Trace' NAME '(' ELEMENTNAME (',' ELEMENTNAME)+ ')'
19              (',' NAME '(' ELEMENTNAME (',' ELEMENTNAME)+ ')')* ;
20  Constraint: 'constraint:' '~'? (ELEMENTNAME|NAME)
21              (',' '~'? (ELEMENTNAME|NAME))* ANNOTATION? ;
22  NegativeConstraint: 'negative constraint:' (ELEMENTNAME|NAME)
23              (',' (ELEMENTNAME|NAME))* ANNOTATION? ;
24  Action: ('abstract action:' | 'action:' ('~'? (ELEMENTNAME|NAME)
25              (',' '~'? (ELEMENTNAME|NAME))* ) ) ANNOTATION? ;
26  TURelation: (TURTYPE ('START' | (NAME ('[' NAME '=' ('true' | 'false')']')?) )
27              (',' ('END' | NAME) ('[' NAME '=' ('true' | 'false')']')?) + )
28              | Decision;
29  Decision: NAME '?' DecisionBlock ':' DecisionBlock;
30  DecisionBlock: ('END' | NAME) ('[' ('END' | NAME) '=' ('true' | 'false')']') ?
31              (',' ('END' | NAME) ('[' ('END' | NAME) '=' ('true' | 'false')']') ? )* ;
32  terminal NAME: ('a'..'z'|'A'..'Z') ('a'..'z'|'A'..'Z'|'0'..'9')* ;
33  terminal ELEMENTNAME: NAME '.' NAME ('[' NAME '=' ('true'|'false')
34              (',' NAME '=' ('true'|'false'))* ']')? ;
35  terminal ANNOTATION: '#' (!'#')* '#' ;
36  terminal TURTYPE: ('Sequence' | 'Random') ':' ;
```

We opted for a textual concrete syntax for DelTa. Listing 1.1 shows the EBNF grammar implemented in Xtext. The structure of a DelTa design pattern is as follows. A new design pattern is declared using the *mtdp* keyword. This is followed by a list of metamodel names. The rules are defined thereafter. Rules can be contained inside transformation blocks represented by the *tblock* keyword. The '*' next to the name of the rule indicates that the rule is recursive; the application count is single by default. A rule always starts with the declaration of all the variables it will use in its constraints and actions. Then, the *constraint* pattern is constructed by enumerating the variables that constitute its elements. Elements can be prefixed with '~' to indicate their nonexistence. Flags can be defined on elements using the square bracket notation. Optional negative constraints can be constructed, followed by an action. An abstract action may not enumerate elements. The final component of a MTDP is the mandatory TUR definitions. A TUR is defined by its type and followed by a list of rule or transformation block names. As an exception, decision TUR is a single line conditional that creates a branch according to the success or fail of the condition rule. Annotations are enclosed within '#'. Listings 1.2– 1.5 show concrete examples of MTDPs using this notation.

2.3 Informal Semantics

The semantics of MTDP rules is borrowed from graph transformation rules [10], but adapted for patterns. Informally, a MTDP rule is applicable if its constraint can be matched and no negative constraints can. If it is applicable, then the action must be performed. Conceptually, we can represent this by: $constraint \land \neg neg1 \land \neg neg2 \land \dots \to action$. The presence of a negated variable (*i.e.*, with `exists=false`) in a constraint means that its corresponding element shall not be found. Since constraints are conjunctive, negated variables are also combined in a conjunctive way. Disjunctions can be expressed with multiple negative constraints. Actions follow the exact same semantics as the "modify" rules in GrGen.NET [21]. Elements present in the action must be created or have their flags updated. Negated variables in an action indicate the deletion of the corresponding element. Only abstract actions are empty, giving the freedom to the actual implementation of the rule to perform a specific action. Flags are not attributes but label some elements to be reused across rules.

MTDP rules are guidelines to the transformation developer and are not meant to be executed. On one hand, the constraint (together with negative constraints) of a rule should be interpreted as *maximal*: *i.e.*, a MT rule shall find at most as many matches as the MTDP rule it implements. On the other hand, the action of a rule should be interpreted as *minimal*: *i.e.*, a MT rule shall perform at least the modifications of the MTDP rule it implements. This means that more elements in the LHS or additional NACs may be present in the MT rule and that it may perform more CRUD operations. Furthermore, additional rules may be needed when implementing a MTDP for a specific application. Note that the absence of an action in a rule indicates that the rule is side-effect free, meaning that it cannot perform any modifications.

The scheduling of the TUs of a MTDP (or contained inside a transformation block) must always begin with START and end with END. TUs can be scheduled in four ways. The Sequence relation defines a sequencing relation between two or more TUs regardless of their applicability. For example `Sequence:A, B` means that A should be applied first and then B can be applied. The Random relation defines the non-deterministic choice to apply one TU out of a set of TUs. For example `Random:A, B` means that A or B should be applied, but not both. The Decision relation defines a conditional branching and applies the TUs in the success or fail branches according to the application of the rule in the condition. For example `A?B:C` means that if A is applicable then B should be applied after, otherwise C should be applied. Note that the latter TUR can be used to define loop structures. For example, `A?A:A` is equivalent to defining A as recursive, *i.e.*, `A*`. The notion of applicability of a transformation block is determined by the result of its END TU. For example, consider a transformation block T and a rule R and P. The scheduling `T?R:P` means that if `END[result=true]` is reached in T, then R will be applied.

3   Model Transformation Design Patterns

In this section, we illustrate how to use DelTa pragmatically by redefining four existing design patterns for MT. Inspired by the GoF catalog templates, we describe a MTDP using the following characteristics: *motivation* describes the need for and usefulness of the pattern, *applicability* outlines typical situations when the pattern can be applied, *structure* defines the pattern in DelTa and explains the pattern, *examples* illustrates practical cases where the patterns can be used, *implementation* provides a concrete implementation of the pattern in a MTL, and *variations* discusses some common variants of the pattern. For the example characteristic, we use a subset the UML class diagram metamodel with the concepts of class, attributes, and superclasses. For the implementation characteristic, we have implemented all design patterns in five languages: MoTif, AGG, Henshin, Viatra2, GrGen.NET. Although we only show one implementation for each in this paper, the complete implementations can be found in [22]. This is how we validated the expressiveness, usability, and implementability of patterns defined in DelTa.

3.1   Entity Relation Mapping

- **Motivation:** Entity relation mapping (ER mapping) is one of the most commonly used transformation pattern in exogenous transformations encoding a mapping between two languages. It creates the elements in a language corresponding to elements from another language and establishes traceability links between the elements of source and target languages. This pattern was originally proposed in [6] and later refined in [23].
- **Applicability:** The ER mapping is applicable when we want to translate elements from one metamodel into elements from another metamodel.
- **Structure:** The structure is depicted in Listing 1.2. The pattern refers to two metamodels labeled src and trgt, corresponding to the source and target languages. It consists of a MTDP rule for mapping entities first and another for mapping relations. The entityMapping rule states that if an entity e from src is found, then an entity f must be created in trgt as well as a trace t1 between them, if t1 and f do not exist yet. The relationMapping rule states that if there is a relation r1 between e and f in src and there is a trace t1 between e and g, and a trace t2 between f and h, then create a relation r2 between g and h if it does not exist yet. Both rules should be applied recursively.

Listing 1.2. One-to-one Entity Relationship Mapping MTDP

```
mtdp OneToOneERMapping
    metamodels: src, trgt
    rule entityMapping*
        Entity src.e, trgt.f
        Trace t1(src.e, trgt.f)
        constraint: src.e, ~trgt.f, ~t1
        action: trgt.f, t1
    rule relationMapping*
        Entity src.e, src.f, trgt.g, trgt.h
        Relation r1(src.e, src.f), r2(trgt.g, trgt.h)
        Trace t1(src.e, trgt.g), t2(src.f, trgt.h)
        constraint: src.e, src.f, trgt.g, trgt.h, r1, t1, t2, ~r2
        action: r2
    Sequence: START, entityMapping, relationMapping, END
```

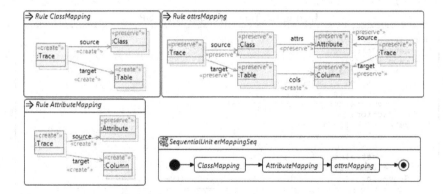

Fig. 2. Rules of ER Mapping in Henshin

– **Examples:** A typical example of ER mapping is in the transformation from class diagram to relational database diagrams, where, for example, a class is transformed to a table, an attribute to a column, and the relation between class and attribute to a relation between table and column.
– **Implementation:** We show the implementation of ER mapping in Henshin in Fig. 2. The pattern states to apply the rules for entities before those for relations. Henshin provides a sequence structure with SequentialUnit. Henshin uses a compact notation for rules together with stereotypes on pattern elements. «preserve» is used for the elements found in the constraint of the MTDP rule and «create» is used to create elements found in the action of the MTDP rule. Here there are two rules corresponding to entityMapping: one for mapping classes to tables and one for mapping attributes to columns. In Henshin, traceability links must be modeled explicitly as a separate class connecting the source and target elements. We did not need to use NACs because Henshin provides a multi-node option that already prevents applying a rule more than once on the same match.
– **Variations:** Sometimes the entities in specific metamodels cannot be mapped one-to-one. It is possible to define one-to-many or many-to-many ER mappings pattern using element groups instead of entities (see [22]). Also, some implementations may require the creation of a trace between the two relations in the relationMapping rule.

3.2 Transitive Closure

– **Motivation:** Transitive closure is a pattern typically used for analyzing reachability related problems with an inplace transformation. It was proposed as a pattern in [3] and in [24]. It generates the intermediate paths between nodes that are not necessarily directly connected via traceability links.
– **Applicability:** The transitive closure pattern is applicable when the metamodels in the domain have a structure that can be considered as a directed tree.
– **Structure:**

Listing 1.3. Transitive Closure MTDP

```
mtdp TransitiveClosure
    metamodels: mm
    rule immediateRelation*
        Entity mm.e, mm.f
        Relation r1(mm.e, mm.f)
        Trace t1(mm.e, mm.f)
        constraint: mm.e, mm.f, r1, ~t1
        action: t1
    rule recursiveRelation*
        Entity mm.a, mm.b, mm.c
        Trace t1(mm.a, mm.b), t2(mm.b, mm.c), t3(mm.a, mm.c)
        constraint: mm.a, mm.b, mm.c, t1, t2, ~t3
        action: t3
    Sequence: START, immediateRelation, recursiveRelation, END
```

The structure is depicted in Listing 1.3. The pattern operates on single metamodel. First, the immediateRelation rule creates a trace element between entities connected with a relation. It is applied recursively to cover all relations. Then, the recursiveRelation rule creates trace elements between the node indirectly connected. That is if entities a-b and b-c are connected with a trace, then a and c will also connected with a trace. It is also applied recursively to cover all nodes exhaustively.

- **Examples:** The transitive closure pattern can be used to find the lowest common ancestor between two nodes in a directed tree, such as finding all superclasses of a class in UML class diagram.
- **Implementation:** We have implemented the transitive closure in AGG. Fig. 3 depicts the corresponding rules. AGG rules consist of the traditional LHS, RHS, and NACs. The LHS and NACs represent the constraint of the MTDP rule and the RHS encodes the action. The immediateSuperclass rule creates a traceability link between a class and its superclass. The NAC prevents this traceability link from being created again. The recursiveSuperclass rule creates the remaining traceability links between a class and higher level superclasses. AGG lets the user assign layer numbers to each rule and starts to execute from layer zero until all layers are complete. Completion criteria for a layer is executing all possible rules in that layer until none

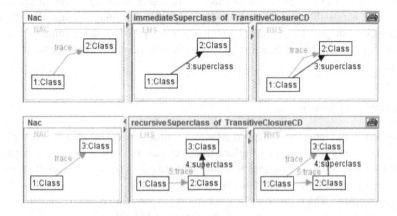

Fig. 3. Transitive Closure rules in AGG

are applicable anymore. Therefore, we set the layer of immediateSuperclass to 0 and recursiveSuperclass to 1 as the design pattern structure stated these rules to be applied in a sequence.

- **Variations:** In some cases, a recursive selfRelation rule may be applied first, for example when computing the least common ancestor class of two classes, as in [5].

3.3   Visitor

- **Motivation:** The visitor pattern traverses all the nodes in a graph and processes each entity individually in a breadth-first fashion. This pattern is similar to the "leaf collector pattern" in [3] that is restricted to collecting the leaf nodes in a tree.
- **Applicability:** The visitor pattern can be applied to problems that consist of or can be mapped to any kind of graph structure where all nodes need to be processed individually.
- **Structure:**

Listing 1.4. Visitor MTDP

```
mtdp Visitor
    metamodels: mm
    rule markInitEntity
        Entity mm.e
        constraint: mm.e # e is a predetermined entity #
        action: mm.e[marked=true]
    rule visitEntity*
        Entity mm.e
        constraint: mm.e[marked=true,processed=false]
        action: mm.e[processed=true] # Process current entities #
    rule markNextEntity*
        Entity mm.e, mm.f
        Relation r1(mm.e, mm.f)
        constraint: mm.e[processed=true], mm.f[marked=false], r1
        action: mm.f[marked=true]
    Sequence: START, markInitEntity, visitEntity, markNextEntity
    markNextEntity ? visitEntity : END
```

As depicted in Listing 1.4, the visitor pattern makes use of flags. The markInitEntity rule flags a predetermined initial entity as "marked". Note that in actual implementation, this rule maybe more complex. This rule is applied first and once. The next rule to be applied is the visitEntity rule. It visits the marked but unprocessed nodes by changing their processed flags to true. The actual processing of the node is left at the discretion of the implementation. Then, the markNextEntity rule marks the nodes that are adjacent to the processed nodes. Marking and processing are split into two steps to reflect the breadth-first traversal. The markNextEntity rule then initiates the loop to visit the remaining nodes. Visiting ends when markNextEntity is not applicable, *i.e.,* when all nodes are marked and have been processed.

- **Examples:** The visitor pattern helps to compute the depth level of each class in a class inheritance hierarchy, meaning its distance from the base class.
- **Implementation:** We have implemented visitor in GrGen.NET as depicted in Fig. 4. This MTL provides a textual syntax for both rules and scheduling mechanisms. In a rule, the constraint is defined by declaring the elements of the pattern and conditions on attributes are checked with an if statement. Actions are written in

```
rule markBaseClass {          rule visitSubclass {          rule markSubclass {
    e:Class;                      d:Class;                      e:Class;
    negative {                    e:Class;                      f:Class;
        d:Class;                  d-:subclass->e;               e-:subclass->f;
        d-:subclass->e;           if {                          if {
    }                                 e.marked==true;               e.processed==true;
    modify {                          e.processed==false;           f.marked==false;
        eval {                    }                             }
            e.marked=true;        modify {                      modify {
            e.processed=true;         eval {                        eval {
        }                                 e.processed=true;             f.marked=true;
    }                                     e.depth=d.depth+1;        }
}                                     }                         }
                                  }                         }
                              }
```

```
exec markBaseClass
exec ([visitSubclass] ;> [markSubclass])*
```

Fig. 4. Visitor rules and scheduling in GrGen.NET

a modify or replace statement for new node creation and eval statements are used for attribute manipulation. The markBaseClass rule selects a class with no super-class as the initial element to visit. Since this class already has a depth level of 0, we flag it as processed to prevent the visitSubclass rule from increasing its depth. This is a clear example of the minimality of a MTDP rule, where the implementation extends the rule according to the application. The visitSubclass rule processes the marked elements. Here, processing consists of increasing the depth of the sub-class by one more than the depth of the superclass. The markSubclass rule marks subclasses of already marked classes. The scheduling of these GrGen.NET rules is depicted in the bottom of Fig. 4. As stated in the design pattern structure, mark-BaseClass is executed only once. visitSubclass and markSubclass are sequenced with the ;> symbol. The * indicates to execute this sequence as long as markSub-class rule succeeds. At the end, all classes should have their correct depth level set and all marked as processed. Note that in this implementation, visitSubclass will not be applied in the first iteration of the loop.

- **Variations:** It is possible to vary the traversal order, for example a depth-first strategy may be implemented. It is also possible to visit relations instead of entities. Another variation is to only have one recursive rule that processes all entities if the order in which they processed is irrelevant.

3.4 Fixed Point Iteration

- **Motivation:** Fixed point iteration is a pattern for representing a "do-until" loop structure. It solves the problem by modifying the input model iteratively until a condition is satisfied. We previously identified this pattern in [5]. Asztalos *et al.* [25] also identified a similar structure named traverser model transformation analysis pattern.
- **Applicability:** This pattern is applicable when the problem can be solved itera-tively until a fixed point is reached. Each iteration must perform the same modi-

fication on the model, possibly at different locations: either adding new elements, removing elements, or modifying attributes.

− **Structure:**

Listing 1.5. Fixed Point Iteration MTDP

```
mtdp FixedPointIteration
    metamodels: mm
    rule initiate
        ElementGroup mm.eg1
        constraint: mm.eg1
        action: mm.eg1[selected=true] # Initiate the element group #
    rule checkFixedPoint
        ElementGroup mm.eg1
        constraint: mm.eg1
        abstract action: # Process the element group #
    rule iterate
        ElementGroup mm.eg1
        constraint: mm.eg1[selected=true]
        abstract action: # Advance the initiated group #
    Sequence: START, initiate, checkFixedPoint
    checkFixedPoint ? END[result=true] : iterate
    iterate ? checkFixedPoint : END[result=false]
```

The structure is depicted in Listing 1.5. The fixed point iteration consists of rules that have abstract actions because processing at each iteration entirely depends on the application. Nevertheless, it enforces the following scheduling. The pattern starts by selecting a predetermined group of elements in the initiate rule and checks if the model has reached a fixed point (the condition is encoded in the constraint of the checkFixedPoint rule). If it has, the checkFixedPoint rule may perform some action, *e.g.,* marking the elements that satisfied the condition. Otherwise, the iterate rule modifies the current model and the fixed point is checked again.

− **Examples:** In [5], we showed how to solve three problems with this pattern: computing the lowest common ancestor (LCA) of two nodes in a directed tree, which adds more elements to the input model; finding the equivalent resistance in an electrical circuit, which removes elements from the input model; and finding the shortest path using Dijkstra's algorithm, which only modifies attributes.

− **Implementation:** Fig. 5 shows the implementation of the LCA from [5] in MoTif using the fixed point iteration pattern. The initiate rule is extended to create traceability links on the input nodes themselves with the LinkToSelf rules and with their parents with the LinkToParent rules. The GetLCA rule implements the check-FixedPoint rule and tries to find the LCA of the two nodes in the resulting model following traceability links. This rule does not have a RHS but it sets a pivot to the result for further processing. The LinkToAncestor rules implement the iterate rule by connecting the input nodes to their ancestors. The MoTif control structure reflects exactly the same scheduling of Listing 1.5.

− **Variations:** In some cases, the initiate rule can be omitted when, for instance, the iterate rule deletes selected elements such as in the computation of the equivalent resistance of an electrical circuit [5].

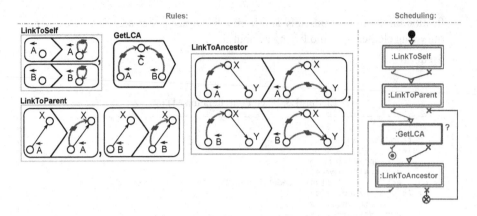

Fig. 5. Rules and Scheduling in MoTif

4   Related Work

The first work that proposed design patterns for model transformation was by Agrawal *et al.* [3]. They defined the *transitive closure* pattern which is similar to what we showed in Section 3.2, except that we create traceability links whereas they reuse the same association type from the input metamodel. The *leaf collector* pattern traverses a hierarchical tree to find and process all leaves. This can be considered as an application of the visitor pattern in Section 3.3 where the visitEntity rule is only applied on leaves. The *proxy generator* idiom is not a general design pattern, since that it is specific to languages modeling distributed systems where remote interactions to the system need to be abstracted and optimized.

Iacob *et al.* [6] defined five other design patterns for outplace transformations. Similar to the ER mapping pattern in Section 3.1, the *mapping* pattern dictates to first map entities and then relations. Since it is described using QVT-R, we consider it as an implementation of our ER mapping pattern. The *refinement* pattern proposes to transform an edge into a node with two edges in the context of a refinement so that the target model contains more detail. The *node abstraction* pattern abstracts a specific type of node from the target model while preserving the original relations. The *flattening* pattern removes the composition hierarchy of a model along by replacing the containment relations. We plan to generalize these three patterns and define them in DelTa. The *duality* pattern is not a general design pattern, since it is specific to languages for data control flow modeling by changing by converting edges to nodes and vice versa.

Bézivin *et al.* [7] mined ATL transformations and ended up with two design patterns. The *transformation parameters* pattern suggests to model explicitly auxiliary variables needed by the transformation in an additional input metamodel, instead of hard-coding them in ATL helpers. The *multiple matching* pattern shows how to match multiple elements in the from part of an ATL rule. Newer versions of ATL already support this feature and therefore this pattern is obsolete now.

The first issue with these three previous works is that all the design patterns are defined using GReAT, QVT-R, and ATL respectively. Therefore, they should not be considered as design patterns for model transformation, but as implementations of design patterns in a specific MTL. The second issue is that they are all defined as model transformations, rather than patterns, and use specific input and output metamodels. Therefore, it is not clear how to reuse these patterns for different application domains. On the contrary, DelTa is independent from any MTL and defines the patterns using abstracted elements independent from the input and output metamodels.

Lano *et al.* [23] proposed other useful patterns using UML class diagrams and OCL constraints (first-order logic) to specify model transformations. Each transformation is described with a set of *assumptions* that represent the precondition of a rule, *constraints* that represent the postcondition of a rule, *ensures* for additional constraints, and *invariants*. The design patterns are for exogenous transformations only. The *conjunctive-implicative form* pattern dictates to separate the creation target entities that are at different hierarchical levels into different phases. For example, the *map objects before links* pattern, essentially our ER mapping pattern, is an instance of this generic pattern. Another instance of this pattern is the *recurrent constraints* pattern where the creation of a target entity may require a fixed point computation. The fixed point iteration pattern in Section 3.4 can be used in one of the creation phases here. Two other instances of the conjunctive-implicative form pattern are the *entity splitting* and *entity merging* patterns that essentially correspond to the one-to-many and many-to-one variants of the ER mapping pattern respectively. The *auxiliary metamodel* pattern suggests to use an auxiliary metamodel when the mapping from elements of one language to another is too complex.

In Lano *et al.*'s approach, the choice of the design pattern language hinders the understandability of the patterns. This also makes them hard to implement in MTLs other than UML-RSDS. Additionally, they defined implementation patterns. In contrast with design patterns, they are guidelines to implement the assumptions and constraints of transformation specifications in a MTL. The description is done on an abstract implementation language that supports sequencing, branching, looping and operation calls, which is similar to what the TURs of DelTa offer.

Guerra *et al.* [1] proposed a collection of languages to engineer model transformations and, in particular, for the design phase. Rule diagrams (RD) are used to describe the structures of the rules and what they do in the low level implementation phase. Like DelTa, RD is defined at a level of abstraction that is independent from existing MTLs. But its purpose is to generate a transformation rather than to define design patterns. Therefore, there are some similarities and differences between RD and DelTa. In RD, rules focus on mappings rather than constraints and actions. Hence, they specify designs for both unidirectional and bidirectional rules. The execution flow of RD supports sequencing rules, branching in alternative paths based on a constraint which is similar to the decision TUR in DelTa, or non-deterministically choosing to apply one rule which is similar to the random TUR. They also allow rules to explicitly invoke the application of other rules. RD is inspired from QVT-R and ETL and is therefore more easily implementable in these language, whereas DelTa currently focuses on graph-based MTLs.

Levendovszky *et al.* [24] proposed domain-specific design patterns for model transformation as well as other DSLs. In their approach, they defined design patterns with a specific MTL, VMTS, where rules support metamodel-based pattern matching. They proposed two design patterns: the *helper constructs in rewriting rules* pattern explicitly produces traceability links, and the *optimized transitive closure* pattern, which is similar to the transitive closure pattern in Section 3.2.

5 Conclusion

In this paper, we proposed DelTa as candidate for a design pattern language for model transformations. DelTa is a language for describing patterns, rather than transformations. It is independent from any MTL yet directly implementable in most graph-based MTLs. To validate the language, we described four known design patterns for model transformation and implemented them in five different languages (the complete implementations can be found in [22]).

As stated in Section 1, a design pattern language must also be understandable and suited to verify correct implementations. For the former, we plan to empirically evaluate DelTa by running user studies. The verifiability requirement remains to be investigated. A formal specification language such as in [23] can then be used, but at the price of the understandability and ease of implementability. Furthermore, identifying additional design patterns will help us evolve the DelTa language and further validate its expressiveness.

When implementing the design patterns, we realized that some patterns are easier to implement in some languages than in others due the constructs they offer for transformation units and for scheduling. In particular, when implementing a pattern that involves more complex scheduling (such as the fixed point iteration) in MTLs with very limited scheduling policies (such as AGG), several tricks need to be used, such as modifying the metamodel or making use of temporary elements or attributes. The lack of a standard paradigm for model transformations is the main source of this difficulty that the model transformation community has to agree on. We plan to extend DelTa to cover non-graph-based MTLs, such as QVT-OM and ATL, and possibly bi-directional MTLs, such as QVT-R and triple graph grammars.

References

1. Guerra, E., de Lara, J., Kolovos, D., Paige, R., dos Santos, O.: Engineering model transformations with transML. Software and Systems Modeling 12, 555–577 (2013)
2. Gamma, E., Helm, R., Johnson, R., Vlissides, J.: Design Patterns: Elements of Reusable Object-oriented Software. Addison-Wesley, Boston (1995)
3. Agrawal, A.: Reusable Idioms and Patterns in Graph Transformation Languages. In: International Workshop on Graph-Based Tools. ENTCS, vol. 127, pp. 181–192. Elsevier (2005)
4. Bézivin, J., Rumpe, B., Tratt, L.: Model Transformation in Practice Workshop Announcement (2005)
5. Ergin, H., Syriani, E.: Identification and Application of a Model Transformation Design Pattern. In: ACM Southeast Conference, ACMSE 2013, Savannah GA. ACM (2013)
6. Iacob, M.E., Steen, M.W.A., Heerink, L.: Reusable Model Transformation Patterns. In: EDOC Workshops, pp. 1–10. IEEE Computer Society (September 2008)
7. Bézivin, J., Jouault, F., Paliès, J.: Towards model transformation design patterns. In: Proceedings of the First European Workshop on Model Transformations, EWMT 2005 (2005)

8. Syriani, E., Gray, J.: Challenges for Addressing Quality Factors in Model Transformation. In: IEEE Software Testing, Verification and Validation, ICST 2012, pp. 929–937 (April 2012)
9. Syriani, E., Gray, J., Vangheluwe, H.: Modeling a Model Transformation Language. In: Domain Engineering: Product Lines, Conceptual Models, and Languages. Springer (2012)
10. Ehrig, H., Ehrig, K., Prange, U., Taentzer, G.: Fundamentals of Algebraic Graph Transformation. EATCS. Springer (2006)
11. Kühne, T., Mezei, G., Syriani, E., Vangheluwe, H., Wimmer, M.: Explicit Transformation Modeling. In: Ghosh, S. (ed.) MODELS 2009. LNCS, vol. 6002, pp. 240–255. Springer, Heidelberg (2010)
12. Syriani, E., Vangheluwe, H.: A Modular Timed Model Transformation Language. Journal on Software and Systems Modeling 12(2), 387–414 (2011)
13. Agrawal, A., Karsai, G., Shi, F.: Graph transformations on domain-specific models. Journal on Software and Systems Modeling (2003)
14. Varró, D., Balogh, A.: The model transformation language of the VIATRA2 framework. Science of Computer Programming 68(3), 214–234 (2007)
15. Syriani, E., Vangheluwe, H., LaShomb, B.: T-Core: A framework for custom-built model transformation engines. Software & Systems Modeling, 1–29 (2013)
16. Arendt, T., Biermann, E., Jurack, S., Krause, C., Taentzer, G.: Henshin: Advanced Concepts and Tools for In-Place EMF Model Transformations. In: Petriu, D.C., Rouquette, N., Haugen, Ø. (eds.) MODELS 2010, Part I. LNCS, vol. 6394, pp. 121–135. Springer, Heidelberg (2010)
17. Czarnecki, K., Helsen, S.: Feature-Based Survey of Model Transformation Approaches. IBM Systems Journal 45(3), 621–645 (2006)
18. Taentzer, G.: AGG: A graph transformation environment for modeling and validation of software. In: Pfaltz, J.L., Nagl, M., Böhlen, B. (eds.) AGTIVE 2003. LNCS, vol. 3062, pp. 446–453. Springer, Heidelberg (2004)
19. Lengyel, L., Levendovszky, T., Mezei, G., Charaf, H.: Model Transformation with a Visual Control Flow Language. International Journal of Computer Science 1(1), 45–53 (2006)
20. Syriani, E., Vangheluwe, H.: De-/Re-constructing Model Transformation Languages. EASST 29 (March 2010)
21. Geiß, R., Kroll, M.: GrGen. net: A fast, expressive, and general purpose graph rewrite tool. In: Schürr, A., Nagl, M., Zündorf, A. (eds.) AGTIVE 2007. LNCS, vol. 5088, pp. 568–569. Springer, Heidelberg (2008)
22. Ergin, H., Syriani, E.: Implementations of Model Transformation Design Patterns Expressed in DelTa. SERG-2014-01, University of Alabama, Department of Computer Science (February 2014), http://software.eng.ua.edu/reports/SERG-2014-01.pdf
23. Lano, K., Rahimi, S.K.: Constraint-based specification of model transformations. Journal of Systems and Software 86(2), 412–436 (2013)
24. Levendovszky, T., Lengyel, L., Mészáros, T.: Supporting domain-specific model patterns with metamodeling. Software & Systems Modeling 8(4), 501–520 (2009)
25. Asztalos, M., Madari, I., Lengyel, L.: Towards formal analysis of multi-paradigm model transformations. SIMULATION 86(7), 429–452 (2010)

Synchronization of Models of Rich Languages with Triple Graph Grammars: An Experience Report[*]

Dominique Blouin[1], Alain Plantec[2], Pierre Dissaux[3], Frank Singhoff[2], and Jean-Philippe Diguet[1]

[1] Lab-STICC, Université de Bretagne-Sud, Centre de recherche, BP 92116
56321 Lorient CEDEX, France
{dominique.blouin,jean-philippe.diguet}@univ-ubs.fr
[2] Lab-STICC, Université de Bretagne-Occidentale, 20 av. Le Gorgeu,
29238 Brest CEDEX, France
{alain.plantec,singhoff}@univ-brest.fr
[3] Ellidiss Technologies, 24 Quai de la Douane, 29200 Brest, France
pierre.dissaux@ellidiss.com

Abstract. We report our experience of using Triple Graph Grammars (TGG) to synchronize models of the rich and complex Architecture Analysis and Design Language (AADL), an aerospace standard of the Society of Automotive Engineers. A synchronization layer has been developed between the OSATE (Open Source AADL Tool Environment) textual editor and the Adele graphical editor in order to improve their integration. Adele has been designed to support editing AADL models in a way that does not necessarily follow the structure of the language, but is adapted to the way designers think. For this reason, it operates on a different meta-model than OSATE. As a result, changes on the graphical model must be propagated automatically to the textual model to ensure consistency of the models. Since Adele does not cover the complete AADL language, this must be done without re-instantiation of the objects to avoid losing the information not represented in the graphical part. The TGG language implemented in the MoTE tool has been used to synchronize the tools. Our results provide a validation of the TGG approach for synchronizing models of large meta-models, but also show that model synchronization remains a challenging task, since several improvements of the TGG language and its tool were required to succeed.

Keywords: Model Transformation, Model Synchronization, TGG, MoTE, AADL.

1 Introduction

Model-Driven Development (MDD) often requires the use of many models to cover the various aspects of the system being developed. It is often the case that designers

---

[*] This work has been supported by the US Army Research, Development and Engineering Command (REDCOM).

D. Di Ruscio and D. Varró (Eds.): ICMT 2014, LNCS 8568, pp. 106–121, 2014.

need to describe the same system with different modeling languages to benefit from the assets of each language. For example, an embedded system model of the Architecture Analysis and Design Language (AADL) [1] may need to be translated into Simulink [2] for functional validation of the system through simulation. Users often want to be able to modify both the AADL and Simulink models and have their changes automatically propagated to maintain consistency of the models. In general, the information content of each model is not the same. One of the models may contain information that is not reflected in the other model because it is irrelevant for the purpose of the model. For example, an AADL model may include power consumption related properties, which are essential for power analysis of the system, but totally useless for functional validation with Simulink. Conversely, a simulation model may include details regarding the simulation, which are not needed on the AADL side. Hence, it is essential to be able to maintain the consistency of the models without the loss of the information that is not shared by both models. This is called model synchronization [19], which is a particular type of model transformation, as it operates on parts of the models at a finer level of granularity.

The need for model synchronization is becoming more and more important for the AADL community, and for model-based engineering in general, since more and more heterogeneous models are used together. For example, batch model transformations have been implemented between AADL and SysML [3], and between AADL and MARTE [4]. Another example is the Adele graphical editor [5], which implements the graphical syntax of AADL and operates on a meta-model of its own. It is the subject of our case study.

Although the need for model synchronization is widely spread, only transformation tools based on Triple Graph Grammars (TGG) can currently perform such type of transformation. Hence, the purpose of this paper is to report on our experiment on applying TGGs on a large and rich language such as the AADL. Our experiment validates the TGG approach for model synchronization, despite the many shortcomings that were identified during the work. Our contributions are:

- A synchronization layer between two AADL editors using different meta-models to represent AADL specifications.
- The new concept of generic TGG rules allowing to drastically reduce the number of rules needed for transforming models of large meta-models, thus improving scalability.
- A method to reuse existing model objects during synchronization thus avoiding information loss.
- Other minor improvements related to the expressivity of the TGG language.

This paper is structured as follows. Section 2 presents our model synchronization case study. Section 3 justifies the selection of the MoTE tool for our experiment. Next, an overview of the implemented solution is presented in Section 4. Section 5 briefly describes the Adele-AADL TGG and our contributions to the TGG language and MoTE tool. Section 6 discusses the tests that were performed on the synchronization layer, and suggests other potential improvements. Section 7 introduces the related work and finally, Section 8 concludes the paper.

2   Case Study

2.1   AADL

AADL is a rich component-based architecture description language that allows the capture of many aspects of an embedded system. The goal is perform model analysis in order to detect design errors early in the life cycle. AADL supports the specification of systems as an assembly of software and hardware components divided into categories. Software categories are thread, thread group, data, process and subprogram. Hardware categories are processor, virtual processor, memory, device, bus and virtual bus. Hardware and software components classifiers can be declared in libraries or hierarchically organized in systems for reuse. AADL components interact through features (interaction points) and connections, which together model data or control flows between components.

One advantage of AADL compared to languages such as UML is that it has both a textual and a graphical syntax. Users can therefore use the syntax they are more comfortable with, or the syntax that is best suited for whatever has to be edited in the model. Unfortunately, there has never been any usable graphical editor developed for the language, and it is a major drawback for the adoption of AADL. Graphical editors are complex, and every attempt to develop a graphical editor for AADL resulted in partially implemented tools that were barely usable.

2.2   AADL Editors

For instance, this was the case of the Adele graphical editor [5]. It stores AADL specifications using a meta-model of its own, which facilitates the edition of models by providing a choice of two edition modes. For example, Adele models can be edited in a top-down intuitive approach that does not follow the structure of the AADL language. Textual AADL specifications are generated from the Adele models for being processed by other tools.

Among these other tools, the Open Source AADL Tool Environment (OSATE) [6] is the main textual editor for AADL. It also provides model analysis facilities. Both Adele and OSATE can be deployed in the Eclipse environment for their simultaneous use. Unfortunately, Adele was never developed to the point where all constructs of the AADL language were managed. Constructs such as modes, flows, prototypes etc. have never been implemented, and sooner or later, Adele users were forced to use OSATE for editing these constructs through textual syntax. The result is that regenerating the textual files from the graphical model was then destroying the unhandled constructs. This was a serious issue because users were soon or later required to synchronize the models by hand. Three options could be envisaged to solve this problem:

- Implement the language constructs which are missing in Adele.
- Rebuild an editor that operates directly on the OSATE meta-model.
- Build a synchronization layer between OSATE and Adele.

Because model synchronization is an important need for the AADL community, the third solution was chosen. It would also provide a first case study of model synchronization with the AADL. In addition, it would allow preserving the more intuitive edition modes specific to Adele, and hardly supported by editors working on the OSATE meta-model directly.

2.3   The OSATE Meta-model

The OSATE meta-model contains 260 classes and is strongly typed. This is well illustrated by the way rules for components decomposition in terms of subcomponents are encoded in the meta-model. For example, an AADL system can contain subcomponents of many categories such as buses, data, devices, memories, processes, etc, as represented by the subcomponent containment references of Fig. 1. For each category (e.g.: *processor*), the containing class declares a specific reference to contain the subcomponents (*ownedProcessorSubcomponent*), and a specific subcomponent class for the category (*ProcessorSubcomponent*). AADL features (component interaction points), which are contained in component types are handled in a similar manner. As it will be explained in Section 5, this structure of the OSATE meta-model revealed several scalability issues, which were so important that they required implementing several improvements of the TGGs to validate their use.

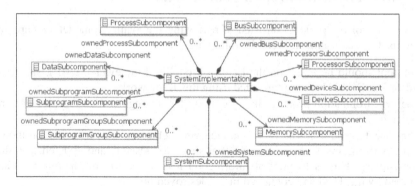

Fig. 1. A diagram of the AADL system implementation class showing distinct containment references and classes for every allowed subcomponent category

2.4   The Adele Meta-model

The Adele editor offers two modes to edit an AADL specification supported by two different types of diagrams. The declarative mode (package diagram) consists of declaring classifiers that can be instantiated later on to produce a system instance specification. Conversely, the instance mode (instance diagram) consists of creating a system instance specification, and to postpone the declaration of subcomponent classifiers to the time when they need to be reused for modeling other systems. In addition, a system diagram specification contains all subcomponents in a single tree.

To support these two edition modes, the Adele meta-model is used in two different ways. Package diagrams are edited according to the left part of Fig. 2, where the hierarchy ends at the subcomponent level, and subcomponents of a subcomponent are declared in the classifier of the subcomponent. Instance diagrams are edited according to the right hand side of the figure, where all subcomponents are contained in a single tree whose root is the parent component implementation.

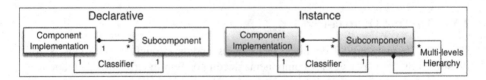

Fig. 2. The Adele meta-model and its uses for the declarative and instance edition modes

Compared to OSATE, the Adele meta-model is weakly typed and contains much fewer classes (48 compared to 260). For a given component category, the same class is used for representing component types, component implementations and subcomponents, where OSATE will declare three distinct classes (*ProcessorType*, *ProcessorImplementation* and *ProcessorSubcomponent*).

3   Model Synchronization Tool Selection

The first task of the project consisted of reviewing the available model synchronization tools. Our requirements were the following:

- The tool should be based on the Eclipse Modeling Framework (EMF), since both Adele and OSATE are implemented using this framework.
- The synchronization process should execute fast enough so that the user does not notice it.
- The objects should not be re-instantiated when changes are performed on the objects, with the instances being reused as much as possible and updated to restore consistency. This is to prevent information losses due to information not transformed by the TGG and contained in the destroyed object.

Several tools have been developed for model transformation. Well-known tools are ATL [9], Epsilon [10], Kermeta [11], Tom [12], and tools implementing the OMG Query View Transformation (QVT) language [13]. However, these tools only support classical one-way batch transformations. Model synchronization, where only part of a model is transformed (incremental transformation) is not supported. These tools are therefore not suitable to solve our problem, even though the relational part of QVT (QVT-R) is promising for model synchronization.

3.1   Approaches for Model Synchronization

As explained in [14], two main approaches exist for model synchronization. The first one considers that inconsistencies will naturally occur during design (e.g., the user modifies one specification without taking care of performing the corresponding modification on the other side), and means are provided to detect the inconsistencies and automatically generate a set of actions to be applied on the models to restore consistency. This set of actions is called a repair plan, and inconsistencies are typically expressed by a set of constraints whose evaluation to true identifies inconsistent models.

The second approach uses coupled graph grammars. Consistency is characterized by membership of the models in the resulting graph language. Automatically generated operational transformations deal with maintaining the models consistent in case one model is changed. The most widely known language for this approach is the Triple-Graph Grammar [15]. Its power comes from the fact that the relation between the two models can be made operational so that models can be transformed / synchronized in either direction. While a graph grammar can be used for defining the dynamic evolution of a single model, a triple graph grammar allows to define the relation between two different kinds of models by defining and coupling three graph grammars (Fig. 4): one grammar for each type of model to be transformed, and a third grammar for a correspondence model whose purpose is to maintain traceability links between elements of the two models to be synchronized.

3.2   Tool Selection

Among the two approaches, only the TGG appeared to be mature enough. We could not find any tool implementing the first approach. On the opposite, TGGs have been around for more than 15 years, and several model synchronization experiments have been performed such as [16] and [17]. Our selection of the TGG tool has been strongly based on [19], which presents a survey of the three most widely known TGG tools still actively developed: (1) *The Model Transformation Engine* (MoTE) [7], (2) *The TGG Interpreter* [20] and (3) *The eMoflon* tool suite [21].

Both MoTE and eMoflon compile TGG rules into story diagrams. For MoTE, the story diagrams are interpreted to transform the models, while for eMoflon, Java code is generated from the story diagrams, which is then executed to perform the transformations. The TGG interpreter works differently as it directly interprets the TGG rules to perform the transformation. This has the advantage of allowing testing the transformation at development time, but has the drawback of reduced performance. Indeed, the survey indicated that that the TGG interpreter is the slowest, while MoTE and eMoflon have similar performances, with eMoflon being slightly faster than MoTE.

All three tools impose restrictions on the input TGGs for being able to prove correctness, and to increase performance in pattern matching in the case of MoTE. MoTE imposes the strongest restrictions on the TGGs. Both MoTE and eMoflon have proven completeness[1]. However, a serious drawback of eMoflon is that it did not support incremental transformations at the time of the survey, which prevented its use.

---

[1] Completeness means that every graph of a graph language $\mathcal{L}$(TGG) of a given TGG can be generated by the tool's forward/backward transformation from a graph of the translator's input domain.

While the survey did not strongly favor any of the three tools, MoTE appeared to be the best choice to synchronize Adele and OSATE. It supports incremental transformation, is fairly fast, has good formal properties and is completely based on EMF. Although a new version of MoTE (MoTE 2) improving performance and expressivity is currently under development, our work was performed with the version 1. This is because at the time we did this work, no TGG graphical editor was available for MoTE 2. At some point during the project, we considered porting our grammar to MoTE 2, but ran into several problems with the MoTE2 development tools and runtime execution. For this reason, we decided to complete the work with MoTE 1 first, and to postpone migration to MoTE 2 to a next phase of the project.

4   Overview of the Implemented Solution

This section introduces the architecture of the Adele-OSATE synchronization layer and its integration in the Eclipse-based modeling environment. We adopted an approach inspired from the work of [22], [23] and [24], where model synchronization is viewed as a specific task of Global Model Management (GMM). We have therefore developed a GMM language allowing formalization and interpretation of the various relations that can exist between models of a modeling environment. This includes the consistency relation between Adele and OSATE models, implemented as a synchronization relation using the MoTE TGG engine.

Fig. 3 presents the architecture of the Adele-OSATE synchronization relation and its deployment into the Eclipse workbench. A GMM controller listens for resource change events, which are sent by the resources manager of the Eclipse platform when users save the models through the editor. For a given changed resource, the GMM controller calls the GMM engine that processes the relations that concern the resource. These relations are declared in a GMM specification. The editor adapter layer is used to provide direct access to the internal resource of any opened editor of the resources to be synchronized, thus making the results of synchronization immediately visible in opened editors.

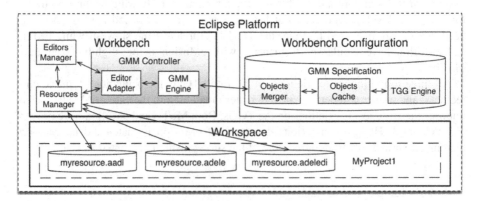

Fig. 3. The architecture of the Adele-OSATE synchronization layer, implemented as a synchronization relation of the Global Model Management language

Note that the MoTE synchronization relation makes use of a cache of the model objects, which are linked through the correspondence models for being synchronized. Changes made by any tool to the changed resource are merged into the cache, thus ensuring the objects traced by the correspondence models are not destroyed whatever the way the tool performed the changes[2]. Despite the fact that the merge operation increases complexity, it has the advantage but isolating the model objects to ensure that synchronization will work independently of the way the objects are modified. The merge layer is implemented using EMF Compare [25], which had to be tuned for merging models correctly as presented in Section 5.

5   The Adele-OSATE TGG

The TGG that was developed for synchronizing Adele and OSATE contains a total of 60 rules, as detailed in Table 1. The major portion of the AADL language has been covered, which makes our experience a relevant case study for applying TGGs to complex and rich languages. Most rules could be easily expressed, except for the connection rules, which required improvements of the TGG language and MoTE tool, and even modifications of the Adele meta-model. Therefore, this section focuses on these improvements, which unfortunately cannot all be presented due to the lack of space.

Table 1. Statistics of the Adele-OSATE

AADL Construct	# of Rules / Contexts	AADL Construct	# of Rules / Contexts
Package and public package section (axiom)	1	Subcomponents	11
Component Types	2	Connections	20
Component Type Features	10	Flows	Not Handled
Feature Group Types	4	Modes	Not Handled
Feature Group Type Features	10	Properties	Not Handled
Component Implementation	2	Prototypes	Not Handled
		Total	**60**

5.1   TGG Language Improvements

Generic TGG Rules

A first encountered problem relates to scalability of both the development and runtime tools, which could be fixed by introducing the concept of generic TGG rules. Indeed, while MoTE scales very well in transforming large models [19], we discovered limitations in handling complex languages like AADL. As illustrated in Fig. 4, a constraint on TGG rules is that the class of the created elements (green) must

---

[2] As a matter of fact, this need was initially discovered because the OSATE textual editor, which is based on the Xtext framework [8], systematically re-parses the AST as soon as any modification is made to the textual file.

be concrete (can be instantiated), and that the references to the created elements must be changeable. Without our improvement, the rule of Fig. 4 is not valid, since both the Adele component and AADL subcomponent classes are abstract, and the *ownedSubcomponent* reference is not changeable being derived. As introduced in section 2.3, the OSATE meta-model is strongly typed, and only the specific classes of each subcomponent category (Fig. 1) should have been used in TGG rules.

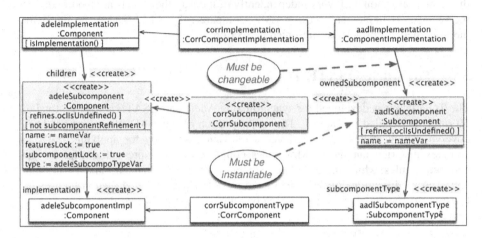

Fig. 4. The Adele-OSATE TGG rule for typed subcomponents

However, this quickly leads to an explosion of the number of required TGG rules. In order to meet the TGG "instantiability" constraints, a TGG rule would be required for each pair of parent component category and subcomponent category. For example, for the system parent category, 9 rules would be required to cover all allowed sub-component categories. In addition, a subcomponent can be created in several contexts, which must all be covered by the rules. A subcomponent can be created with a type as illustrated in Fig. 4, or untyped as shown in Fig. 5, or typed as its parent, or with the subcomponent being inherited and refined to a more specialized type, according to the AADL subcomponent refinement mechanism. In total, the AADL language implies a number of 11 different creation contexts for a subcomponent of a given category. Hence, this implies that in order to cover only the system component implementation, 99 TGG rules are needed. However there are 14 component categories in AADL, and a simple calculation shows that more than 700 TGG rules would actually be required just for specifying the transformation of subcomponents!

Such a large number of rules cannot be handled by MoTE. First, the Story Diagram (SD) generator did not scale well with the number of TGG rules. It was observed that when a TGG reaches a number of roughly 300 rules, SD generation would require too much memory and would not complete on the computer used for this project, which had about 3.5 GB of RAM memory. Furthermore, the disk space required to store such a large number of SDs would make the release of the synchronization layer not manageable (about 3GB for 250 TGG rules). As a matter of fact, the space taken for a given synchronization SD increases with the total number of TGG rules, making the size of the total SDs not growing linearly with the number of TGG rules. SDs are generated in a way that when a rule that produced a given set of objects is not matched anymore due to changes of the objects, a call is placed to all other rules of the entire grammar in order to discover a potentially matching rule. As a result, when the total number of rules increases in a TGG, the number of calls of the synchronization SDs increases and can potentially lead to performance issues.

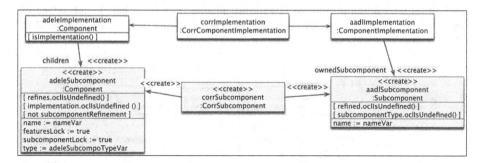

Fig. 5. The TGG rule for untyped subcomponents

To avoid these scalability issues, our first attempt was to optimize the SD generator to avoid consuming too much memory. But that turned out to be unnecessary after we implemented the concept of generic TGG rule allowing reducing the number of required rules for subcomponents from more than 700 to 11. This is shown in Fig. 4, which is the actual rule used in our Adele-OSATE TGG, and where the class *Subcomponent* of the created model element on the AADL side is abstract, and the containing reference (*ownedSubcomponent*) is not changeable in the AADL meta-model. The solution consisted of modifying the MoTE TGG language so that the TGG designer can provide an expression attached to model objects whose class is abstract, and to unchangeable model links. The SD interpreter then evaluates these expressions at runtime to determine which concrete class has to be instantiated, and which changeable reference has to be updated. In our specific case, the expression is a call action providing a static method of a transformation helper class called to determine the concrete class to be instantiated from the actual concrete class of the model element on the other side. A similar method is provided to determine the changeable reference from the types of the parent model element and the subcomponent.

Reuse of Objects to Avoid Information Loss
We also encountered problems with model objects being re-instantiated when synchronizing changes, despite the fact that MoTE had already been improved regarding this aspect. MoTE implements the algorithm presented in [26], which avoids re-instantiating the entire set of objects created in the sub-tree of the changed object.

However, changing a reference from an object to another model object caused re-instantiation of the object. For example, consider the rule of Fig. 4, which describes the creation of a subcomponent of a given type. When the subcomponent type is changed to null, the MoTE engine will detect that the rule that created the model element is not matched anymore due to the changes. In such case, it will try to match all other rules of the TGG. In our example, the rule of Fig. 5 (when the subcomponent is untyped) will obviously be matched. MoTE will then repair the corresponding object by marking it as deleted, and by instantiating a new subcomponent and setting its properties according to the newly matched rule. This operation is performed with a dedicated SD named *repair structure*. While this is an improvement compared to the original algorithm, it is not sufficient for our use case. Elements such as AADL properties contained in subcomponents and declared on only one side of the TGG must be preserved. We therefore developed an original solution to avoid this re-instantiation (Fig. 6). It has the advantage of simplicity and limited overhead compared to other solutions such as that presented in [27].

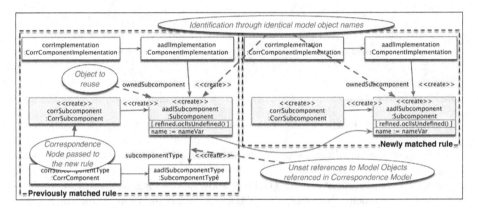

Fig. 6. The process of reusing an existing model object after changes

The objective is to be able to find the existing object that has changed so that it can be reused when applying the newly matched rule instead of instantiating a new object. Fortunately, when the repair structure SD of the newly matched rule is called, the correspondence node that refers to the changed object is always passed to the rule. We then simply need to identify the existing object to be reused from the set of objects referred by the correspondence node. For this, we can first discard all objects whose class is not the same as that of the object to be re-created. However, this criterion is not sufficient since there could be many objects with the same class created for a given correspondence node. To uniquely identify the changed object, we require an additional constraint to be verified by the TGG rules at the time they are defined. Comparing the rules of Fig. 4 and Fig. 5, we notice that their patterns are quite similar, and the only difference between them is that for the first one, there is a link to the type of the subcomponent, while for the second one, this link is removed and a constraint stating that the subcomponent type is null is added. If we require that the created subcomponent model objects have identical names for both rules (*adeleSubcomponent* and *aadlSubcomponent*), which is typically the case when good practices are used in TGG rules definition, we can then identify the existing object to be reused from the name of its model object in the newly matched rule. However, to make this possible, the way the correspondence model is represented has to be changed to associate with each created object the name of the model object of the creation rule. This is easily implemented in MoTE.

Now that the existing object is identified, two additional steps must be performed. First all references of the reused object to objects that are already mapped in the correspondence model must be removed. This is because the proper references will be set as if the object was newly created when the repair structure SD is applied. So we avoid setting the same object twice in case of multiple cardinality references. Conversely, objects that are not mapped in the correspondence model such as properties will not be reset by this process and will be preserved as desired.

This simple solution appears to work quite well for our Adele-OSATE TGG and ensures that whatever was contained by the subcomponent and not handled by the TGG is preserved. The only drawback is that it enforces using the same name in the created model objects of all rules for a given type of created model object. However, this can be ensured by adding constraints to the TGG meta-model.

Other Improvements
Other improvements were implemented but only briefly mentioned due to lack of space. We enhanced the MoTE global pattern matching constraints, by adding an applicability clause to the constraint. It states whether it is to be applied only during forward or reverse transformations. We also added the capability to specify an additional reference to a model object link to be used for matching purposes. In some cases, MoTE tries to match a pattern from the inverse direction of a model object link, starting from the target object to the source object. If the reference of the link has an opposite reference or is a containment reference, MoTE uses the opposite or the container reference to navigate to the source object. However, for some references of the OSATE meta-model, opposite references exist but are not explicitly specified in the meta-model. We therefore added a property on the TGG model object link class to specify this reference, and modified the SD interpreter for making use of it.

5.2   Tooling Improvements

Cross-Resource References Management
Another major issue with MoTE is that cross-resource references are not handled. For example, if a component refers to a component contained in a different resource, its reference property will not be handled during transformations. Such a shortcoming is more than enough to prevent a tool from being used. For languages like AADL, which provide packages declared in separate files to better organize a specification, this is a blocking limitation.

To overcome this problem, we modified the MoTE TGG engine so that it takes care of pre-building the correspondence model with correspondence nodes of external model elements. This fix slightly increases execution time, since a complete correspondence model has to be recursively created for each cross resource. However, each correspondence model is stored in the TGG engine cache so that the impact on performance is limited.

EMF Compare Improvements
As illustrated in Fig. 3, the integration of MoTE in our modeling environment is achieved through the use of a model object cache. This is needed to ensure that the model elements traced by the correspondence model are maintained. EMF Compare

1.3 has been used to merge the changes detected in the resources of the workspace into the resources of the cache.

Again, a few improvements were needed for being able to merge the models correctly. The first issue relates to the way EMF Compare merges changes in which cross resource references are involved. Our synchronization layer requires that if a reference to an external element is set, then the external model element should be contained in a resource of the cache on the cache side, because it may already be referred by a correspondence model. However, the default behavior of EMF Compare is to set the same referenced object in the target object as that of the source object, and EMF Compare had to be adapted to take this into account.

Another problem is related to the order in which the merge operations are performed. To avoid unnecessary re-instantiation of objects, the delete operations, which are received as model change events by the TGG engine, should be added at the end of the transformation queue. In this way, the references to the object to be deleted can be moved to other objects before the object is deleted during synchronization. Hence, this implied modifying the order of the merge operations in EMF Compare to ensure that deletion operations are performed at the end. Other minor merging issues were also identified and corrected but cannot be presented due to the lack of space.

Other Improvements

Other improvements to MoTE were required as well, such as the implementation of post-creation actions, which were declared in the TGG language but not implemented in the TGG compiler. The same is true for position constraints used to define whether an element is to be added at the first or the last position in a list. This feature was handled in the SD interpreter but not in the TGG language. We also introduced the *between* constraint used when the element should neither be the first and nor the last element, provided that there are at least two elements in the list. We also had a few issues with the MoTE change listener that receives model changes events to be added as modifications to the TGG engine transformation queue for synchronization.

6   Discussion

6.1   Implemented Synchronization Layer

The concrete result of this work is a synchronization layer between Adele and OSATE, solving the problem of integrating tools that are essential for the growing AADL community. Experience gained during this project supports the ongoing work of integrating other languages and tools with the AADL such as VHDL.

Automated tests were developed for the synchronization layer for testing bidirectional batch transformations and synchronization transformations, and for consistency checks performed by creating and analyzing correspondence models. In addition, we have tested our synchronization layer with several realistic and complex AADL models such as electronic hardware systems using all constructs of the AADL language handled by Adele. Such systems require up to 7 levels of recursive component extensions declared in different files, which was used to validate our fix of the MoTE for the cross-resource references problem.

6.2   Suggestions for Further Improvements

Based on our experiment, we found that current TGG approaches require further improvements for being suitable for industrial use. These would increase the usability of TGGs and ease the development of model synchronization layers. For example, it would be useful to have a mechanism to allow reusing one side of an existing TGG (for instance the AADL side) and complete the other side according to the new language to be synchronized with AADL (e.g., VHDL). Another improvement could be to provide a "soft" reference mechanism for model links of graph patterns, instead of requiring the reference to be declared in the class of the source model object. In our experiment, this would have avoided the need to add references to the Adele meta-model, which are used only for TGG rule matching purposes. This is even more important for the cases where the modeling languages cannot be modified (e.g.: the AADL). In addition, other improvements published in the literature would really need to be implemented in MoTE. These are described in the related work section.

It was also found that the use of TGGs could be made much easier if better documentation was provided. In the actual state, the transformation designer needs to understand the generated SDs to be able to define correct TGGs, and several additional TGG validation rules would need to be enforced. For example, when defining constraints, beginners have no clue which model objects can be used in constraints. The bound model objects depend on the specific type of transformation (mapping, batch or synchronization), and several errors occur at runtime due to unbound model objects being referenced in constraint expressions.

7   Related Work

To our knowledge, no experience has been made to assess the usability of TGGs for synchronizing models of complex and rich languages such as the AADL, with a real need to integrate tools used by an active community. However, a few similar works can be compared to ours.

In [19], a set of benchmarks has been performed for large models to compare three TGG tools (MoTE, eMoflon and the TGG Interpreter). However, the meta-models are extremely simple. In [16], synchronization has been implemented with MoTE between SysML and AUTOSAR, but only subsets of the languages were covered. A work closer to ours is presented in [17], where the synchronization of Modal Sequence Diagrams (MSDs) with networks of Timed Game Automata (TGA) using the TGG Interpreter is presented. Like for us, their experiment lead to the development of several improvements such as:

- The integration of OCL in TGGs, which is already implemented in MoTE.
- TGG rule generalization / inheritance, which is also introduced in [18] for eMoflon, and would be worth implementing in MoTE.
- Reusable patterns, which allow declaring in a single TGG rule several contexts of creation of a given graph of model elements. This would have helped in MoTE by reducing the number of required rules for handling the numerous creation contexts (e.g., 11 for subcomponents).

- Global constraints, which are already implemented in MoTE, to which we added an applicability clause for specific transformation directions (forward / reverse).

Furthermore, in [27], a new algorithm is presented and implemented in the TGG Interpreter to allow further reuse of model elements during synchronization. It avoids the loss of the information not handled by the TGG rules. We provided a different solution to this problem, which appears to be simpler but requires additional constraints to be met by a set of TGG rules describing the contexts of creation of a given model object class.

8   Conclusion and Perspectives

In this paper, we reported our experience in synchronizing models of two different meta-models for the complex feature-rich AADL language. Our experiment shows that applying state of the art model synchronization techniques remains challenging, despite the good quality of the MoTE tool that was used. This case study allowed the development of several improvements of TGGs to account for the size of the AADL meta-model and its properties. However, the fact that we succeeded in synchronizing the tools validates the TGG approach and opens interesting perspectives.

A future work will consist of porting our improvements and our Adele-OSATE TGG to MoTE 2, in order to benefit from the MoTE 2 improvements. In addition, we are currently working on improving other aspects of TGGs and MoTE through the development of an endogenous refinement transformation for AADL, and an AADL-VHDL transformation. We also plan to write a cookbook to help developers get acquainted with TGG development.

References

1. SAE International, Architecture Analylsis and Design Language (AADL), http://standards.sae.org/as5506b/
2. MathWorks, MathLab Simulink, http://www.mathworks.fr/products/simulink/
3. OMG, Systems Modeling Language (SysML), http://www.omgsysml.org/
4. OMG, Modeling and Analysis of Real-Time Embedded Systems (MARTE), http://www.omgmarte.org/
5. The Adele Graphical Editor for AADL, https://wiki.sei.cmu.edu/aadl/index.php/Adele/
6. Open Source AADL Tool Environment (OSATE), http://www.aadl.info/aadl/currentsite/tool/osate-down.html
7. The Model Transformation Engine (MoTE), http://www.mdelab.de/mote/
8. The Xtext Framework, http://www.eclipse.org/Xtext/
9. The Atlas Transformation Language (ATL), http://www.eclipse.org/atl/
10. The Epsilon Project, http://www.eclipse.org/epsilon/
11. The Kermeta Project, http://www.kermeta.org/
12. The Tom Project, http://tom.loria.fr
13. OMG, Query View Transformation (QVT), http://www.omg.org/spec/QVT/

14. Boronat, A., Meseguer, J.: Automated Model Synchronization: A Case Study on UML with Maude. Proc. of the ECEASST (41) (2011)
15. Schürr, A.: Specification of graph translators with triple graph grammars. In: Mayr, E.W., Schmidt, G., Tinhofer, G. (eds.) WG 1994. LNCS, vol. 903, pp. 151–163. Springer, Heidelberg (1995)
16. Giese, H., Hildebrandt, S., Neumann, S.: Model Synchronization at Work: Keeping SysML and AUTOSAR Models Consistent. In: Engels, G., Lewerentz, C., Schäfer, W., Schürr, A., Westfechtel, B. (eds.) Nagl Festschrift. LNCS, vol. 5765, pp. 555–579. Springer, Heidelberg (2010)
17. Greenyer, J., Rieke, J.: Applying Advanced TGG Concepts for a Complex Transformation of Sequence Diagram Specifications to Timed Game Automata. In: Schürr, A., Varró, D., Varró, G. (eds.) AGTIVE 2011. LNCS, vol. 7233, pp. 222–237. Springer, Heidelberg (2012)
18. Klar, F., Königs, A., Schürr, A.: Model Transformation in the Large. In: Proc. of the 6th Joint Meeting of the European Software Engineering Conference and the ACM SIGSOFT Symposium on the Foundations of Software Engineering (ESEC-FSE 2007), pp. 285–294 (2007)
19. Hildebrandt, S., Lambers, L., Giese, H., Rieke, J., Greenyer, J., Schafer, W., Lauder, M., Anjorin, A., Schürr, A.: A Survey of Triple Graph Grammar Tools. In: Proc. of the 2nd International Workshop on Bidirectional Transformations (2013)
20. TGG-Interpreter,
    http://www.cs.upb.de/index.php?id=tgg-interpreter/
21. eMoflon, http://www.emoflon.org/
22. Hebig, R., Seibel, A., Giese, H.: On the Unification of Megamodels. In: Proc. of the 4th International Workshop on Multi-Paradigm Modeling (MPM 2010). ECEASST, vol. 42 (2011)
23. Vignaga, A., Jouault, F., Bastarrica, M.C., Brunelière, H.: Typing in Model Management. In: Paige, R.F. (ed.) ICMT 2009. LNCS, vol. 5563, pp. 197–212. Springer, Heidelberg (2009)
24. Seibel, A., Neumann, S., Giese, H.: Dynamic hierarchical mega models: comprehensive traceability and its efficient maintenance. Softw. Syst. Model 9(4), 493–528 (2010)
25. EMF Compare, http://www.eclipse.org/emf/compare/
26. Giese, H., Hildebrandt, S.: Efficient Model Synchronization of Large-Scale Models, Tech. Rep. 28, Hasso Plattner Institute at the University of Potsdam (2009)
27. Greenyer, J., Pook, S., Rieke, J.: Preventing information loss in incremental model synchronization by reusing elements. In: France, R.B., Kuester, J.M., Bordbar, B., Paige, R.F. (eds.) ECMFA 2011. LNCS, vol. 6698, pp. 144–159. Springer, Heidelberg (2011)
28. Giese, H., Hildebrandt, S., Seibel, A.: Improved Flexibility and Scalability by Interpreting Story Diagrams. ECEASST (18) (2009)

Triple Graph Grammars in the Large for Translating Satellite Procedures

Frank Hermann[1], Susann Gottmann[1], Nico Nachtigall[1], Hartmut Ehrig[2],
Benjamin Braatz[1], Gianluigi Morelli[3], Alain Pierre[3],
Thomas Engel[1], and Claudia Ermel[2]

[1] Interdisciplinary Centre for Security, Reliability and Trust,
Université du Luxembourg, Luxembourg
firstname.lastname@uni.lu
[2] Technische Universität Berlin, Germany
firstname.lastname@tu-berlin.de
[3] SES, Luxembourg
firstname.lastname@ses.com

Abstract. Software translation is a challenging task. Several requirements are important – including automation of the execution, maintainability of the translation patterns, and, most importantly, reliability
concerning the correctness of the translation.

Triple graph grammars (TGGs) have shown to be an intuitive, well-
defined technique for model translation. In this paper, we leverage TGGs
for industry scale software translations. The approach is implemented using the Eclipse-based graph transformation tool Henshin and has been
successfully applied in a large industrial project with the satellite operator SES on the translation of satellite control procedures. We evaluate
the approach regarding requirements from the project and performance
on a complete set of procedures of one satellite.

Keywords: model transformation, software translation, refactoring,
triple graph grammars, Eclipse Modeling Framework (EMF).

1 Introduction

Migration of software systems is an important but complex task, especially for
enterprises that are highly dependent on the reliability of their running systems.
The general problem is to translate the source code of a software that is currently in use into corresponding source code that shall run on the new system.
Up to now, this problem was addressed based on manually written converters,
parser generators, compiler-compilers or meta-programming environments using
term rewriting or similar techniques. Model transformation based on triple graph
grammars (TGGs) is a general, intuitive and formally well-defined technique for
the translation of models [25,26,13]. While previous concepts and case studies
were focused mainly on visual models of software and systems, this paper shows
that model transformation based on TGGs provides a powerful technique for

D. Di Ruscio and D. Varró (Eds.): ICMT 2014, LNCS 8568, pp. 122–137, 2014.
© Springer International Publishing Switzerland 2014

software translation as well. Since software systems are on average much larger than visual models, we provide a general technique for efficiency improvement and show its applicability within a large scale industrial project.

The general idea of TGGs is to specify a language of integrated models. Such an integrated model consists of a model of the source domain, a model of the target domain, and explicit correspondence structures in the middle component. The source and target models in the present scenario are abstract syntax trees of source code. The operational rules for executing the translation are generated from the specified TGG and executed via the graph transformation tool Henshin [7]. TGGs are equivalent to a restricted class of plain graph transformation systems [8,13]. This restriction ensures the existence of the explicit correspondence structures and formal properties concerning correctness and completeness [14]. In this paper, we use rather simple and intuitive but non-trivial translation patterns. The full translation contains several more complex ones, e.g., for the reordering and regrouping of blocks. Translation strategies that are solely based on finding and replacing words (like e.g. Awk[1]) will fail due to the highly context-sensitive structural dependencies in the source code.

Within the research project *PIL2SPELL* with the industrial partner SES (Société Européenne des Satellites), we developed the general approach for software translation in this paper. SES is operating a fleet of 56 satellites manufactured by different vendors that often use their own proprietary programming language for automated operational satellite procedures. In order to reduce the high complexity and efforts during operation caused by this heterogeneity, SES developed the open source satellite language SPELL [27] (Satellite Procedure Execution Language & Library), which is nowadays used by more and more operators and may become a standard in this domain. The main aim of the project was to provide a fully automated translation of existing satellite control procedures written in PIL (Procedure Intermediate Language) of the satellite manufacturer ASTRIUM into satellite control procedures in SPELL.[2] Since the PIL procedures are already validated, the translation has to ensure a very high level of reliability in terms of fidelity, precision and correctness in order to minimise the efforts for revalidation. In our first contribution of this paper we propose and validate the use of TGGs for software translation in the *PIL2SPELL* project. Since the *PIL2SPELL* project is an industrial application of rather large size (more than 200 translation rules were specified), a technique was needed to improve the efficiency of the TGG rewriting method and tool. Hence, the second contribution of this paper is a general approach for improving efficiency of graph transformation systems applied to leverage TGGs for software translations in industry and we evaluate the implementation in Henshin [7]. The corresponding technical report [16] for this paper provides full technical details on the formal constructions and full proofs.

Sec. 2 introduces our running example, Sec. 3 presents the general concept and Sec. 4 describes the applied TGG techniques. Thereafter, Sec. 5 presents results

---

[1] Awk Community: http://awk.info/

[2] In [15], we present a short overview of the *PIL2SPELL* project.

```
 1 SELECT
 2   CASE ($BATT = "HIGH")
 3       CHECKTM(TEMP_C1)
 4       CHECKTM(VOLT_D2 = 4)
 5   ENDCASE
 6   CASE ($BATT = "LOW")
 7     SEND SWITCH_B1_B2
 8         CHECKTM(VOLT3 = 5)
 9       ENDSEND
10     ENDCASE
11 ENDSELECT
```

```
1 if (BATT == 'HIGH'):
2   GetTM('T TEMP_C1')
3   Verify([['T VOLT_D2', eq, 4]])
4 elif (BATT == 'LOW'):
5   Send(command = 'C SWITCH_B1_B2',
6         verify  = [['T VOLT3', eq, 5]])
7 #ENDIF
```

Fig. 1. Procedure written in *PIL* (left) and translated procedure in *SPELL* (right)

for improving the efficiency and scalability, and Sec. 6 evaluates the approach. Sec. 7 discusses related work and Sec. 8 provides a conclusion and discusses aspects of future work.

2   Case Study *PIL2SPELL*

We illustrate the methodology for software translation on some details of the project *PIL2SPELL*. Fig. 1 presents a simplified *PIL* procedure for battery maintenance and its translation in *SPELL*. Structures of the form SELECT-CASE-ENDSELECT are translated into structures of the form if-elif-#ENDIF. SEND instructions (lines 7-9) for sending telecommands to the satellite are mapped to corresponding Send statements with the same command-id as argument prefixed with a C (lines 5-6). Instructions for checking telemetry values (*PIL* instruction CHECKTM) are handled in three ways:

1. CHECKTM(X) (line 3): parameter checks without condition are used to retrieve and display a telemetry value from the satellite. They are translated into GetTM statements, where prefix T is added to the parameter (line 2).
2. CHECKTM(X = Y) (line 4): parameter checks with additional condition are used to verify telemetry values and are mapped to Verify statements with a corresponding condition (line 3).
3. CHECKTM(X = Y) (line 8): parameter checks within a SEND instruction are translated into a verify argument of the corresponding Send statement (line 6). △

Note that the translation is context-sensitive as it treats e.g. a CHECKTM instruction inside a SEND instruction differently from a not nested CHECKTM instruction. Moreover, PIL and SPELL use different concepts for calling subroutines. In order to respect the execution semantics, block structures of the form STAGE..ENDSTAGE in PIL have to be translated into two SPELL structures. The first one is a function call that remains in the main part and the second one is a function definition containing the translated body of the block structure and it is placed at the beginning of the SPELL procedure. This restructuring and reordering of information motivates to perform a separation of concerns by splitting the translation into parsing, translation and serialisation instead of using an integrated approach, where some of the phases are merged.

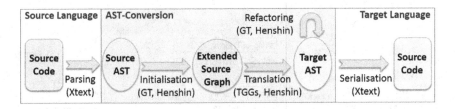

Fig. 2. Concept for software translation

3   Concept for Software Translation

The general concept for software translation in Fig. 2 consists of the phases *parsing*, *AST conversion* (main phase), and *serialisation*. It is executed using the Eclipse Modeling Framework (EMF) tools *Xtext* [6] and *Henshin* [7]. Xtext supports the syntax specification of textual domain specific languages (DSLs), in particular of programming languages. Based on the EBNF (Extended Backus-Naur Form) grammar specification of a DSL and an additional formatting configuration, the Xtext framework generates the corresponding parser and serialiser. The parser checks that the input source code is well-formed and the serialiser ensures that the generated output source code is well-defined. The Xtext serialiser enables us to check and ensure that the output conforms to the given EBNF for the target language and that additional AST-specific formatting guidelines are respected. SES explicitly required the conformance to the SPELL EBNF and to SES formatting guidelines (e.g. alignment of list entries and semantic indentation), which goes beyond the power of generic template specification. Henshin is an Eclipse plugin supporting the visual specification and execution of EMF transformation systems, which is used for the main phase (AST conversion).

Example 1 (Parsing & Serialisation). Fig. 3 (left) shows a fragment of the AST obtained by parsing the *PIL* source code example in Fig. 1 (left, lines 7-9). Root node : Send_PIL represents the SEND – ENDSEND structure (lines 7-9) with telecommand-id (SWITCH_B1_B2, left branch) and telemetry parameter check (CHECKTM, right branch). Fig. 3 (right) shows the obtained SPELL AST fragment after translation. The serialisation of the SPELL AST yields the corresponding source code in Fig. 1 (right, lines 5-6). Root node : Send represents the Send statement with telecommand-id (C SWITCH_B1_B2) in the left branch and telemetry parameter verification argument (verify) in the right branch.   △

The AST-conversion consists of three phases (see Fig. 2). The first and third phases (initialisation and refactoring) are general in-place transformations and are performed via plain graph transformation (GT) systems. The second phase (translation) is performed using a triple graph grammar (TGG), which is presented in detail in Sec. 4. Note that TGGs can be fully encoded as plain graph transformations [13]. The initialisation phase is used to extend the given AST of the source language with additional structures that simplify the specification of the translation rules in Phase 2. The refactoring phase refines the resulting AST

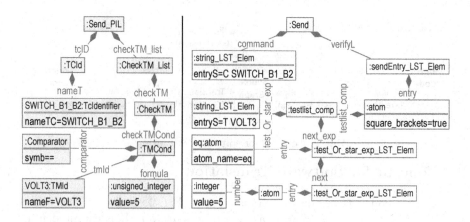

Fig. 3. Fragment of source AST (left) and target AST (right)

in order to satisfy certain coding guidelines required in the target domain. These refactorings are specified by compact GT rules that also delete substructures. Employing a TGG for the refactoring phase instead would drastically increase the amount of rules.

To reduce the complexity of the translation rules, the initialisation phase is used to pre-process information and to create additional helper structures that store this information locally in the source AST. In our case study, the initialisation rules are used, e.g., to compute a global numbering for the subcomponents of a satellite procedure that are needed in SPELL. Moreover, we create explicit pointers from complex instructions to their subcomponents (see, e.g. Ex. 2).

As TGGs are non-deleting, the source model is preserved completely during the translation. The translation markers ensure that each element is translated exactly once. At each translation step, a substructure of the given AST is translated and trace links are created. The resulting fragments in the target domain are connected according to the tree structure of the input AST. These properties help to ensure that the resulting output graph has a tree structure and is in fact an AST.

4   Triple Graph Grammars with Henshin

In the following, we briefly review main concepts for model transformation based on TGGs [10]. A triple graph is an integrated model consisting of a source model, a target model and explicit correspondences between them. More precisely, it consists of three graphs G^S, G^C, and G^T, called source, correspondence, and target graphs, respectively, together with two mappings (graph morphisms) $s_G\colon G^C \to G^S$ and $t_G\colon G^C \to G^T$. The two mappings in G specify a correspondence relation between elements of G^S and elements of G^T.

Triple graphs are related by triple graph morphisms $m : G \to H$ [25,10] consisting of three graph morphisms that preserve the associated correspondences (i.e., left diagrams in Fig. 4 commute). Triple graphs are typed over a

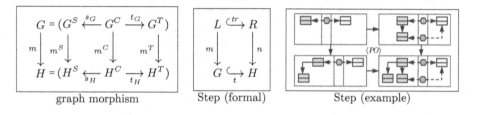

| graph morphism | Step (formal) | Step (example) |

Fig. 4. Triple graph morphism and transformation step

triple type graph TG and attributed according to [10]. For a triple type graph $TG = (TG^S \leftarrow TG^C \rightarrow TG^T)$, we use $\mathcal{L}(TG)$, $\mathcal{L}(TG^S)$, and $\mathcal{L}(TG^T)$ to denote the classes of all graphs typed over TG, TG^S, and TG^T, respectively.

A triple graph grammar $TGG = (TG, S, TR)$ consists of a triple type graph TG, a triple start graph S and a set TR of triple rules, and generates the triple graph language of consistently integrated models $\mathcal{L}(TGG) \subseteq \mathcal{L}(TG)$ with consistent source and target languages $\mathcal{L}(TGG)^S = \{G^S \mid (G^S \leftarrow G^C \rightarrow G^T) \in \mathcal{L}(TGG)\}$ and $\mathcal{L}(TGG)^T = \{G^T \mid (G^S \leftarrow G^C \rightarrow G^T) \in \mathcal{L}(TGG)\}$. TG^C differentiates the possible types of correspondences.

A triple rule specifies how a given consistently integrated model can be extended simultaneously on all three components yielding again a consistently integrated model. It is non-deleting and therefore, can be formalised as an inclusion from triple graph L (left hand side) to triple graph R (right hand side), represented by $tr : L \hookrightarrow R$ with $tr = (tr^S, tr^C, tr^T)$. Applying a triple rule tr means to find a match morphism $m : L \rightarrow G$ and to perform a triple graph transformation step $G \xrightarrow{tr, m} H$ yielding triple graph H defined by the gluing construction[3] in Fig. 4 where the occurrence of L in G is replaced by the occurrence of R in H and glued to the remaining graph elements) [26]. Moreover, triple rules can be extended by application conditions for restricting their application to specific matches [13].

The operational forward translation rules for executing forward model transformations are derived automatically [13] from the TGG. A forward translation rule tr_{FT} and its original triple rule tr differ only on the source component: elements (nodes, edges or attributes) created by tr become elements that are preserved and marked as "translated" by the forward translation rule.

Example 2 (Operational Triple Rules). Fig. 5 shows screenshots (tool Henshin [7]) of some generated forward translation rules of the TGG for *PIL2SPELL* in short notation. Left- and right-hand side of a rule are depicted in one triple graph and the elements to be created have the label $\langle$++$\rangle$. Translation attributes are indicated by label $\langle$tr$\rangle$. The depicted rules are typical operational rules of average rule size. Rule (1) translates an existing `Instruction_LST_Elem` node into its corresponding `stmt_LST_Elem` node. Both node types are containers for

---

[3] Formally, this is a pushout diagram (PO) in the category of triple graphs.

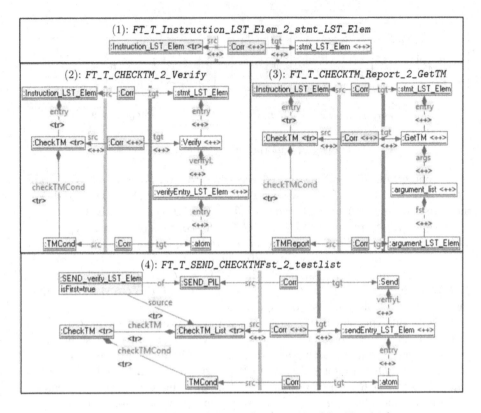

Fig. 5. Forward translation rules (generated by Henshin)

specific instructions and statements. Rules (2) and (3) depend on rule (1) as they use the stmt_LST_Elem nodes as context.

Rules (2)-(4) are some of the rules that translate CHECKTM instructions. They depend on further rules for the translation of their parameters (TMCond or TMReport). Depending on the parameter type, the respective SPELL statement is created, i.e., telemetry conditions (TMCond) yield a Verify statement, telemetry reports (TMReport - label without condition) yield a GetTM statement and telemetry conditions within a SEND instruction become an argument in a verify list of the corresponding Send statement. This corresponds to items 1–3 in Sec. 2. Rules (2) and (3) translate CHECKTM instructions that are not embedded within a specific context while rule (4) translates CHECKTM instructions within a SEND instruction.

Note that the node type SEND_verify_LST_Elem is created in the initialisation phase as helper structure and used to mark exactly those CheckTM elements that handle a telemetry condition (TMCond). The remaining CheckTM elements of a SEND instruction are translated to GetTM statements outside the scope of the SPELL Send statement.   △

A *forward translation sequence* $(G^S, G_0 \xmapsto{tr^*_{FT}} G_n, G^T)$ is given by an input source model G^S, a transformation sequence $G_0 \xmapsto{tr^*_{FT}} G_n$ obtained by executing the forward translation rules TR_{FT} on $G_0 = (G^S \leftarrow \varnothing \rightarrow \varnothing)$, and the resulting target model G^T obtained as restriction to the target component of triple graph $G_n = (G^S \leftarrow G^C \rightarrow G^T)$. A *model transformation* based on forward translation rules $MT : \mathcal{L}(TG^S) \Rightarrow \mathcal{L}(TG^T)$ consists of all forward translation sequences. Note that a given source model G^S may correspond to different target models G^T. In order to ensure unique results, we presented in [13] how to use the automated conflict analysis engine of AGG for checking functional behaviour of model transformations.

5 Leveraging TGGs for Software Translations in Industry

As described in the previous section, the basic execution algorithm for forward translations based on TGGs does not use any kind of pre-defined order on rules. For medium and large scale projects, the application of rules in a non-deterministic way would result in poor efficiency. In this section, we present a general approach for graph transformation systems, with which we leverage TGGs for larger software translations. This concerns grammars containing more than 200 rules, like the manually specified rules for the *PIL2SPELL* project that were derived from a document of correspondence patterns (small corresponding source code fragments). The approach is orthogonal to the analysis and reduction of conflicts via filter NACs for TGGs [13]. Both approaches can be combined - the second one improves the rules directly while the first provides a structuring technique on them.

The main observation is that the efficiency of the execution can be improved significantly by analysing the potential dependencies. For example, rules (2) and (3) in Fig. 5 can only be applied after rule (1) was applied to translate the node of type `Instruction_LST_Elem`. Our strategy is partly inspired by several existing optimisations in TGG implementations [17] and dependency analysis for graph transformation systems [12]. It generalises the idea of precedence triple graph grammars [22] from node type dependencies towards general rule dependencies and works also for TGGs with attributes. It uses the general formal results on critical pair analysis [9,21] including the case of transformation rules with application conditions. Practically, we use the critical pair analysis engine of the tool AGG [28] for determining the dependencies and conflicts between the rules. Based on the results, we group those rules together that show cyclic dependencies or conflicts. The resulting set of groups of rules shows a partial order that we linearise to a complete order. Finally, we apply this grouping and ordering technique to the set of forward translation rules.

In order to group the rules of a given rule set R, their sequential dependencies and conflicts are represented by a dependency-conflict graph $DCG(R)$ containing the rules as nodes and rule dependencies/conflicts as edges. A pair of rules (r_1, r_2) is in conflict if there exists a critical pair for (r_1, r_2) [9], i.e., there are two parallel dependent transformation steps $t_1 = G_0 \xRightarrow{r_1} G_1$, $t_2 = G_0 \xRightarrow{r_2} G_2$. A pair of rules (r_1, r_2) is sequentially dependent if there is a transformation sequence $t = (t_1; t_2) = G_0 \xRightarrow{r_1} G_1 \xRightarrow{r_2} G_2$, where t_2 sequentially depends on t_1 (produce-use or forbid-create dependency). Note that the order is relevant for sequential dependencies. Both concepts can be analysed statically using the tool AGG [28]. The graph $DCG(R)$ may contain cycles. These cycles are used to define non-overlapping clusters of rules leading to the acyclic dependency-conflict cluster graph $CLG_{DC}(R)$. By $N(G)$ we denote the set of nodes of a graph G.

Definition 1 (Dependency-Conflict Cluster Graph). *Let R be a set of rules, then we define:*

- *dependency-conflict graph $DCG(R)$ with nodes $N(DCG(R)) = R$ and edges $E_{DCG} = \{(r \to r') \mid (r, r')$ is a sequentially dependent pair $\} \cup \{(r \to r'), (r' \to r) \mid \exists$ a critical pair for $(r, r')\}$,*
- *for $r \in R$ the dependency-conflict cluster $[r]_{DC} = \{r\} \cup \{r' \in R \mid \exists$ a path $(r \to \ldots r' \ldots \to r)$ in $DCG(R)\}$,*
- *dependency-conflict cluster graph $CLG_{DC}(R)$ with nodes $N(CLG_{DC}(R)) = \{c \mid c = [r]_{DC} \wedge r \in R\}$ and edges $E = \{(c \to c') \mid \exists\ r \in c, r' \in c' : (r \to r')$ in $DCG(R)\}$.*   △

A DC-Layered Transformation System (DC-LTS) linearises the partial order on clusters of a given $CLG_{DC}(R)$ to a complete order where each cluster becomes a layer and the sequential order of the layers respects the dependencies between the clusters. Formally, a layered transformation system $LTS = (R, S)$ consists of a set of rules R and a sequence $S = (S_i)_{i \in I}$ of subsets of R as layers. Given a graph G, then an execution of LTS is performed by applying each layer consecutively according to the sequence S, where the rules in each layer S_i are applied exhaustively.

Definition 2 (DC-Layered Transformation System). *Let $CLG_{DC}(R)$ be the derived dependency-conflict cluster graph for R, then $LTS = (R, S)$ with $S = (S_i)_{i \in I}$ is a DC-layered transformation system, if the following conditions hold*

1. *S is a permutation of the clusters in $N(CLG_{DC}(R))$ (cluster compatibility)*
2. *$\forall$ edges $(a \to b)$ in $CLG_{DC}(R)$: $a = S_k \wedge b = S_l \Rightarrow k < l$ (sequential order)* △

The construction of a DC-layered transformation system LTS for a set of rules R reduces the amount of rules to be checked for applicability at each step. By definition, the execution of a layer in an LTS concerns only rules in that layer. Thm. 1 below ensures preservation of the input-output behaviour. All terminated sequences via R (i.e., no more rules are applicable) can be performed via LTS. Each rule only depends on rules in a preceding layer and rules in the same layer. The input-output relation IO_{TS} of a transformation system TS contains all pairs (G_I, G_O) with a terminated transformation sequence $G_I \Rightarrow^* G_O$ via TS.

Theorem 1 (Completeness of DC-LTS). *Let R be a set of rules and LTS be a DC-layered transformation system for R, then: $IO_R = IO_{LTS}$, i.e.*
($\exists$ terminated $(G_0 \Rightarrow^* G_n)$ via R) $\Leftrightarrow$ ($\exists$ terminated $(G_0 \Rightarrow^* G_n)$ via LTS).   △

Proof (Idea). The proof (see [16]) uses the general results of completeness of critical pairs and the local Church-Rosser Theorem to stepwise shift the steps in s for obtaining sequence s' that respects the order in S. Using the construction of S, this ensures by induction that there is no rule in a cluster S_i which depends on a rule in cluster S_j with $j > i$. We obtain that s' can be divided into subsequences s_i' for each cluster S_i. Since for each rule of a cluster, the cluster also contains all conflicting rules, we can again apply completeness of critical pairs and the local Church-Rosser Theorem and show by contraposition that an extending step in any subsequence implies an extended step in the original sequence s, which contradicts the precondition that s is terminated.   □

A DC-LTS can reduce the effort for backtracking. By Thm. 2 below, functional behaviour of the layers eliminates the need for backtracking of transformation steps that are not in the current layer. A transformation system TS has functional behaviour, if IO_{TS} is right unique, i.e. for each input graph, there is at most one output graph up to isomorphism. A layer S_i of an $LTS = (R, S)$ has functional behaviour, if the induced transformation system with rules S_i has functional behaviour, which can be analysed statically with the tool AGG [13,28].

Theorem 2 (Reduction of Backtracking). *Let LTS be a DC-layered transformation system, where each layer has functional behaviour. Then, there is no need to backtrack already completed layers during the computation of a terminated sequence $G_0 \Rightarrow^* G_n$ via LTS. Moreover, LTS has functional behaviour.*   △

Proof. Assume we backtrack already completed layers, then we will obtain the same output graphs for these layers due to functional behaviour and thus, we derive the same input graph for the current layer. $LTS = (R, S)$ has functional behaviour, because each layer has functional behaviour and the layers are executed via the fixed sequence S.   □

The effect of Thm. 2 is that the effort for checking functional behaviour of the whole system is reduced to the analysis of each layer separately. Note that application conditions for rules are an appropriate method to ensure functional behaviour [13]. Our approach can be combined with the generation of filter NACs [13], which eliminates some types of rule conflicts, but not all.

We improve the performance of a model transformation MT by applying the concept of a DC-LTS to the set of operational rules of MT. By $TRAFOS(MT)$ we denote the set of all model transformation sequences $TRAFOS(MT) = \{s \mid s = (G^S, G_0 \Rightarrow^* G_n, G^T)$ is a model transformation sequence via $MT\}$ for a model transformation MT.

Definition 3 (DC-optimised Model Transformation). *Let $LTS = (TR_{FT}, S)$ be a DC-layered transformation system for the forward translation rules TR_{FT} of a TGG with induced model transformation MT. The DC-optimised model transformation $MT_{LTS}: \mathcal{L}(TG^S) \Rightarrow \mathcal{L}(TG^T)$ is obtained from*

MT by restriction to the LTS-compatible model transformation sequences, i.e.,

$$TRAFOS(MT_{LTS}) = \{s \in TRAFOS(MT) \mid s = (G^S, G_0' \xrightarrow{tr_{FT}^*} G_n', G^T) \text{ and}$$

$G_0' \xrightarrow{tr_{FT}^*} G_n'$ *is a transformation sequence via LTS*}.   △

By Thm. 3 below, we show that the execution of the DC-LTS does not affect the existing results for TGGs concerning the notion of correctness and completeness (see Def. 4 below according to [13]).

Definition 4 (Correctness and Completeness). *A model transformation MT is* correct, *if for each MT-sequence* $(G^S, G_0 \Rightarrow^* G_n, G^T)$ *there is a triple graph* $G = (G^S \leftarrow G^C \rightarrow G^T) \in \mathcal{L}(TGG)$. *It is called* complete, *if for each* $G^S \in \mathcal{L}(TGG)^S$, *there is an MT-sequence* $(G^S, G_0 \Rightarrow^* G_n, G^T)$.   △

Theorem 3 (Correctness and Completeness). *Each DC-optimised model transformation* $MT_{LTS} : \mathcal{L}(TG^S) \Rightarrow \mathcal{L}(TG^T)$ *is correct and complete.*   △

Proof. By Thm. 1 in [13], we know that model transformations *MT* based on forward translation rules are correct and complete. By Thm. 1, we derive that *MT* and MT_{LTS} have the same input/output relation and thus, MT_{LTS} is correct and complete.   □

6   Evaluation

Fig. 6 shows the evaluation of the efficiency improvement using a standard consumer laptop (CPU: i7-2860QM, RAM: 8GB, Java: 1.7U25, OS: 64-bit version of Windows 7) for translating all control procedures (202 files, 199,853 lines of code (LOC)) that were developed by ASTRIUM for the satellite ASTRA 1N. The construction of the dependency conflict clusters is performed once statically for the TGG and thus, not contained in the execution times. The left chart shows the translation via the TGG without efficiency improvement for the smallest 126 files[4] (<50KB) – file no. 127 reached a timeout of 10 hours. The amount of nodes of an AST graph is on average about 4 times the amount of LOC of the file. The execution of the DC-layered TGG (right chart) is faster (approximately 100 times as fast for graphs with 4,000 nodes) - mainly due to the massively reduced amount of rule match computations at each step. Fig. 6 shows the execution times for translating each input file separately. The effective translation of the full set of files at SES is performed by distributing the files to eight parallel Java threads (four physical cores). This leads to an additional average speed up factor of three such that the translation for one satellite takes about five minutes. SES appreciated the obtained speed as it is largely above what is needed for practical use.

Table 1 provides an overview of the evaluation of the translator concerning the industrial requirements of SES. The implementation has been delivered to

---

[4] A file contains the code for one satellite control procedure.

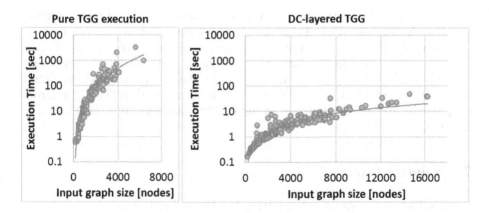

Fig. 6. Measurements for satellite ASTRA 1N (logarithmic scale) using Henshin

Table 1. Evaluation of requirements

Requirement	Evaluation
Syntactical correctness and completeness	Ensured for Phase 2 of the AST conversion by Thm. 3; TGGs simplify the guarantee of a resulting tree structure
Precision/fidelity, minimal efforts for revalidation	TGG rules are obtained from DSL mapping document that was specified by domain experts containing pairs of corresponding source and target code fragments
Complete automation	Yes: no user interaction, no manual editing of output files.
Maintainability	- Visual and intuitive GUI for TGG rules - No complex control structures for execution - Automated check of rule dependencies with AGG [28]
Readability	- The output source code in SPELL is well aligned - Output is compliant with SPELL coding guidelines - All header entries and comments are generated adequately
Efficiency, scalability	- Metamodels of generated Xtext plugins: >140 types - Rules: 484 (TGG: 249, initialisation + refactoring: 235), - Internal XML representation: ~50,000 LOC (lines of code) - Benchmark: ~5:00 min. for satellite Astra 1N (see Fig. 6)
Direct savings	1–2 man years per satellite (estimated by SES, compared to manual conversion and validation)

SES and was successfully assessed and validated by SES and the satellite manufacturer ASTRIUM. According to Thm. 3, the translation ensures syntactical correctness and completeness for Phase 2 of the AST conversion via the TGG. TGGs simplify the challenge to ensure that the resulting graph of the model transformation forms an AST. The source model is always preserved and the execution ensures that elements are translated exactly once. This reduces the challenge of checking that the rules translate each path or subtree of the source

AST into a path or subtree in the target graph attached to the corresponding parent node. The size of the TGG, the processed input files and the corresponding execution times in Table 1 show that the presented approach is applicable for large scale applications. Currently, the following six satellites are running on the generated control procedures: Astra-1M, Astra-1N, Astra-2E, Astra-2F, Astra-3B, and SES-6. Moreover, SES is validating two further TGG-translators for the satellite control languages of the satellite manufacturers THALES and BOEING.

7   Related Work

Other solutions for software translation include manually writing a converter, using a compiler-compiler or meta-programming based on term rewriting or similar techniques. In fact, a fully manual rewrite in the target language, using the source language artefact only as a reference, is also feasible in some situations and even has been the preferred approach for the mission-critical satellite control procedures at SES, before the approach presented in this paper has been taken into account.

Compiler-compilers or parser generators, such as ANTLR [24], can be used to generate a parser based on the grammar of a source language. Then, the generation of the target language has to be programmed either in annotation to the source grammar or by traversing the generated abstract syntax tree. In both cases, only the source language can be specified in an adequate way by its grammar, while the target language is implicit in the manually written code.

Source transformation systems based on term rewriting include the DMS system [2], TXL [4], the Rascal language [19] and the Spoofax language workbench [18] with the Stratego/XT engine [3]. Using these systems is quite similar to our approach, which can be seen, e. g., in the Extract-Analyze-Synthesise (EASY) Paradigm for Rascal [20]. Both, the source and the target language, are specified in some form of grammar formalism and the transformation between the languages is given by a set of transformation rules, where all the above-mentioned systems use some sorts of rewriting rules, which are specified in a textual syntax.

While these systems aim at providing integrated systems, we are using separate building blocks that are already available in the EMF ecosystem – Xtext for parsing and serialising and Henshin for transformation. Parsers and/or serialisers can also be generated from XML Schema Definition (XSD) files by the core EMF system if the language is an XML dialect. Source and/or target language can also be visual languages implemented by EMF-based tools like the Graphical Modeling Framework (GMF). This provides for a seamless integration of heterogeneous languages. Moreover, the basic language definitions – Xtext grammars, XSD files, GMF projects – and the resulting plugins are reusable for all translation, refactoring and model transformation projects involving the same language.

The textual programming of a specific term rewriting language has quite a steep learning curve [5], while we experienced that the visual specification of pattern-based graph transformation rules on EMF models provides more intuitive access. Our division of the conversion by graph transformation into the three phases – initialisation, forward translation based on triple graph grammars, and refactoring of the result – yields a separation of concerns that additionally helps in keeping the solution comprehensible. Our example from Sec. 4 already shows non-trivial structural differences between the abstract syntax structures of source and target language. In our industrial case study, the visual representation provided a more intuitive access to those structural differences than a textual, tree-oriented representation.

Several performance improvements for TGGs have been proposed for restricted kinds of TGGs using dependency information on nodes only [22,11]. The present paper provides a general technique for arbitrary TGGs and yields a layered transformation system, where functional input/output behaviour avoids the need for backtracking of already executed layers. We use the general notion of rule conflicts and dependencies - in particular, we take into account dependencies on edges, attributes and application conditions. We are confident that the existing approaches can be integrated in the new one by applying them locally to each layer.

Regarding performance of model transformations in general, Mészáros et al. [23] have proposed manual and automatic optimizations based on overlapping of matches. Specifically for Henshin, Tichy et al. [29] have identified several "bad smells", i. e., features of transformation rules that possibly result in poor transformation performance and should be avoided if possible. During the development of the *PIL2SPELL* translation, in addition to our dependency-based strategy, we followed the guidelines from [29].

8 Conclusion

In this article, we presented a formal and fully automated approach to industrial software source code translation. We provided a general concept for efficiency improvement of graph transformation systems (Thms. 1 and 2). In our main result (Thm. 3), we have shown the correctness of the approach. We evaluated the approach within a safety critical industrial application: the translation of satellite control procedures. In particular, we evaluated the industrial requirements, including reliability, efficiency and code readability. Our approach considerably improves the rewriting efficiency of the used triple graph transformation approach while guaranteeing the correctness. As an effective result, six communication satellites are running on the generated procedures.

Regarding the Henshin tool, work is in progress to implement the critical pair analysis directly instead of using AGG. The performance results achieved by our proposed approach shall be further evaluated by making use of recently developed benchmarks [17,1].

In future work, we will employ the rich formal foundation of TGGs and apply them for the synchronisation between source code and possible visualisations of software. We also plan to apply graph transformation techniques for analysing test coverage and generating valid test cases.

Acknowledgments. This project is part of the Efficient Automation of Satellite Operations (EASO) project supported by the European Space Agency (ESA)[5].

Supported by the Fonds National de la Recherche, Luxembourg (3968135, 4895603).

References

1. Anjorin, A., Cunha, A., Giese, H., Hermann, F., Rensink, A., Schürr, A.: Benchmarx. In: Bidirectional Model Transformations 2014. CEUR-Workshop Proceedings, vol. 1133, pp. 82–86. CEUR (2014)
2. Baxter, I., Pidgeon, P., Mehlich, M.: DMS: Program transformations for practical scalable software evolution. In: Software Engineering (ICSE 2004). IEEE Press (2004)
3. Bravenboer, M., Kalleberg, K.T., Vermaas, R., Visser, E.: Stratego/XT 0.17. a language and toolset for program transformation. Science of Computer Programming 72(1-2), 52–70 (2008)
4. Cordy, J.R.: The TXL source transformation language. Science of Computer Programming 61(3), 190–210 (2006)
5. Cordy, J.R.: Excerpts from the TXL cookbook. In: Fernandes, J.M., Lämmel, R., Visser, J., Saraiva, J. (eds.) GTTSE 2009. LNCS, vol. 6491, pp. 27–91. Springer, Heidelberg (2011)
6. The Eclipse Foundation: Xtext – Language Development Framework – Version 2.2.1 (2012),
http://www.eclipse.org/Xtext/
7. The Eclipse Foundation: EMF Henshin – Version 0.9.4 (2013),
http://www.eclipse.org/modeling/emft/henshin/
8. Ehrig, H., Ehrig, K., Hermann, F.: From model transformation to model integration based on the algebraic approach to triple graph grammars. ECEASST 10, 14 (2008)
9. Ehrig, H., Ehrig, K., Prange, U., Taentzer, G.: Fundamentals of Algebraic Graph Transformation. Springer (2006)
10. Ehrig, H., Ehrig, K., Ermel, C., Hermann, F., Taentzer, G.: Information preserving bidirectional model transformations. In: Dwyer, M.B., Lopes, A. (eds.) FASE 2007. LNCS, vol. 4422, pp. 72–86. Springer, Heidelberg (2007)
11. Giese, H., Wagner, R.: From model transformation to incremental bidirectional model synchronization. Software and Systems Modeling 8(1), 21–43 (2009)
12. Hegedüs, Á., Horváth, Á., Varró, D.: Towards guided trajectory exploration of graph transformation systems. ECEASST 40 (2010)
13. Hermann, F., Ehrig, H., Golas, U., Orejas, F.: Efficient analysis and execution of correct and complete model transformations based on triple graph grammars. In: Model Driven Interoperability (MDI 2010), pp. 22–31. ACM (2010)
14. Hermann, F., Ehrig, H., Orejas, F., Golas, U.: Formal analysis of functional behaviour of model transformations based on triple graph grammars. In: Ehrig, H., Rensink, A., Rozenberg, G., Schürr, A. (eds.) ICGT 2010. LNCS, vol. 6372, pp. 155–170. Springer, Heidelberg (2010)
15. Hermann, F., Gottmann, S., Nachtigall, N., Braatz, B., Morelli, G., Pierre, A., Engel, T.: On an Automated Translation of Satellite Procedures Using Triple Graph Grammars. In: Duddy, K., Kappel, G. (eds.) ICMB 2013. LNCS, vol. 7909, pp. 50–51. Springer, Heidelberg (2013)

---

[5] http://www.esa.int/ESA

16. Hermann, F., Gottmann, S., Nachtigall, N., Ehrig, H., Braatz, B., Morelli, G., Pierre, A., Engel, T., Ermel, C.: Triple Graph Grammars in the Large for Translating Satellite Procedures – Extended Version. Tech. rep. TR-SnT-2014-7, University of Luxembourg, SnT (2014), http://orbilu.uni.lu/
17. Hildebrandt, S., Lambers, L., Giese, H., Rieke, J., Greenyer, J., Schäfer, W., Lauder, M., Anjorin, A., Schürr, A.: A survey of triple graph grammar tools. In: Stevens, P., Terwilliger, J.F. (eds.) Bidirectional Transformations 2013. ECEASST, vol. 57. European Association of Software Science and Technology (2013)
18. Kats, L.C.L., Visser, E.: The Spoofax language workbench. rules for declarative specification of languages and IDEs. In: Object-Oriented Programming, Systems, Languages, and Applications, OOPSLA 2010 (2010)
19. Klint, P., Vinju, J.J., van der Storm, T.: RASCAL: A domain specific language for source code analysis and manipulation. In: Source Code Analysis and Manipulation. pp. 168–177. IEEE Computer Society (2009)
20. Klint, P., van der Storm, T., Vinju, J.: EASY meta-programming with Rascal. In: Fernandes, J.M., Lämmel, R., Visser, J., Saraiva, J. (eds.) GTTSE 2009. LNCS, vol. 6491, pp. 222–289. Springer, Heidelberg (2011)
21. Lambers, L.: Certifying Rule-Based Models using Graph Transformation. Ph.D. thesis, Technische Universität Berlin (2009)
22. Lauder, M., Anjorin, A., Varró, G., Schürr, A.: Bidirectional model transformation with precedence triple graph grammars. In: Vallecillo, A., Tolvanen, J.-P., Kindler, E., Störrle, H., Kolovos, D. (eds.) ECMFA 2012. LNCS, vol. 7349, pp. 287–302. Springer, Heidelberg (2012)
23. Mészáros, T., Mezei, G., Levendovszky, T., Asztalos, M.: Manual and automated performance optimization of model transformation systems. International Journal on Software Tools for Technology Transfer 12(3-4), 231–243 (2010)
24. Parr, T., Fisher, K.: LL(*): the foundation of the ANTLR parser generator. ACM SIGPLAN Notices 46(6), 425–436 (2011)
25. Schürr, A.: Specification of graph translators with triple graph grammars. In: Mayr, E.W., Schmidt, G., Tinhofer, G. (eds.) WG 1994. LNCS, vol. 903, pp. 151–163. Springer, Heidelberg (1995)
26. Schürr, A., Klar, F.: 15 years of triple graph grammars. In: Ehrig, H., Heckel, R., Rozenberg, G., Taentzer, G. (eds.) ICGT 2008. LNCS, vol. 5214, pp. 411–425. Springer, Heidelberg (2008)
27. SES Engineering: SPELL - Satellite Procedure Execution Language & Library – Version 2.3.13 (2013), http://code.google.com/p/spell-sat/
28. TFS-Group, TU Berlin: AGG (2014), http://www.tfs.tu-berlin.de/agg
29. Tichy, M., Krause, C., Liebel, G.: Detecting performance bad smells for Henshin model transformations. In: Proc. Analysis of Model Transformations (AMT 2013). CEUR-Workshop Proceedings, vol. 1077, pp. 82–86. CEUR (2013)

Developing eMoflon with eMoflon

Erhan Leblebici[1,*], Anthony Anjorin[1,**], and Andy Schürr[2]

[1] Graduate School of Computational Engineering, Technische Universität Darmstadt
{leblebici,anjorin}@gsc.tu-darmstadt.de
[2] Real-Time Systems Lab., Technische Universität Darmstadt
andy.schuerr@es.tu-darmstadt.de

Abstract. eMoflon is a Model-Driven Engineering (MDE) tool that supports rule-based unidirectional and bidirectional model transformation.
eMoflon is not only being used successfully for both industrial case studies and in academic research projects, but is also consequently used to
develop itself. This is known as *bootstrapping* and has become an important test, proof-of-concept, and success story for us. Interestingly,
although MDE technologies are inherently self-descriptive and higher-
order, very few actively developed MDE tools are bootstrapped. In this
paper, we (i) report on the current state and focus of eMoflon, (ii) share
our experience with bootstrapping in an MDE context, and (iii) provide a
scalability analysis of a core component in eMoflon implemented as both
a unidirectional and bidirectional model transformation with eMoflon.

Keywords: eMoflon, MDE, model transformation, bootstrapping.

1 Introduction and Motivation

eMoflon[1] is a graph transformation tool that supports the rule-based specification of model transformations, which play a central role in Model-Driven Engineering (MDE). eMoflon builds upon the Eclipse Modelling Framework (EMF),
using *Ecore* for metamodelling, *Story Driven Modelling* (SDM) [3] (a dialect
of programmed graph transformations) for unidirectional model transformation,
and *Triple Graph Grammars* (TGGs) [6] for bidirectional model transformation. eMoflon consists of an Eclipse plugin as backend, and two frontends: a set
of Eclipse-based editors supporting a *textual* syntax, and a plugin for Enterprise
Architect (EA), a professional UML tool, supporting a *visual* syntax.

Besides industrial case studies and academic research projects, an important
proof-of-concept for eMoflon is its own self-development. This is often referred
to as *bootstrapping* and will be used in the rest of this paper to present the main
features supported by eMoflon. Figure 1 depicts a schematic overview of the
chain of model transformations employed internally by eMoflon.

* Supported by the 'Excellence Initiative' of the German Federal and State Govern-
ments and the Graduate School of Computational Engineering at TU Darmstadt.
** The project on which this paper is based was funded by the German Federal Ministry
of Education and Research, funding code 01IS12054. The authors are responsible for
all contents.
[1] www.emoflon.org

D. Di Ruscio and D. Varró (Eds.): ICMT 2014, LNCS 8568, pp. 138–145, 2014.

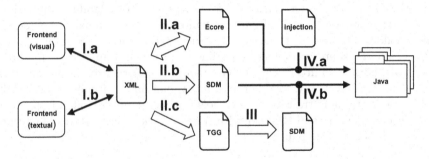

Fig. 1. An overview of the main model transformations used in eMoflon

Ecore, SDM and TGG models are specified in either a visual or textual concrete syntax using the respective frontend. The first step in the chain (marked as I.a, I.b in Fig. 1) maps the frontend-specific representation to and from a common, frontend-independent XML tree structure. This is realized with C# code in the case of EA, and with standard (un)parsers in the case of our textual syntax. The tree structure is used as a generic exchange format decoupling the backend from its different frontends. It is kept as simple as possible to shift the complexity of the transformation to the subsequent steps in the chain.

The second step (marked as II.a, II.b, and II.c in Fig. 1) is to transform the generic tree structure to actual instances of our Ecore, SDM, and TGG metamodels. These transformations are bootstrapped (depicted as bold white arrows) meaning that they are implemented with eMoflon itself. The transformation II.a is bidirectional to enable importing external Ecore instance models (e.g., as provided by the Transformation Tool Contest[2]). A unidirectional version of II.a is also available in the XML-Ecore direction with SDM, as support for SDM in eMoflon was implemented *before* TGGs. The two versions of II.a provide for an interesting qualitative and quantitative comparison of SDM and TGGs, and we shall use excerpts of transformation II.a as our running example throughout the paper. The transformations II.b and II.c transform a tree structure to SDM and TGGs, respectively. These transformations are currently unidirectional, but bidirectionalizing them is work in progress as it would, for example, enable transforming generated models (result of III) back into the respective concrete syntax.

TGGs are *operationalized* by *compiling* them to SDM with the transformation III, which is bootstrapped with SDMs as a unidirectional model transformation. Bidirectionality is not absolutely necessary in this case as the SDM generated from a TGG represents low-level operationalization details and is not an artifact meant for further user adjustments. Finally, unidirectional model-to-text transformations IV.a and IV.b generate Java projects from Ecore and SDM, with the option of *injecting* hand-crafted (Java) code into the generated files.

In this paper, our contribution is to share and discuss our experience of bootstrapping in an MDE context. For this, we use excerpts from the import/export mechanism of eMoflon as our running example, which is developed with SDMs

---

[2] http://www.transformation-tool-contest.eu/

and TGGs in two different versions. We also provide a scalability comparison of these two versions. That is of particular interest in the context of bootstrapping eMoflon. The rest of the paper is structured as follows: Section 2 introduces eMoflon's support for metamodelling with Ecore. Support for unidirectional (SDMs) and bidirectional (TGGs) model transformation is presented in Sect. 3 and 4, respectively, together with an evaluation of runtime scalability in Sect. 5. Bootstrapping transformation tools in general, and eMoflon in particular, is discussed in Sect. 6 together with related work. Sect. 7 states our future focus and concludes the paper.

2   Metamodelling with Ecore

eMoflon supports Ecore-conform metamodelling used to specify the data structures to be manipulated with model transformations. An excerpt of the metamodel used to represent the generic exchange format in eMoflon is depicted as a class diagram to the left of Fig. 2, consisting basically of labelled Nodes with children and Attributes. To demonstrate how this tree structure is used, the tree metamodel itself is represented as a generic tree to the right of Fig. 2 (as an object diagram). Only the tree structure for representing EClasses and EReferences is shown, i.e., EAttributes as well as multiplicities and containment are omitted. The EClasses "Node" and "Attribute" are represented as nodes in the tree labelled as "EClass" with attributes for their names and a global ID used for cross references in the tree. EReferences are represented analogously, placed in the tree as children of a "references" node of the respective "EClass" node.

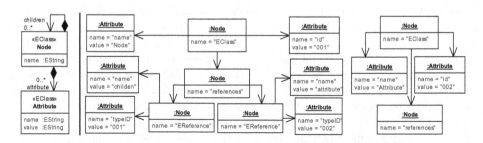

Fig. 2. Metamodel used as an exchange format and its representation as a generic tree

3   Unidirectional Model Transformations with SDM

Story Driven Modelling (SDM) [3] is used in eMoflon to specify unidirectional model transformation. SDM combines graph patterns with control flow structures consisting of a start node, connected activity nodes, and stop nodes. Figure 3 depicts the SDM **handleReferences** that transforms the tree structure representing a reference to an actual instance of **EReference** in Ecore. The SDM, simplified for presentation purposes, takes a related node and class (**classNode** and **eClass**) as parameters, and consists of two activity nodes.

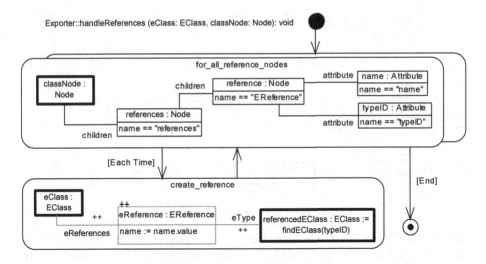

Fig. 3. SDM for exporting references of an EClass

Starting with a *for-each* activity node (`for_all_reference_nodes`) that determines *all* occurrences of the specified pattern in the tree, the SDM iterates over all subtree structures that represent references in the given root node `classNode`. Fixed elements in the pattern such as `classNode` (bound to the given parameter) are depicted with a bold frame, while all other elements are determined via pattern matching, such that all constraints are satisfied (e.g., `name == "typeID"`). For each occurrence of the pattern, the SDM executes the second activity `create_reference`. This activity creates a new `EReference` (depicted green with a "++" markup) between `eClass`, fixed to the given parameter, and `referencedEClass`, determined by invoking a helper method that returns the class referenced by `typeID`. Binding an object over a method call (possibly with parameters as in our case) is a standard language feature in SDM as defined in [4]. Such helper methods can be implemented again with SDM or with plain Java (e.g., using a pre-filled hash table for efficiency reasons). This enables recursion and the integration of hand-crafted code in SDM.

4 Bidirectional Model Transformations with TGGs

Triple Graph Grammars (TGGs) [6] are a declarative, rule-based technique to specify bidirectional model transformation. A TGG is a set of rules that describe how consistent *triples* of source and target models (*graphs*), connected by a correspondence model, are built up simultaneously. All *operational* transformations such as forward, backward and update propagation, are automatically derived from the single specification. In the following, the same transformation implemented with SDMs in Fig. 3, i.e., handling references in the tree, is presented as a TGG rule (depicted in Fig. 4). Black elements represent the pre-condition of the rule, i.e., an occurrence of these elements must be found in order to apply the

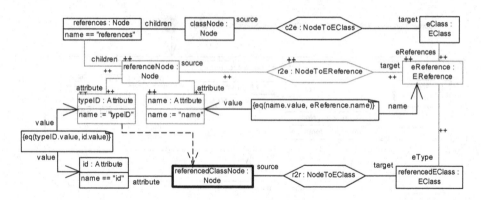

Fig. 4. TGG rule for handling references

rule. Green elements with a ++ markup state the post-condition that must hold after the rule has been applied. The rule, therefore, states that an **EReference** is created together with the depicted subtree structure. TGGs are declarative in the sense that no explicit control structure or rule dependencies are specified. The underlying algorithm figures out automatically the correct choice and sequence of rules to apply for each operational scenario. *Attribute constraints* such as eq(name.value, eReference.name) are specified with a bidirectional extensible textual constraint language, and ensure that eReference is named correctly using the appropriate attribute in the tree, and that referenceNode has the correct typeID value corresponding to the referenced class node in the tree.

In case of a forward transformation, the TGG rule in Fig. 4 is modified by adding all source elements to its context. This means that the required tree structure is "parsed" and only the correspondence link and the target elements are created when applying the rule. Unfortunately, finding the referenced class node might be very time-consuming as no direct connection exists from the reference node to the referenced class node in the tree. In the worst case, one must iterate over all class nodes in the tree to find the correct one. As an optimization technique for such cases, we propose *binding expressions* to *bind* an element directly from another via an auxiliary method, which can be implemented with SDM or plain Java. In our example, the binding expression (depicted as a dashed arrow in the rule) takes the type id attribute of the reference node as input and returns the referenced class node, which should have the same type id. Analogously to the helper method for the SDM (Fig. 3), this is realized in constant time as a table lookup in a lazy cache. Integrating such hand-crafted components seems to contradict the declarative nature of TGG rules, but they serve as a crucial and pragmatic means of dealing with performance issues at critical points.

In our example, a second rule is required to handle self-references and would only differ slightly from the rule depicted in Fig. 4. For such cases, eMoflon supports *rule refinements*, a modularity concept for TGGs. Using refinements, an *abstract* rule covering the commonalities of both rules can be specified and refined appropriately in the concrete rules. Rule refinement avoids pattern duplication and greatly improves the readability and maintainability of TGG specifications.

5   Scalability

The plots on the left and right side of Fig. 5 show our runtime measurements in linear and logarithmic scale, respectively, for the import with TGGs and the export with TGGs and SDM. The y-axis shows the time in seconds, the x-axis the number of elements of randomly generated Ecore models. Vertical dashed lines indicate a change in step size in the x-axis. The logarithmic plot shows two additional measurement points for very large models containing up to 300.000 elements. All measurements were repeated 10 times (the median is plotted) and executed on an Intel i5-3550 (3.30 GHz) processor with 8 GB RAM running Windows 7 and Eclipse 4.3.

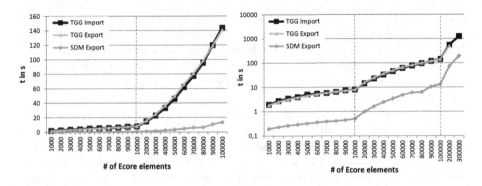

Fig. 5. Runtime measurements in linear and logarithmic scale

Our TGG algorithm is in theory polynomial with respect to model size, and our results back this claim (showing even almost linear behaviour for up to 10.000 elements). Our results also show that both directions (import and export) exhibit very similar runtime behaviour, reflecting the bidirectional and symmetrical nature of TGGs. On the other hand, the TGG-based transformations are 10-15 times slower than the SDM implementation and run out of memory as from 200.000 elements for the export, and 300.000 for the import (this difference is due to the tree being much larger than the corresponding Ecore model).

6   Discussion and Related Work

MDE technologies are inherently self-descriptive and higher-order but, to the best of our knowledge, very few model transformation tools are actually developed with bootstrapping. ATL [5] and FUJABA [3], however, are examples for tools/toolsuites that do practice bootstrapping. Although the bootstrapped FUJABA code generator CodeGen2 is actually reused in eMoflon to generate

Java code from SDMs, it is only used as a well-tested black-box component and is no longer bootstrapped. Figure 1 in the introduction reflects our pragmatic decision on what is to be bootstrapped in eMoflon after considering our current research foci and the advantages/challenges of bootstrapping.

Bootstrapping is a common technique in compiler construction for General Purpose Languages (GPLs) such as C++. SDM and TGGs, however, are Domain Specific Languages (DSLs) for model transformation, and cannot replace a GPL. Nevertheless, we are convinced that it is just as advantageous to use such transformation languages for defining suitable parts of their compilers. Barzdins et al. [1] demonstrate this by obtaining model transformation languages from existing ones via bootstrapping. A transformation language L_i is compiled to a lower-level language L_{i-1} with a compiler written in L_{i-1}. This corresponds to TGGs being compiled to SDMs with SDMs (cf. Fig. 1). In addition to their arguments for usability and efficiency of bootstrapped languages, our experience shows the following advantages: (i) the tool itself is a non-trivial test that cannot be skipped, (ii) a proof-of-concept is established regarding the capabilities of the developed transformation languages, and (iii) both functional and non-functional requirements are equally considered due to intensive self-usage. Regarding the last point, language-related features such as binding expressions and modularity concepts (cf. Sect. 4), as well as non-functional qualities such as user-friendliness and performance are constantly being improved on the basis of our self-usage experience.

Buchmann et al. [2] challenge the added value of graph-based model transformations in general and SDMs in particular, referring to the bootstrapping of CodeGen2. Some of the drawbacks they identify are indeed relevant for our bootstrapping, including a lack of means for low-level details such as exception handling, and missing modularity concepts for patterns. Moreover, our experience reveals further challenges of bootstrapping with SDMs: (i) increased complexity when making changes as they must be tested before and after building a new version of the tool, (ii) an increased dependency on underlying code generators and their shortcomings, and (iii) redundant implementations of components (initial versions with Java, later versions with SDMs, and in some cases finally with TGGs).

7   Conclusion and Future Focus

In this paper, we have reported on the current state of eMoflon, conducted a scalability analysis of a core component in eMoflon implemented with eMoflon, and shared our experience with bootstrapping. For the future, the focus of TGGs in eMoflon will be *synchronization* of concurrently changed models, a special case of model transformation where models are no longer created from scratch, but are updated incrementally to reflect the changes. Moreover, work on a new pattern matching engine is in progress to replace CodeGen2 and improve the code generation capabilities of eMoflon and, therefore, our development experience.

References

1. Barzdins, J., Kalnins, A., Rencis, E., Rikacovs, S.: Model Transformation Languages and their Implementation by Bootstrapping Method. In: Avron, A., Dershowitz, N., Rabinovich, A. (eds.) Pillars of Computer Science. LNCS, vol. 4800, pp. 130–145. Springer, Heidelberg (2008)
2. Buchmann, T., Westfechtel, B., Winetzhammer, S.: The Added Value of Programmed Graph Transformations A Case Study from Software Configuration Management. In: Schürr, A., Varró, D., Varró, G. (eds.) AGTIVE 2011. LNCS, vol. 7233, pp. 198–209. Springer, Heidelberg (2012)
3. Fischer, T., Niere, J., Torunski, L., Zündorf, A.: Story Diagrams: A New Graph Rewrite Language Based on the Unified Modeling Language and Java. In: Ehrig, H., Engels, G., Kreowski, H.-J., Rozenberg, G. (eds.) Graph Transformations. LNCS, vol. 1764, pp. 296–309. Springer, Heidelberg (2000)
4. Heinzemann, C., Rieke, J., Detten, M.V., Travkin, D., Lauder, M.: A new Meta-Model for Story Diagrams. In: 8th International Fujaba Days, pp. 2–6 (2011)
5. Jouault, F., Kurtev, I.: Transforming Models with ATL. In: Bruel, J.-M. (ed.) MoDELS 2005. LNCS, vol. 3844, pp. 128–138. Springer, Heidelberg (2006)
6. Schürr, A.: Specification of Graph Translators with Triple Graph Grammars. In: Mayr, E.W., Schmidt, G., Tinhofer, G. (eds.) Graph-Theoretic Concepts in Computer Science. LNCS, vol. 903, pp. 151–163. Springer, Heidelberg (1995)

ChainTracker, a Model-Transformation Trace Analysis Tool for Code-Generation Environments

Victor Guana and Eleni Stroulia

Department of Computing Science
University of Alberta
Edmonton, Canada
{guana,stroulia}@ualberta.ca

Abstract. Model-driven engineering is advocated as an effective method for developing families of software systems that systematically differ across well defined dimensions. Yet, this software construction paradigm is rather brittle at the face of evolution. Particularly, when building code-generation environments, platform evolution scenarios force developers to modify the generated code of individual generation instances in an ad-hoc manner. Thus violating the systematicity of the original construction process. In order to maintain the code-generation environment synchronized, code refinements have to be traced and backwardly propagated to generation infrastructure, so as to make these changes systematically possible for all systems that can be generated. This paper presents *ChainTracker*, a general conceptual framework, and model-transformation composition analysis tool, that supports developers when maintaining and synchronizing evolving code-generation environments. *ChainTracker* gathers and visualizes *model-to-model*, and *model-to-text* traceability information for ATL and Acceleo model-transformation compositions.

1 Introduction

Code-generation environments automate and systematize the process of building families of software systems. They typically rely on one or more domain-specific languages, and a set of model transformations that reify the abstractions expressed in the domain models and generate executable code [1]. The transformations work by injecting execution semantics into the initial problem specification, through a composition of *model-to-model* and *model-to-text* transformation modules.

Like all software, code-generation environments are bound to evolve [2]. Recent empirical studies revealed that practitioners face challenges when new requirements arise, and changes have to be introduced in either the source code of a generated application, or the domain-specific languages and the model-transformation compositions involved in the code-generation process [3].

Although, in principle, developers avoid modifying the code of a system after it is generated, approximately 40% end up having to do so [3][2] and, when they do, they have to spend copious amounts of time inspecting how changes

D. Di Ruscio and D. Varró (Eds.): ICMT 2014, LNCS 8568, pp. 146–153, 2014.

impact models and transformations, so changes can be backwardly propagated to the generation environments, and later reused in the generation of future systems. So far, little progress has been made towards supporting developers when performing these modifications during the construction and maintenance of code-generation environments.

The work we describe in this paper makes two novel contributions. The first is a general conceptual framework that formalizes how to model and collect traceability information in code-generation environments with model-transformation compositions that use (i) rule-based transformation languages to implement *models-to-model* transformations, an (ii) template-based languages to implement *model-to-text* transformations, distinguishing between explicit and implicit traceability links. The second contribution of our work is *ChainTracker*, a model-transformation composition analysis tool that supports developers when maintaining and synchronizing evolving code-generation environments. *ChainTracker* gathers and visualizes *model-to-model*, and *model-to-text* traceability information for ATL [4] and Acceleo [5] model-transformation compositions (as examples of the above rule-based *model-to-model* and template-based *model-to-code* transformation languages).

2   Background and Related Work

In principle, traceability information can be used in multiple ways, including to assess metamodel coverage in a code-generation environment, to verify model-transformation correctness, and to reduce the cognitive challenges when understanding a model-transformation chain [6][7]. However, most of the time, traceability information is collected manually or through experimental tools. More importantly, all current tools are unable to examine the *model-to-text* transformations, ignoring the last step in the model-transformation composition and effectively relying on developers for mapping code changes to their upstream dependent generation infrastructure.

Let us now review in some detail current approaches to traceability in model-driven engineering. Falleri, et al. [8] propose an imperative language in order to create trace models inside individual model-transformation modules. In this proposal, developers have to insert traceability constructs inside the transformation code to gather the traceability information of a transformation module. Similarly, Jouault [9] presents a strategy to keep track of ATL trace links by extending model-transformation rules with ATL constructs that build a traceability model conforming to a traceability metamodel proposed by the same author.

Van Amstel et al. [10] present a tool that gathers and visualizes traceability information of transformation compositions. In this case, the implemented tool makes explicit the mappings between source and target elements of a transformation, highlighting the hierarchical structure of both metamodels and ATL transformation modules. Jouault's proposal does not provide insights on possible visualization mechanisms to reduce the cognitive challenges of coping with massive amounts of information derived from complex model-transformation compositions. Furthermore, none of the proposals presented above provide any type of support to collect or visualize traceability information for *model-to-text* transformations.

In Section 3 we present *ChainTracker*'s implementation architecture and visualization mechanisms. *ChainTracker* works as a third-party tool that analyses model-transformation compositions (that include *model-to-text* mappings), keeping the semantics of transformation rules intact, and providing an orthogonal set of metamodels that contain traceability information by statically interpreting a set of transformation rules that have been composed in order to generate code. In Section 3, we also introduce the concept of implicit traceability links (not covered by the current proposals). Implicit traceability links augment the traceability analysis by identifying indirect relations between source and target metamodels. This information provides additional support to developers when analysing the impact of changes in metamodels and transformations, that need to be synchronized after generated code refinements.

3   The ChainTracker Architecture

As shown in Figure 1, the architecture of *ChainTracker* consists of four main components: the *ATL Parser*, the *Tuple Extractor*, the *Acceleo Parser*, and the *Tuple Visualizer*. *ChainTracker* receives as input all the relevant transformations of a model-transformation composition to be analysed (ATL scripts for *model-to-model* and Acceleo scripts in the case of *model-to-text* transformations).

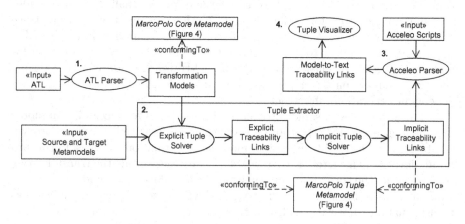

Fig. 1. ChainTracker Implementation Architecture

3.1   A Transformation Composition Example

We will illustrate the *ChainTracker* process using a simple model-transformation composition example. The goal of the composition is to refactor the elements of a model conforming to the *MetamodelA*, and produce a model conforming to *MetamodelB*, both portrayed in Figure 2. Then, the composition generates a

Java class that contains attributes initialized using elements of the latter model. Listings 1.1 and 1.2 present our *model-to-model* and *model-to-text* transformation examples respectively.

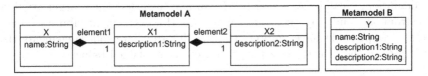

Fig. 2. Metamodel A (source) and Metamodel B (target) examples

3.2 The ATL Parser

The main functionality of the *ATL Parser* is to read, parse, and simplify a set of ATL transformation scripts. *ChainTracker* uses the reflexive capabilities of ATL's virtual machine to obtain the XMI-AST representation of a set of ATL scripts. *ChainTracker* implements a programmatic transformation that takes the XMI model of an ATL script, and produces a simplified representation that contains all the information relevant for the traceability link recollection. The resulting model conforms to *MarcoPolo*, a metamodel that we have designed in order to highlight transformation mappings in rule-based and template-based transformation languages (Figure 3). *MarcoPolo* is composed by two main packages, *MarcoPolo Core* and *MarcoPolo Tuple*. In this particular case, *MarcoPolo Core* is conceived to manage the complexity of transformation tuples that represent ATL transformation mappings. Effectively, we use *MarcoPolo "to find our way"* through the traceability links of a model-transformation composition.

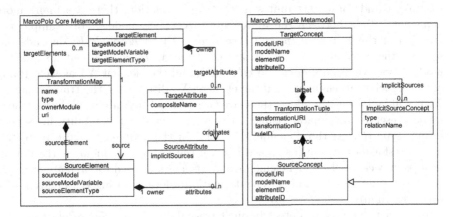

Fig. 3. MarcoPolo Metamodel

In *MarcoPolo Core*, we see each transformation module as a 3-tuple (TM, TE, se), where TM is the set of transformation rules, and TE a collection of its target-model elements. TE is defined as a tuple (TA, se) in which TA is a set of target attributes *ta*, and *se* a unique source-model element. Furthermore each source-model element *se* contains a set, namely *SA*, that represent multiple source attributes *sa*. Finally, *ta* is modelled as a nested tuple (ta, sa) establishing a one-to-one mapping from a target attribute to a source attribute. Following this definition, it can be seen that in *MarcoPolo* the origins of a target attribute come from one, and only one, source attribute. However, the attribute's *implicit source* concept could have pointers to other intermediate source elements that participate in the creation of a target element as explained below.

```
1  module A2B;
2  create OUT : B from IN : A;
3  rule X2Y {
4    from
5      x : A!X
6    to
7      y : B!Y (
8        name <- x.name,
9        description1 <- x.element1.description1,
10       description2 <- x.element1.element2.description2)}
```

Listing 1.1. ATL - A2B Transformation Module Example

In our example, after the $X2Y$ matched rule is parsed (Listing 1.1), a model conforming to *MarcoPolo Core* is produced with the following (ta, sa) tuples:

- $(Y : name, (X : name))$
- $(Y : description1, (X : element1/description1))$
- $(Y : description2, (X : element1/elenment2/description2/))$

On cursory examination, these tuples would be identified as all the traceability links that map the elements of the *MetamodelA* into elements in of the *MetamodelB*. However, even though there are one-to-one mappings between the target and source attributes in the transformation, there are many more dependency links between the source and target metamodels. For example, the creation of the $Y : description2$ attribute in the *MetamodelB*, depends not only on the attribute $X2 : description2$ of the *MetamodelA*, but also on the model associations *element1* and *element2*, and the element $X1$ as well. If any of the associations changes, or if the element $X1$ disappears, the transformation $X2Y$ will be broken. In effect, there are two types of traceability links that need to be preserved and made visible: *explicit* and *implicit* traceability links. The former type reflects the dependencies between the endpoints of the mappings in a transformation rule (as shown above); the latter type includes the dependencies between metamodel elements and associations used to navigate or query the source metamodel, and select information relevant during the creation of a target attribute.

In order to be able to detect implicit traceability links, *MarcoPolo Core* includes the *implicit source* attribute as a part of the source attribute concept. The *implicit source* represents the relative path that a mapping rule follows when navigating source model concepts in order to create a target attribute (see Figure 3). After the ATL modules are parsed, the *implicit source* contains a chain of meta-associations and meta-attributes, often extracted from OCL expressions.

For example, in the context of the $X2Y$ rule, the *implicit source* value for the source attribute $X2 : description2$ is $X : element1/element2/description2/$. Notice how the *implicit source* does not include information about where the *element1* and *element2* associations come from, and if there is an intermediate element that binds them, in this case $X1$. Given that both OCL and ATL model-navigation expressions are solved in execution time, this information is not explicitly available in the ATL abstract syntax model. *ChainTracker's Tuple Extractor* implements an ATL interpreter that takes the source attribute context together with its *implicit source*, in order to identify where the intermediate associations and intermediate attributes come from.

3.3 The Tuple Extractor

The main functionality of the *Tuple Extractor* component is to analyze every source-to-target mapping and identify sets of explicit and implicit traceability links. For that purpose, the *Tuple Extractor* takes as input a set of models conforming to *MarcoPolo Core* that represent all the mappings between source and target models implemented in a transformation script. It also takes all the intermediate metamodels used in the composition as input and output patterns.

The *Tuple Extractor* consists of two sub-modules (Figure 1). While the *explicit tuple solver* takes a set of *MarcoPolo* instances and extracts all the explicit transformation links for a given transformation mapping. The *implicit tuple solver* finds the intermediate or navigated concepts involved in a given transformation rule. These concepts can be either metamodel elements or associations. In our example, the *implicit tuple solver* will take a (ta, sa) tuple such as $(Y : description2, (X : element1/elenment2/description2/))$, and through a recursive exploration of the $A2B$ source metamodel, it will discover the three implicit traceability links:

- $(Y : description2, X : element1)$ Association *element1* that belongs to X
- $(Y : description2-> X1 : element2)$ Association *element2* that belongs to X1
- $(Y : description2-> X2 : description2)$ Element $X2$ and *description2* attribute

The final result of the *Tuple Extractor* module is a set of *MarcoPolo Tuple* instances that portray the explicit and implicit traceability links of a given set of ATL transformation scripts.

3.4 The Acceleo Parser

So far we have described how *ChainTracker* collects traceability information from *model-to-model* transformations. The *Acceleo Parser* identifies transformation tuples that map model elements into text artifacts. It takes an Acceleo script together with the metamodel that the script uses as input, and statically analyses its code-injection statements. *Model-to-text* traceability links are modelled in the form of tuples with the following structure $((startLineID, endLineID), (moduleID, fileID, sourceModelID, source ElementID))$. In the tuples, *startLineID* and *endLineID* specify the initial and final code line identifiers where a specific source element is queried for a code injection statement, or used in an Acceleo model navigation construct.

```
1  [module B2Java('http://ualberta.edu.cs.ssrg.cge.b')]
2  [template public generateElement(yB : Y)]
3  [comment @main/]
4  [file ('Generated.java', false, 'UTF-8')]
5  public class Generated {
6    [for (it : Y | yB)]
7      private Y [it.name/];
8    [/for]
9      public Generated (){
10     [for (it : Y | yB)]
11        [it.name/] = new Y([it.description1/], [it.description2/]);
12     [/for]}}
13 [/file]
14 [/template]
```

Listing 1.2. Acceleo 3.0 - B2Java Transformation Module Example

After analysing the Acceleo *model-to-text* transformation script presented in Listing 1.2, the *Acceleo Parser* identifies traceability links such as $((13, 13),$ $(B2Java, Generated.java, MetamodelB, Y : description1))$

3.5   The Tuple Visualizer

In order to communicate the traceability information to developers, *Chain-Tracker* includes a web-based traceability-visualization tool implemented in the *Tuple Visualizer*. Figure 4 presents the visualization of the traceability link tuples obtained using *ChainTracker's Tuple Extractor*, and the *Acceleo Parser* for our *A2B (model-to-model)* and *B2Java (model-to-text)* composition example.

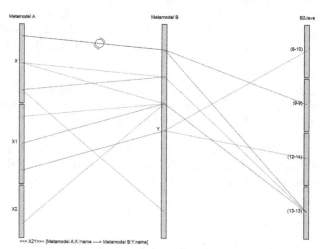

Fig. 4. Model-Transformation Composition Traceability Visualization

In Figure 4, red lines represent explicit traceability links according to *MarcoPolo*'s definition, and blue lines represent implicit traceability information of the composition. The details of the transformation tuples behind the links can be obtained by hovering the cursor over a link.

4 Conclusions and Future Work

In this paper we described *ChainTracker*, a tool designed to support the maintenance and evolution of code-generation environments. In the face of an environment's platform evolution, *ChainTracker* can support developers to trace ad-hoc modifications, from the generated code to is generation environment, thus enabling corresponding changes to the generation infrastructure so as to make these changes systematically possible for all systems that can be generated. *ChainTracker* is currently aware of the ATL and Acceleo transformation syntaxes, which it parses to extract traceability information in its syntactically simpler *MarcoPolo* metamodel. The second contribution of our work, beyond *ChainTracker* itself, is the conceptual framework underlying the design of the tool that formalizes how we model, and collect traceability information in code-generation environments, distinguishing between explicit and implicit links and capturing both in *MarcoPolo*. We believe that this framework is general and can support the extension of *ChainTracker* to deal with other transformation technologies, beyond ATL and Acceleo.

References

1. Czarnecki, K.: Overview of generative software development. In: Banâtre, J.-P., Fradet, P., Giavitto, J.-L., Michel, O. (eds.) UPP 2004. LNCS, vol. 3566, pp. 326–341. Springer, Heidelberg (2005)
2. Van Deursen, A., Visser, E., Warmer, J.: Model-driven software evolution: A research agenda. In: Proceedings 1st International Workshop on Model-Driven Software Evolution, pp. 41–49 (2007)
3. Hutchinson, J., Whittle, J., Rouncefield, M., Kristoffersen, S.: Empirical assessment of mde in industry. In: Proceedings of the 33rd International Conference on Software Engineering, pp. 471–480. ACM (2011)
4. Jouault, F., Kurtev, I.: Transforming models with ATL. In: Bruel, J.-M. (ed.) MoDELS 2005. LNCS, vol. 3844, pp. 128–138. Springer, Heidelberg (2006)
5. Musset, J., Juliot, É., Lacrampe, S., Piers, W., Brun, C., Goubet, L., Lussaud, Y., Allilaire, F.: Acceleo user guide (2006)
6. Guana, V.: Supporting maintenance tasks on transformational code generation environments. In: Proceedings of the 2013 International Conference on Software Engineering, pp. 1369–1372. IEEE Press (2013)
7. Guana, V., Stroulia, E.: Backward propagation of code refinements on transformational code generation environments. In: 2013 International Workshop on Traceability in Emerging Forms of Software Engineering (TEFSE), pp. 55–60 (2013)
8. Falleri, J., Huchard, M., Nebut, C., et al.: Towards a traceability framework for model transformations in kermeta (2006)
9. Jouault, F.: Loosely coupled traceability for atl. In: Proceedings of the European Conference on Model Driven Architecture (ECMDA) Workshop on Traceability, Nuremberg, Germany, vol. 91. Citeseer (2005)
10. van Amstel, M., Serebrenik, A., van den Brand, M.: Visualizing traceability in model transformation compositions. In: Pre-Proceedings of the First Workshop on Composition and Evolution of Model Transformations (2011)

Tracing Program Transformations with String Origins[*]

Pablo Inostroza[1], Tijs van der Storm[1,2], and Sebastian Erdweg[3]

[1] Centrum Wiskunde & Informatica, Amsterdam, The Netherlands
[2] INRIA Lille, France
[3] TU Darmstadt, Germany
{Pablo.Inostroza.Valdera,Tijs.van.der.Storm}@cwi.nl,
erdweg@informatik.tu-darmstadt.de

Abstract. Program transformations play an important role in domain-specific languages and model-driven development. Tracing the execution of such transformations has well-known benefits for debugging, visualization and error reporting. In this paper, we introduce *string origins*, a lightweight, generic and portable technique to establish a tracing relation between the textual fragments in the input and output of a program transformation. We discuss the semantics and the implementation of string origins using the Rascal meta programming language as an example. We illustrate the utility of string origins by presenting data structures and operations for tracing generated code, implementing protected regions, performing name resolution and fixing inadvertent name capture in generated code.

1 Introduction

Program transformations play an important role in domain-specific language (DSL) engineering and model-driven development (MDD). In particular, DSL compilers are often structured as a sequence of transformations, starting with an input program and eventually generating code. It is well-known that origin tracking [16] and model traceability [1,8,12,13,14] provide valuable information for debugging, error reporting and visualization.

In this paper, we focus on traceability for transformations that generate (fragments of) text. We propose *string origins*, a lightweight technique that links each character in the generated text to its origin. A string either originates directly from the input model, occurs as a string literal in the transformation definition, or is synthesized by the transformation (e.g., by string concatenation or substitution). We represent string origins using a combination of unique resource identifiers (URIs) and offset and length values that identify specific text fragments in a resource. We propagate string origins through augmented versions of standard string operators, such that the propagation is fully transparent to transformation writers. In particular, parsing and unparsing retains string origins for text fragments that appear in the AST, such as variable names.

Through applications of string origins we further confirm the usefulness of model traceability by realizing generic solutions to common problems in program-transformation design. First, string origins allow us to link generated elements back

---

[*] This research was supported by the Netherlands Organisation for Scientific Research (NWO) Jacquard Grant "Next Generation Auditing: Data-Assurance as a service" (638.001.214).

D. Di Ruscio and D. Varró (Eds.): ICMT 2014, LNCS 8568, pp. 154–169, 2014.

to their origin. In Section 3.1, we show how this enables the construction of editors with embedded hyperlinks to inspect generated code. Second, we present an example of attaching additional information to generated code via string origins. Section 3.2 describes how this enables protected regions in generated code. Third, string origins can be interpreted as unique pointers that identify subterms. In Section 3.3, we use the origins of symbolic names (variables, type names, method names, etc.) to implement name resolution. Finally, string origins can be used to systematically replace fragments of the generated code that have the same origin. In Section 3.4, we show a generic solution for circumventing accidental variable capture (hygiene) by systematic renaming of generated names.

In Section 4, we discuss the implementation of string origins in the context of Rascal [9]. Overall, we found that string origins have a number of important benefits that can improve the design of program transformations and transformation engines:

- Totality: Unlike existing work in origin tracking and model traceability [12], string origins induce an origin relation which is total. That is, the origin relation maps every character in the output text of a transformation back to its origin.
- Portability: Since the origin relation is based on string values and string operations instead of inferred from transformation code, the structure or style of the transformation language is largely irrelevant. As a result, string origins are portable across transformation systems, transformation styles, and technological spaces. Even in the case of graphical modeling languages, embedded strings (e.g., names, labels, etc.) could be annotated with their location in the serialization format used to store such models.
- Universality: String origins are independent of the source or target language, since they only apply to the primitive type string. In particular, origin propagation is independent of the AST structure or meta model.
- Extensibility: String origins are automatically propagated as annotations of substrings. As such, string origins can serve as general carriers of additional, domain-specific information. Marking certain subsstrings as protected (Section 3.2) is an example of this.
- Non-invasiveness: Transformation languages that support string manipulation during program transformation can support string origins by modifying the internal representation of strings, without changing the programming interface of strings. The only visible change is at input boundaries where strings are constructed.

We have implemented string origins as an experimental feature of Rascal, a meta programming language for source code analysis and transformation [9]. The applications and example code of this paper have all been prototyped in Rascal. The full code of the examples can be found online at `https://github.com/cwi-swat/string-origins`.

2 String Origins

We illustrate the basic idea of string origins in Figure 1. The code in the middle shows a simple transformation which converts name and email address specifications to the

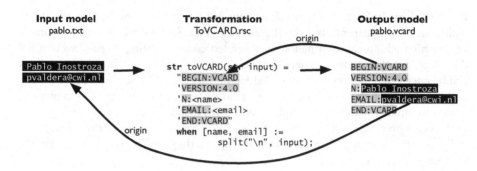

Fig. 1. Example of a simple Rascal transformation with trace links

VCARD format. Arrows and shading indicate the origin relation. The white-on-black substrings in the output are introduced by the transformation; their origins point to the string template in the transformation code in the middle. In contrast, the substrings with gray backgrounds (name and email) are copied over from the input to the output, and hence point back to the input model. The substrings in the result are partitioned according to the origin relation: a fragment originates in either the input, or the transformation.

Note that the transformation processes the input by splitting the string. It is important to realize that this does not break the origin relation, but instead makes it more fine-grained: the output fragments "Pablo Inostroza" and "pvaldera@cwi.nl" have distinct origins pointers to the exact corresponding substrings in the input.

2.1 Representing String Origins

Many transformations take text files as input and, eventually, produce text files as output. Moreover, the transformations themselves are expressed often as transformation code that is stored in text files as well. String origins exploit this fact by representing origins as *source locations*. Conceptually, a source location is a tuple consisting of a URI identifying a particular resource and an *area* identifying a text fragment within the resource. We represent an area by its start offset and length.

In the context of Rascal, source locations are represented by the built-in **loc** data type. To give an example, |file:///etc/passwd|(0, 50) identifies the first 50 characters in the file /etc/passwd, starting at offset 0. Rascal's source locations also represent begin and end line and column numbers, but for the remainder of this paper we will abstract from this technical detail. Although source locations are built into Rascal, they are easily implemented in any other transformation system.

The propagation of string origins is transparent: The transformation writer can fully ignore their presence and simply uses standard string operations such as concatenation or substitution. We discuss the details of the propagation in Section 4. Here, we want to highlight how to build generic tools on top of origin information. To this end, we provide an API for accessing locations and origins of substrings. First, we provide a function for decomposing a string into its atomic substrings (called chunks):

```
alias Index = rel[loc pos, str chunk];
Index index(str x, loc output);
```

Function index constructs an Index by collecting the atomic substrings of a string at a given location (e.g., a file path). The type Index is defined as a binary relation from the location of a substring to the corresponding chunk. The relation type **rel** is native in Rascal and is equivalent to a set of tuples. Second, each of the chunks in an Index has an associated origin which can be retrieved with the function origin.

loc origin(**str** x); // require: x is a chunk

For example, we can call index on the generated VCARD shown in Fig. 1. Assuming the output location is |file:///pablo.vcard|, we get the following index:

```
{<|file:///pablo.vcard|(0,28), "BEGIN:VCARD\nVERSION:4.0\nN:">,
 <|file:///pablo.vcard|(28,14), "Pablo Inostroza">,
 <|file:///pablo.vcard|(42,7), "\nEMAIL:">,
 <|file:///pablo.vcard|(49,14), "pvaldera@cwi.nl">,
 <|file:///pablo.vcard|(63,9), "\nEND:VCARD">}
```

Applying the origin function on any of the chunks retrieves the location where that particular chunk of text was introduced. Combining both functions gives us the origin relation, modeled by the Trace data type, which relates output locations to their corresponding origins:

alias Trace = **rel**[**loc** pos, **loc** org];
Trace trace(**str** s, **loc** out) = {<l, origin(chunk)> | <l, chunk> ← index(s, out)}

Function trace maps function origin over all chunks of the index. Considering again the example of Fig. 1, the trace relation of the generated VCARD looks as follows:

```
{<|file:///pablo.vcard|(0,28), |file:///ToVCARD.rsc|(28, 28)>,
 <|file:///pablo.vcard|(28,14), |file:///pablo.txt|(0,14)>,
 <|file:///pablo.vcard|(42,7), |file:///ToVCARD.rsc|(66, 7)>,
 <|file:///pablo.vcard|(49,14), |file:///pablo.txt|(15,14)>,
 <|file:///pablo.vcard|(63,9), |file:///ToVCARD.rsc|(86, 9)>}
```

Note that the URIs in the origins distinguishes chunks originating in the input (pablo.txt) from chunks introduced by the transformation (ToVCARD.rsc). Both the index and trace relations are the stepping stones for the generic tools developed in the subsequent section.

2.2   String Origins in M2T and M2M Transformations

The previous example illustrates the use of string origins for text-to-text transformations. However, string origins are also useful in model-to-text and model-to-model transformations. More specifically, when parsing text into an AST, the string fragments that appear as leaves of the AST have string origins attached, pointing to the corresponding text fragment in the input file. Model-to-model transformations preserve the origins of strings copied from the input model and generate new origins for synthesized string fragments. Similarly, unparsing and other model-to-text transformations preserve the origins of strings in the AST. Again, the origin propagation is transparent to transformation writers, parsing and unparsing because origins are propagated through standard string operators.

```
state opened
  close => closed
end
state closed
  open => opened
  lock => locked
end
state locked
  unlock => closed
end
```

(a) An example state machine

```
controller(
  [ ... /* event declarations */ ... ],
  [state("opened"@{linput|(62,6)}, [],
    [transition("close"@{linput|(70,5)},
                "closed"@{linput|(79,6)})]),
   state("closed"@{linput|(100,6)},[],[],
    [transition("open"@{linput|(108,4)},
                "opened"@{linput|(116,6)}),
     transition("lock"@{linput|(124,4)},
                "locked"@{linput|(132,6)})]),
   state("locked"@{linput|(152,6)},[],[],
    [transition("unlock"@{linput|(160,6)},
                "closed"@{linput|(170,6)})])])
```

(b) Parsed AST of the state machine

```
prog([
  fdef("opened"@{linput|(62,6)},[],val(nat(0))),
  fdef("closed"@{linput|(100,6)},[],val(nat(1))),
  fdef("locked"@{linput|(152,6)},[],val(nat(2))),
  ... // dispatch functions per state
  fdef( // main dispatch
    "main"@{lmeta|(1280,13)},
    ["state"@{lmeta|(1307,5)},
     "event"@{lmeta|(1316,5)}],
    cond(equ(var("state"@{lmeta|(1515,5)}),
             call("opened"@{linput|(62,6)}, [])),
         call("opened-dispatch"
             @{lmeta|(1565,9),linput|(62,6)},
             [var("event"@{lmeta|(1583,5)})])),
    cond(equ(var("state"@{lmeta|(1515,5)}),
             call("closed"@{linput|(100,6)},[])),
         call("closed-dispatch"
             @{linput|(100,6),lmeta|(1565,9)},
             [var("event"@{lmeta|(1583,5)})])),
    cond(equ(var("state"@{lmeta|(1515,5)}),
             call("locked"@{linput|(152,6)},[])),
         call("locked-dispatch"
             {lmeta|(1565,9),linput|(152,6)},
             [var("event"@{lmeta|(1583,5)})])),
    val(error("UnsupportedState"
             @{lmeta|(1375,16)}))))))))], [])
```

(c) Generated AST of the compiled state machine

Fig. 2. The names in the state machine code (a) end up as strings in the AST (b), the origins of which are propagated to the compiled AST (c). State machine input is represented by URI *input*, the transformation definition by URI *meta*.

Tracing origin information for string fragments in an AST is often useful. For example, variable names typically occur as string fragments in an AST. Figure 2 illustrates tracing of variable names in the context of a DSL for state machines. Figure 2a shows the source code of a state machine. Parsing the state machine produces an abstract syntax tree (AST), which is shown in Figure 2b. Note that all strings in this AST are annotated with their origin, using the pseudo-notation "@". The AST is then translated to an imperative program which is shown in Figure 2c. Some strings have *input* origins (e.g., "opened"), some are introduced by the transformation and have *meta* origins (e.g., "main"), and some strings have origins in both the input and transformation because of concatenation (e.g., "opened-dispatch").

3   Applications of String Origins

3.1   Hyperlinking Generated Artifacts

One of the foremost applications of string origins is relating (sub)strings of the output back to the input of a transformation [10,12]. Applications of this information include embedding links back to the source program in generated code, inspectors, debuggers (e.g., using SourceMaps [15]), or translating back errors produced by further transformations (e.g., general-purpose language compiler errors). In this section we show an

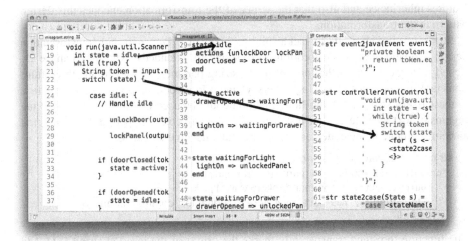

Fig. 3. Three editors showing (1) generated code with embedded hyperlinks (2) the input state machine model and (3) the transformation code. Fragments of the generated code that originate from the input are in bold red.

example of inspecting the result of a program transformation where the output is shown in an editor with embedded hyperlinks to the input or transformation code.

To display hyperlinks for parts of the generated code, the offsets of the chunks in the generated code must be mapped back to the origin associated with each corresponding chunk. Fortunately, the trace relation introduced in Section 2.1 contains exactly this information. The hyperlinks are created by finding the location of a click in the Trace mapping and moving the focus and cursor to the corresponding editor.

A demonstration of this feature is shown in Fig. 3. The screenshot shows three editors in Rascal Eclipse IDE. The first column shows generated Java code. The substrings highlighted in red are the substrings originating from the input, a textual model for state machines (shown in the middle). The other substrings (in black) are introduced by the code generator, which is shown in the right column. Clicking anywhere in the first column will take you to the exact location where the clicked substring originated.

3.2 Protecting Regions of Generated Code

In many cases, a model-to-text transformation is intended to generate just a partial implementation that has to be completed by the programmer. Normally, if the transformation is re-run, the manually edited code is overwritten. In general, this problem is addressed by explicitly marking certain zones of the generated text as *editable*. The MOF Models to Text Standard [11], for instance, introduces the unprotected keyword at the transformation level to specify whether a region can be editable by the end programmer or not. Another traditional solution is the generation gap pattern [6], in which the generated code and the code that is expected to be handwritten are related by inheritance. This, however, demands that the generated code is written in a language that features inheritance and also that the writer of the transformation encodes this design pattern in the transformation.

String origins allow us to tackle this problem in a language and transformation design agnostic way. Since locations correspond to extended URIs, they can be enriched with meta data in the form of query string parameters. We provide three functions tagString(key,value), getTagValue(key) and isTagged(key), as an abstract interface to these query strings. The tagString function could be used in a transformation to tag regions of text as editable. For instance, the following code snippet marks a substring as being editable in the code generator for a state machine language:

```
str command2java(Command command) =
  "private void <command.name>(Writer output) {
  '    output.write(\"<command.token>\\n\");
  '    <tagString("// Add more code here", "editable", command.name)>
  '}";
```

The function tagString transparently marks the origin of the inserted string ("// Add more code here") to be an editable region and names it as the name of the command input to command2java.

To provide editor support for editable regions, the marked substrings need to be extracted from the generated code. The function extract constructs a map from output location to region name using the index function introduced in section 2.1.

```
alias Regions = map[loc pos, str name];
Regions extract(str s, loc l) =
  (l: getTagValue(x, "editable") | <l, x> ← index(s, l), isTagged(x, "editable") );
```

From the index computed on the generated code s and the target location l, the function extract collects all locations which have an associated string value that is tagged as editable. An editor for s can then use the locations in the domain of this map to allow changes to the regions identified by the locations. In fact, it maintains another map, this time from region name (range of the result of extract) to the contents of each region.

When the code is regenerated, the edited contents of the regions need to be plugged back into the newly generated code, to restore the manual modifications. The function plug performs this task:

```
alias Contents = map[str name, str contents];
str plug(str s, loc l, Contents c) = substitute(s, extract(s, l) o c);
```

The Contents type captures the edits made in the editable regions. The function plug uses a generic substitution function (substitute) which receives a map from location to string and performs substitution based on the locations. To obtain this map, plug composes the map returned by extract with the contents c, where the map composition operator o is similar to relational composition.

As a proof of concept, we have added a feature to the Rascal editor framework that uses the presented infrastructure in order to provide consistent editing of generated artifacts with editable areas. When a transformation that produces editable regions is executed, a file with information about the editable offsets is generated as well. When the user opens a generated file, the editor checks if the region information is available. If so, the editor restricts the editing of text just to the regions marked as editable, ensuring

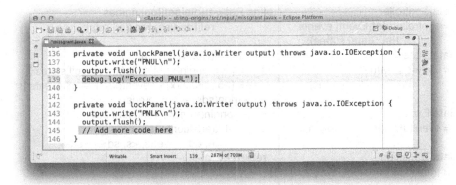

Fig. 4. Editor featuring highlighted editable regions

that the fixed generated code stays as it is. Fig. 4 shows a screenshot of the editor with highlighted editable regions.

3.3   Resolving Symbolic Names

Textual DSLs or modeling languages employ symbolic names to encode references, for instance from variables to declarations. As a result, DSL compilers and type checkers require name analysis to resolve references to referenced entities, in fact imposing a graph structure on top of the abstract syntax tree (AST) of the DSL. The names themselves cannot be used as nodes in this graph, since then different occurrences of the same name will be indistinguishable. A solution to this problem is to assign unique labels to each name occurrence in the source code. Since no two names can occupy the same location in the source code, string origins are excellent candidates to play the role of such labels.

Figure 5a shows the abstract syntax of the state machine language used in Fig. 2. Note that states, events and transitions contain strings. Each of these strings will be annotated with an origin by the state machine parser as in Fig. 2b. Figure 5b shows the generic type Ref for *reference graphs*: a tuple consisting of the set of all name occurrences (names), and a relation mapping uses of names to declarations. The function resolve computes a reference graph by first constructing two relations mapping names of states and events to declarations of states and events, respectively (sds resp. eds). The last comprehension uses the deep matching feature of Rascal (/) to find transitions arbitrarily deep in the controller ctl. Each transition then contributes two edges to the relation e.

Reference graphs such as returned by resolve have numerous generic applications in the context of DSL engineering. For instance, reference graphs can be used to implement jump-to-definition hyperlinking of editors: when the user clicks on the use of a name, the reference graph can be used to find the location of its declaration. Another application is rename refactoring: given a reference graph, and the locations of a name occurrence, it is possible to track other names that reference it or are referenced by it and consistently rename them. Finally, if Ref is slightly modified to distinguish uses from

```
data Controller
  = controller(list[Event] events,
              list[State] states);
data State
  = state(str name,
          list[Transition] trans);

data Event
  = event(str name, str token);

data Transition
  = transition(str event, str state)
```

```
alias Ref = tuple[set[loc] names,
                  rel[loc use, loc def] refs];

Ref resolve(Controller ctl) {
  sds = { <x, origin(x)> | state(x, _) ← ctl.states };
  eds = { <x, origin(x)> | event(x, _) ← ctl.events };
  v = range(sds) + range(eds);
  e = { <origin(e),ed>, <origin(s),sd>
        | /transition(e, s) := ctl,
          <e, ed> ← eds, <s, sd> ← sds};
  return <v, e>;
}
```

(a) AST data type of state machines   (b) Name resolution for state machines

Fig. 5. Implementing name resolution for state machines

declarations in the names component, reference graphs can be used to report unbound names or unused declarations.

3.4   Enforcing a Same Origin Policy for References

A common problem with code generation is that names used in the input (source names) which pass through a transformation and end up in the output might interact with names introduced by the transformation (introduced names). For instance, the declaration of a name introduced by the transformation might capture a reference to a source name, or vice versa. This is the problem that is traditionally solved in the work on macro hygiene [3].

The problem of inadvertent name capture is best illustrated using an example. Figure 6a shows the simple state machine used earlier in Fig. 2a, but this time the last state is named current. The code generator of state machines – partially shown in Fig. 6b – introduces another instance of the name current to store the current state in the generated Java implementation of the state machine. As a result, the declaration of this current captures the reference to the state constant current.

The reference arrows in Fig. 6c show that both current variables in the if-condition are bound by the current state variable declaration. However, the right-hand side of the equals expression should be bound by the constant declaration corresponding to the state current. Moreover, the Java compiler will not signal an error: even though the code is statically correct, it is still wrong.

To avoid name capture, the algorithm described below renames the source names in the output of a transformation if they are also in the set of non-source names. The result can be seen in Fig. 6d: the source occurrences of current are renamed to current0, and inadvertent capture is avoided. Effectively, the technique amounts to enforcing a same origin policy for names, similar to how a same origin policy avoids cross-site scripting

```
str controller2run(Controller ctl) =
"void run(Scanner input, Writer output) {
'    int current = <ctl.states[0]>;
'    while (true) {
'      String tk = input.nextLine();
'      <for (s ← ctl.states) {>
'      <state2if(s)>
'      <}>
'    }
'}";

str state2if(State s) =
"if (current == <s.name>) {
'    <for (transition(e, s2) ← s.transitions) {>
'    if (<e>(tk)) current = <s2>;
'    <}>
'    continue;
'}";
```

```
state opened
  close => closed
end

state closed
  open => opened
  lock => current
end

state current
  unlock => closed
end
```

(a) Input

(b) Excerpt of state machine compiler

```
static final int current = 2;
void run(...) {
  int current = opened;
  ...
  if (current == current) {
    if (unlock(tk)) current = closed;
    continue;
  }
  ...
}
```

(c) Incorrect output

```
static final int current0 = 2;
void run(...) {
  int current = opened;
  ...
  if (current == current0) {
    if (unlock(tk)) current = closed;
    continue;
  }
  ...
}
```

(d) Repaired output

Fig. 6. Example of repairing name capture: the input (a) contains the name **current**, but this name is introduced in the transformation as well (b). Consequently, the introduced variable in the output shadows the constant declaration (c). The **fix** function renames all occurrences of **current** originating in the input to **current0** so that capture is avoided (d). The arrows in (c) and (d) link variable uses to their declarations.

attacks in Web application security[1]: names originating from different artifacts should not reference each other.

In [5] the authors showed how string origins proved to be instrumental in automatically repairing the problem of unintended variable capture. In this section we present a technique that is simpler but also more conservative: it might rename more identifiers than is actually needed. Whereas the method of [5] is parameterized in the scoping rules of both source and target language, the technique of this section is language agnostic, and does not require name analysis of the source or target language.

The key observation is that whenever name capture occurs it involves a source name and a name introduced by the transformation. This difference is reflected in the origins of the name occurrences in the output: the origins' source locations will have different URIs. The same origin policy then requires that for every reference in the generated code from x to y, both x and y originate from the input or neither. The same origin policy is enforced by ensuring that the set of source names is disjoint from the set of names introduced by the transformation. This can be realized by consistently renaming source names in the generated code when they collide with non-source names.

To formalize the same origin policy, let $t = f(s)$ be the result of some transformation f on input program s, inducing a trace relation $\tau \in Trace$, and let $G_s = \langle V_s, E_s \rangle$, $G_t = \langle V_t, E_t \rangle$ be the reference graphs of the source s and target t, respectively. The same origin policy then requires that

$$\forall \langle l_1, l_2 \rangle \in E_t, \langle l_1, o_1 \rangle \in \tau, \langle l_2, o_2 \rangle \in \tau \ : \ o_1 \in V_s \Leftrightarrow o_2 \in V_s$$

---

[1] http://en.wikipedia.org/wiki/Same-origin_policy

```
str fix(str gen, Index names, loc inp) {
  bool isSrc(str x) = origin(x).path == inp.path;
  set[str] other = { x | <_, x> ← names, !isSrc(x) };
  set[str] allNames = { x | <_, x> ← names };
  map[loc,str] subst = ();
  map[str,str] renaming = ();
  for (<l, x> ← names, isSrc(x), x in other) {
    if (x notin renaming) {
      <y, allNames> = fresh(x, allNames);
      renaming[x] = y;
    }
    subst[l] = renaming[x];
  }
  return substitute(gen, subst);
}
```

Fig. 7. Restoring disjointness by fixing source names

To enforce the same origin policy, one more assumption on reference graphs is needed, namely that the locations in every reference edge point to the same textual name. In other words: every use is bound by a declaration with the same name. For instance, the reference edges drawn in Fig. 6c and Fig. 6d satisfy this invariant since variable uses l_1, l_2, l_3 point to occurrences of the name current, which is also the name used in the declaration l_0.

If we assume that the same name invariant is true for E_t, then the same origin policy is satisfied if the set of source names is disjoint from the set of names introduced by the transformation. The same name invariant ensures that for every $\langle l_1, l_2 \rangle \in E_t$, we have that l_1 and l_2 point to the same name. Consequently, it is not possible that one name originates from the input (e.g., through o_1) but the other does not (e.g., through o_2) because that would contradict disjointness of names.

The code for restoring disjointness is shown in Fig. 7. The function fix has three parameters: the generated code gen, the index names capturing the names occurring in gen, and a source location identifying the input program inp. The latter is used by the predicate isSrc to determine whether a name x is a source name by checking if the path in the origin of x is the input path.

The **for**-loop iterates over the index names that represents all names in the generated string gen. If such a name x originates in the source and is also used as an other name, an entry is created in the substitution subst, mapping location l to a new name. The new name is retrieved from the renaming map which records which source names should be renamed to which new name. The function fresh produces a name that is not used anywhere (i.e., it is not in allNames). The variable allNames is updated by fresh to ensure that consecutive renames do not introduce new problems.

Note that fix could also be parameterized with an additional set of external names which might capture or be captured by source names. External names could include the reserved identifiers (keywords) of the target language or (global) names that are always in scope (e.g., everything in java.lang). The only required change is to add the external names to other.

4   Implementation

The implementation of string origins requires changes to the internal representation of strings used by the transformation engine. In this section we discuss the implementation of string origins in Rascal.

As Rascal is implemented in Java, we have implemented string origins in Java as well. Rascal string values (of type **str**) are internally represented as objects conforming to the interface IString. We have reimplemented this interface to support string origins, changing only the internal representation. Instances of IString are constructed through a factory method IString string(java.lang.String) in the Rascal factory interface for creating values (IValueFactory).

To ensure that the propagation of string origins is complete, every created string now needs a location to capture its origin. We have extended IValueFactory with another factory method IString string(java.lang.String, ISourceLocation) to support this. Calls to the original string(...) method were changed to the new one, everywhere in the Rascal implementation. The locations where changes have been made correspond to the following three categories:

- Input: any function that reads a resource into a string must be modified to install origins on the result. In Rascal, these are built-in library functions like readFile(**loc**), readLines(**loc**), parse(**loc**), etc.
- String literals: constant string values that are created as part of a Rascal program get the origin of the string literal in the Rascal file. Whenever a string literal is evaluated, its location is looked up in its AST and passed to the factory method. This category also covers interpolated string templates.
- Conversions: converting a value to a string in Rascal is achieved through string interpolation. For instance, "<x>" returns the string representation of x. If x evaluates to a string, the result of the conversion is that string itself (including origin); otherwise, the newly created string gets the locations of the expression x in the Rascal source.

String origins are propagated through all string operations. As a result, all operations provided in the IString interface have been reimplemented. The two most important operations are concat and substring. Their semantics is illustrated in Fig. 8. The top two string values are annotated with source locations |file:///foo.txt|(0,5) and |file:///bar.txt|(0,5). Concatenating both strings (middle row) produces a new, composite string, where the original arguments to concat are still distinguishable, and have their respective origins. Finally, the substring operation computes a new composite string with the origin of each component updated to reflect which part of the original input is covered. Besides concat and substring, all common string operations such as indexOf, replaceAll, split etc. can be defined on strings with origins, with full propagation.

Internally, Rascal strings with origins are represented as binary trees. A string is either a *chunk* object which has a source location attached to it, or it is a *concat* object which represents two concatenated strings. A string represented as a binary tree can be flattened to a list containing elements with a string value and source location for each chunk object at the leaves. This list is the basis for the functions index and origin introduced in Section 2.1.

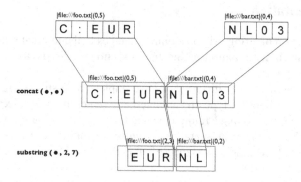

Fig. 8. The concat and substring operations defined on origin strings

Although in our experience the performance penalty introduced by representing strings as binary trees is acceptable in practice, further benchmarking is needed to assess the overall impact. In particular, it will be interesting to see how the choice of representation affects different use cases. For instance, when generating code, concatenation is one of the most frequently executed string operations. The binary tree representation is optimized for that: concatenation is an $O(1)$ operation. On the other hand, analyzing strings (e.g., substring, parsing, matching) is much more expensive if a string is a binary tree. But then again, the penalty will be most significant if these operations apply to strings resulting from concatenation in the first place. We consider investigating these and other aspects of performance an important area for further research.

5   Related Work

String origins are related to previous work in origin tracking, taint propagation and model traceability in model-driven engineering. Below we discuss each of these areas in turn.

Origin Tracking. The main inspiration of string origins is origin tracking [16]. In the context of term-rewriting systems, this technique relates intermediate subterms matched and constructed during a rewriting process. Origin tracking was proposed as a technique to construct automatic error reporting, generic debuggers and visualization in program transformation scenarios. String origins are related in that the result is a relation between input and output terms. However, for string origins, only string valued elements are in this relation. Furthermore, the origin relation of [16] is derived from analyzing rewrite rules. As a result the transformation writer is restricted to this paradigm. With string origins, a transformation can be arbitrary code.

Taint Propagation. In Web applications, untrusted user input might potentially end up as part of a database query, a command-line script execution or web page. Malicious input could thus compromise the system security in the form of code injection attacks. Taint propagation [7] is a mechanism to raise the level of security in such systems by tracking potentially risky strings at runtime. It consists of three main phases: mark certain *sources* of strings as tainted, propagating taint markers across the execution of the program, and disallowing the use of tainted strings at certain specific points called *sinks*. The propagation is achieved by annotating the string values themselves and making sure that string operations propagate taintedness.

Although in general the taint information is coarse-grained: any string that is computed from any number of tainted strings is tainted as well. A finer granularity is employed in character-based taint propagation [2]. String origins are very similar to this approach in that the origin is known for each character in a string. On the other hand, string origins can be considered more general, because origins capture more information than just taintedness. In fact, taint propagation could easily be realized using string origins by considering certain input locations as tainted.

In [4], the authors present an application of taint propagation to the domain of model-to-text transformations, specifically, to support debugging of failures introduced in a transformation. Their approach consists in instrumenting the transformation in order to add so-called *tainted marks* to each identifiable element of the input. On the other hand, the user of the transformation has to identify erroneous sections in the output. Since the taints from the input are consistently propagated by the instrumented transformation, it is possible to relate the errors in the output to specific elements of the input. In this work, the input is an XML document and the transformation, an XSLT file. The granularity of this technique is at the level of XML nodes, which provides quite precise information for the error tracking analysis.

Traceability in Model-Driven Engineering. In model-driven engineering, models are refined through transformations to produce executable artifacts. In [1], the authors argue for the need for automatic generation of trace information in such a setting. Several endeavors towards this goal have been reported in the context of different model transformation systems, such as ATL, MOF, and Epsilon.

For instance, ATL transformations can be manually enriched with traceability rules that conform to a traceability metamodel [8]. Besides the target models, the enriched transformations will also automatically produce trace models when executed. In order to avoid the manual work of adding these specifications to existing transformations, the authors present a technique for automatically weaving the trace rules into the transformation. Unlike string origins, this approach relies on the structure of the ATL rules to derive the trace links, and such links just relate a subset of the elements in the target model to certain elements in the source model, but not to the transformation itself.

Another approach to address traceability is the MOF Models to Text Transformation Language standard [11]. In this specification, transformations can be decorated with a trace annotation so when the transformation is executed, a relation between its output and its input is constructed. As in the case of [8], the transformation conveys the traceability information explicitly. To overcome this, [12] and [13] introduce an alternative technique for managing traceability in MOFScript, a language for defining model to text transformations based on the MOF standard. In this case, "any reference to a model element that is used to produce text output results in a trace between that element and the target file". Like string origins, this technique provides implicit propagation and fine-grained tracing. However, no relation between the output and the text fragments coming from the transformation is created. Just as in the case of ATL, MOFScript depends on the structure of the rules to analyze the transformation and generate trace information.

Finally, The Epsilon Generation Language (EGL) is a model-to-text transformation language defined at the core of the Epsilon Platform [14]. EGL provides an API to construct a transformation trace. However, this API is coarse-grained (file-level).

6   Conclusion

String origins identify the exact origin of a fragment of text. By annotating string values with their origins, the origins are automatically propagated through program transformations, independent of transformation style or paradigm. The result is that for every string valued element in the output of a transformation, we know where it came from, originating in the input program or introduced by the transformation itself.

String origins have diverse applications. They address traditional model traceability concerns by linking output elements to where they were introduced. We have shown two applications in this space, namely hyperlinked editors for generated code and protected regions. Moreover, string origins can be used to uniquely identify sub terms, which is instrumental for implementing name resolution, rename refactoring, jump-to-definition services and error marking. Finally, we have shown that by distinguishing source names from introduced names, accidental name capture in generated code can be avoided in a reliable and language agnostic way.

The implementation of string origins is simple and independent of any specific meta-model, transformation engine or technological space. Any transformation system or programming language that manipulates string values during execution can support string origins by changing the internal representation of strings. The standard programming interface on strings remains the same. As a result, code that manipulates strings does not have to be changed, except for the code that creates strings in the first place. Although conceptually simple, we have shown that string origins, nevertheless, provide a powerful tool to improve the understandability and reliability of program transformations.

References

1. Aizenbud-Reshef, N., Nolan, B.T., Rubin, J., Shaham-Gafni, Y.: Model traceability. IBM Syst. J. 45(3), 515–526 (2006)
2. Chin, E., Wagner, D.: Efficient character-level taint tracking for Java. In: Proceedings of the 2009 ACM Workshop on Secure Web Services, pp. 3–12. ACM (2009)
3. Clinger, W., Rees, J.: Macros that work. In: Proceedings of Symposium on Principles of Programming Languages (POPL), pp. 155–162. ACM (1991)
4. Dhoolia, P., Mani, S., Sinha, V.S., Sinha, S.: Debugging model-transformation failures using dynamic tainting. In: D'Hondt, T. (ed.) ECOOP 2010. LNCS, vol. 6183, pp. 26–51. Springer, Heidelberg (2010)
5. Erdweg, S., van der Storm, T., Dai, Y.: Capture-avoiding and hygienic program transformations. In: Proceedings of European Conference on Object-Oriented Programming (ECOOP). Springer (to appear, 2014)
6. Fowler, M.: Domain-Specific Languages. Addison Wesley (2010)

7. Haldar, V., Chandra, D., Franz, M.: Dynamic taint propagation for Java. In: 21st Annual Computer Security Applications Conference, p. 9. IEEE (2005)
8. Jouault, F.: Loosely coupled traceability for ATL. In: Proceedings of the European Conference on Model Driven Architecture (ECMDA) Workshop on Traceability, pp. 29–37 (2005)
9. Klint, P., van der Storm, T., Vinju, J.: Rascal: A domain-specific language for source code analysis and manipulation. In: Proceedings of Conference on Source Code Analysis and Manipulation (SCAM), pp. 168–177 (2009)
10. Kolovos, D.S., Rose, L., Paige, R., García-Domínguez, A.: The Epsilon book, http://www.eclipse.org/epsilon/doc/book/ (accessed November 13, 2012)
11. Object Management Group (OMG). MOF Model to Text Transformation Language 1.0. formal/2008-01-16 (January 2008)
12. Oldevik, J., Neple, T.: Traceability in model to text transformations. In: 2nd ECMDA Traceability Workshop (ECMDA-TW), pp. 17–26 (2006)
13. Olsen, G.K., Oldevik, J.: Scenarios of traceability in model to text transformations. In: Akehurst, D.H., Vogel, R., Paige, R.F. (eds.) ECMDA-FA. LNCS, vol. 4530, pp. 144–156. Springer, Heidelberg (2007)
14. Rose, L.M., Paige, R.F., Kolovos, D.S., Polack, F.A.C.: The Epsilon generation language. In: Schieferdecker, I., Hartman, A. (eds.) ECMDA-FA 2008. LNCS, vol. 5095, pp. 1–16. Springer, Heidelberg (2008)
15. Seddon, R.: Introduction to JavaScript source maps (2012), http://www.html5rocks.com/en/tutorials/developertools/sourcemaps/
16. van Deursen, A., Klint, P., Tip, F.: Origin tracking. Symbolic Computation 15, 523–545 (1993)

Transformation of UML and OCL Models into Filmstrip Models⋆

Frank Hilken, Lars Hamann, and Martin Gogolla

University of Bremen
{fhilken,lhamann,gogolla}@informatik.uni-bremen.de

Abstract. This contribution presents an automatic transformation from
UML and OCL models into enriched UML and OCL models, so-called
filmstrip models, which embody temporal information when employing
OCL while maintaining the same functionality as the original model.
The approach uses a combination of object and sequence diagrams that
allows for a wide range of possible OCL constraints about sequences of
operation calls and their temporal properties. The modeler does not need
to account for such properties while creating the original model. Errors
found by constraints for the filmstrip model can easily be related back to
the original model, as the elements of the filmstrip model are synchronized with the original model and the backwards calculation is generally
simple. The approach is implemented in a UML and OCL modeling tool.

1 Introduction

In recent years, the Unified Modeling Language (UML) has become the standard
language for modeling IT systems. Among the various UML diagram forms,
UML class diagrams are the most frequently used ones. One way (among other
possibilities) to completely specify structure and behavior of an application is to
enrich class diagrams with class invariants and operation pre- and postconditions
expressed in the Object Constraint Language (OCL). The starting point for this
contribution is an application model solely described by a class diagram and
OCL constraints. In the development process, it is essential to validate and
verify that such an application model meets the informal and formal postulated
requirements.

For structural models with class diagrams and invariants, a number of efficient validation and verification techniques [2,13,4,11,17] are available. These
techniques partly transform UML models including OCL invariants into validation and verification platforms (like SAT or SMT solvers or relational logic)
allowing an efficient check of relevant structural properties of the UML model in
terms of the target platform. However, less attention has been paid to behavioral
model properties, in particular to operation pre- and postconditions.

This contribution proposes a transformation from a UML and OCL application model with pre- and postconditions and invariants into a UML model with

---

⋆ This work was partially funded by the German Research Foundation (DFG) under
grant GO 454/19-1.

D. Di Ruscio and D. Varró (Eds.): ICMT 2014, LNCS 8568, pp. 170–185, 2014.

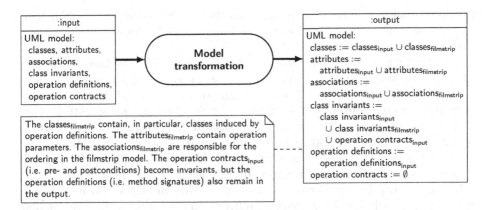

Fig. 1. Inputs and outputs of the filmstrip transformation

OCL invariants only (thus without pre- and postconditions). The intention is that this filmstrip model can then be handled by one of the efficient techniques available for structural models. All behavioral aspects of the original application model are equivalently expressed in a so-called filmstrip model in form of structural constraints, i.e., invariants. Figure 1 gives an overview of the inputs and outputs of the transformation.

There are a number of reasons for us to study the proposed transformation. Alloy [13], for example, has to model temporal system development with explicit relations for objects representing points in time, and these relations have to be described by the developer. Our approach comprises an automatic way to handle temporal system development on the basis of pre- and postconditions. On the other hand, Alloy nicely demonstrates that design flaws concerning dynamics can be successfully detected by structural techniques. A further motivation for us to study the current transformation is a fundamental question about the relationship between structure and behavior and to find out to what extent structural techniques can encode dynamic problems. We also expect that structural automatic validation and verification techniques will show major advances in coming years, as they have shown in recent years.

The challenge of building the filmstrip model is to create a model that does not change the behavior and expressiveness of the application model, but offers more possibilities for validation and verification by employing OCL for checking behavioral properties on the filmstrip model and to automatically translate the detected properties back to the application model: The filmstrip model captures several application model states in one object diagram; it keeps information about successive operation calls and changes between the application model states; pre- and postconditions are transformed into invariants and make behavioral properties from application model sequence diagrams detectable in a single filmstrip model object diagram. The approach allows to give feedback on the application model in form of scenarios and test cases that are directly understandable and analyzable by the application model developer. The filmstrip model also enables the use of temporal logic properties formulated using an extension of standard OCL [20,3,18].

Another feature of our approach is that it can be used for checking properties of model transformations themselves. Let us assume that a model transformation consists of separate operations described with pre- and postconditions (for example, given a graph transformation system, each rule becomes an operation), the filmstripped model transformation can be checked for confluence of rules: within a finite search space our approach can build scenarios for rule applications.

Our work is related to several other papers using filmstrip models for various different tasks. The first known notion of the idea is in [8]. The authors of [10] take the filmstrip idea and employ it as part of three-dimensional visualizations within software design. [19,1] define a different approach for a filmstrip model (called snapshot model or snapshot transition model), which changes more of the original model elements instead of using abstract interface elements. In [5] filmstrips are used as a device for functional testing. [12] shows a less generic approach, with less separation between application model and filmstrip model.

Multiple approaches of an extension of OCL with temporal logic exist in order to verify temporal properties in UML and OCL models, but only a few keep the verification task on the UML and OCL layer. [18] and [14] give a comparison of the different approaches. [6] concentrated on temporal business rules without giving a full semantic definition. [20] gives a semantic definition of linear temporal logic operators. [9] focused on the integration of time bounds in connection with temporal constructs. In [1] temporal OCL expressions are evaluated in state transition systems – a similar form of filmstrip models using a more relational database-like approach.

The rest of this paper is structured as follows. In Sect. 2 the example model for this paper is described, its properties are explained and an example system state is shown. Section 3 covers the transformation of the UML part of the model transformation and Sect. 4 covers the OCL part respectively. Section 5 completes the example and shows further examples of use for the filmstrip model. Section 6 describes the implementation of the transformation and Section 7 finishes the paper with a conclusion and discusses future work.

2   Running Example

The input for the transformation is a UML and OCL model consisting of a class diagram describing an application completely with classes, attributes, associations, operations and invariants. The operations – with their pre- and postconditions – describe the model dynamics, which can be visualized in sequence diagrams. The other characteristics of the model, e.g. invariants and multiplicities describe the allowed system states, which are represented by object diagrams. We call this model the application model.

As an example for this paper, the transformation of a classic process scheduler application model [16,7] into its filmstrip counterpart is demonstrated. Figure 2 shows the class diagram of the transformed model. The original application

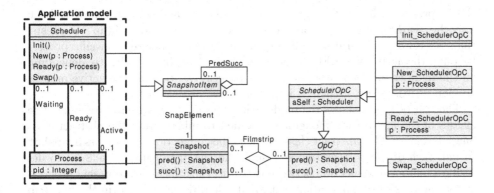

Fig. 2. Scheduler filmstrip model with the contained application model highlighted

model, consisting of the two classes `Scheduler` and `Process` and three associations `Active`, `Ready` and `Waiting`, is completely contained in the filmstrip model and displayed in the dashed box in the left part of the picture. The structure of such model is unchanged.

The class `Process` represents the processes of the system and has one attribute `pid` to distinguish them. The class `Scheduler` represents a scheduler which is connected to the processes via three associations. They link the currently *active* process, which may be none, the ones that are *ready* to be scheduled and the ones *waiting* for an action to become ready again.

Additional constraints, not expressible in UML, are specified using OCL. The OCL constraints marks the sets of ready and waiting processes of a scheduler to always be disjoint, the active process is not simultaneously ready or waiting and when there is no active process, there may not be a ready process. Lastly the process identifiers (`pid`) of the class `Process` must be unique.

The scheduler class has all the functionality of the system. The first operation *initializes* the scheduler into a defined start state. The second operation *New* registers a process to the scheduler and puts it in the list of waiting processes. The third operation moves a process from the list of waiting processes into the list of *ready* processes, unless there is no active process, in which case the process will immediately become the active one. The fourth and last operation *swaps* the active process, putting it into the list of waiting processes and schedules another ready process, if there is any. The general flow of a process therefore is as follows:

$$\text{Unassigned} \xrightarrow{\text{New}} \left(\text{Waiting} \xrightarrow{\text{Ready}} \text{Ready} \xrightarrow{\text{Swap}^*} \text{Active} \xrightarrow{\text{Swap}} \text{Waiting}\right)^*$$

The states represent how a process is connected to the scheduler and the arrows describe operation calls on the scheduler between the state changes. The sequence is focusing on one process. An *Unassigned* process is not connected to any scheduler, yet. It gets assigned to a scheduler by a *New* operation call and is then permanently assigned to this scheduler, where it continues *Waiting*. Here it waits for a *Ready* operation call to get into a *Ready* state. When the scheduler now issues a *Swap* operation call and this process is chosen, it will become the

Active process. The next *Swap* operation call will then bring the process back into the *Waiting* state and the cycle repeats. The notation "Swap*" suggests, that several swap operation calls might be necessary before a specific process becomes the active one. Also the flow of a process might vary slightly depending on the number of ready processes, e.g. a process can become the active process as soon as it is ready, if there is no other active process.

The rest of Fig. 2 shows the model parts specific to the filmstrip model. The classes of the application model are modified to inherit from the abstract class SnapshotItem. This abstract class provides the connection to the class Snapshot to link each object to a certain snapshot and the aggregation PredSucc to describe a temporal connection between two object instances. To represent progression of objects during operation calls, multiple objects are used in the filmstrip model with the delta being the changes applied in the course of an operation invocation. Thus an association is required to guarantee that every object of an application model class is linked to a unique snapshot. The association PredSucc connects objects that represent one instance.

The next class added to the model is the Snapshot class which represents a reference point for a system state in the application model. With the abstract class for representing operation calls (OpC), the snapshot is also linked to its predecessor and successor in the same way as the application model classes are. This ternary association is called Filmstrip and links two snapshot objects and an operation call object together, representing one operation call. The resulting object diagrams of this structure involve a sequence of snapshots (system states) with operation calls linked in between them, like a filmstrip consists of many consecutive pictures that change from frame to frame.

The possible operation calls of the application model are added to the filmstrip model as classes derived from the interface OpC. In the example in Fig. 2 the abstract class SchedulerOpC has an attribute aSelf which saves the object, this operation is invoked on. This is the base class for every concrete class representing an operation of the class Scheduler. These classes store the dynamic information, e.g. parameter values, that occur during an operation call.

An example system state of the filmstrip model is shown in Fig. 3. A scenario in the application model can be represented with an object diagram sequence to show the different states and a sequence diagram to represent the operation calls. The filmstrip model combines this information into a single system state. The main problem is to find a transformation that can reproduce the complete behavior of the application model and nothing more.

Further challenges of the transformation include the consistent handling of: (1) the insertion of new root elements for filmstrip models into the existing model; (2) the change of model classes and operations; and (3) the correct adaptation of OCL constraints.

3   UML Transformation

The process of a filmstrip transformation is an endogenous model transformation. The changes take place solely in the class diagram. This section explains the

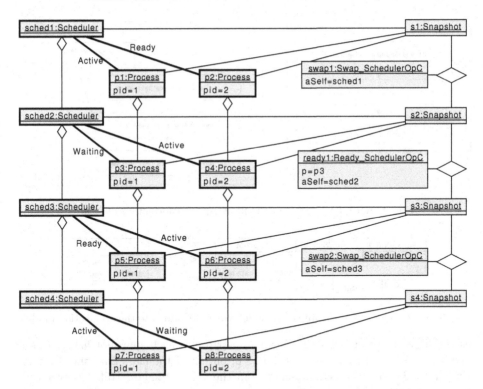

Fig. 3. Example system state of the scheduler filmstrip model with elements from the application model highlighted

steps required to transform an application model into a filmstrip model regarding the UML elements. Further constraints on these elements that are required for a correct behavior, but are not expressible in UML, i.e. OCL invariants, are discussed in Section 4. UML model elements that are not mentioned, e.g. associations and operations, remain the same in the filmstrip model. Figure 4 gives an overview for the steps of the whole transformation process.

3.1   Filmstrip Core Elements

First the core of the filmstrip model is included into the application model. These elements are shown in Fig. 5 and are the same in every filmstrip model. They consist of three classes and three associations and define the functionality of the filmstrip model. They also provide an interface for elements of the application model classes to enable interaction with them (SnapshotItem).

The class Snapshot represents a system state of the application model where any object linked to a snapshot belongs to the system state represented by it. To represent multiple system states in one object diagram multiple snapshot instances are used. An object diagram may contain several snapshots that represent the same system state, i.e. the properties of the linked objects are equal and the system state would be identical in the application model. This is required

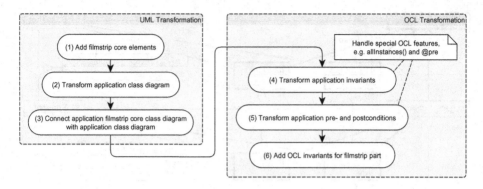

Fig. 4. Activity diagram of the filmstrip transformation process

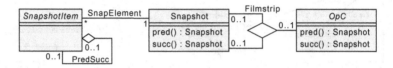

Fig. 5. Static elements of the filmstrip model which are added to the application model

as the filmstrip model shows a linear filmstrip and each snapshot has at most
one predecessor and one successor. The intention of the class **SnapshotItem** is
similar to the class **LocalSnapshot** from the OCL standard [15], however the
handling of the ordering is different there.

Another core element is the abstract class **OpC**. This interface represents the
operation calls that occur between two snapshots and is later extended with the
specific information from the application model operations. This information
includes the object that the operation is called on, the name of the operation,
which is called and the parameters. The operations **pred()** and **succ()** of the
classes **Snapshot** and **OpC** are query operations navigating to the predecessor
snapshot or successor snapshot respectively, returning a single object instead of
a **Set**, which the association end for this navigation indicates. For the class **OpC**
these are the pre and post states of an operation call.

The next element of the filmstrip core is the abstract class **SnapshotItem**. It
is an interface for the classes of the application model and lists functions that
every class has to provide, so the filmstrip elements can work with them. The
first functionality is specified by the association **SnapElement**, being a connection to the snapshot to assign objects to it. The second functionality is specified
by the aggregation **PredSucc**, which connects two objects of the same type with
each other. An aggregation is used to keep the connections cycle free. It defines the successors and predecessors of each object to easily navigate between
different incarnations. These incarnations describe one object from the application model that can change its state during operation calls, whereas in the
filmstrip model each incarnation is a new object in the object diagram. Without
an explicit connection between these objects, another identifier would be necessary to navigate between incarnations, e.g. a key attribute. In contrast with the

alternatives the association provides easier access, which is in particular useful when transforming the OCL expression @pre.

Finally, the ternary association Filmstrip connects two Snapshot objects and an OpC object, to represent the predecessor state and the successor state of an operation call. A ternary association is chosen to provide direct access between the objects and still keep a maximum level of compatibility. An alternative is replacing the abstract class OpC with an abstract association class between two Snapshot classes, which would make the query operations pred() and succ() unnecessary. For an even better compatibility, especially with validation and verification tools in mind, the ternary association OpC can be replaced with two binary associations. One leading from the Snapshot class to the OpC class and one association back to the Snapshot class. These associations can also be represented by aggregations or compositions to inherit their traits, i.e. cycle freeness. All options are interchangeable with minor differences in their usage which affects the transformation process. The constraints on the filmstrip association also need to be adapted. This work concentrates on the transformation using a ternary association, as shown in the class diagram in Fig. 5.

3.2   Application Model Classes

The next step in the transformation process handles the application model classes. These classes remain mostly the same, i.e. the name, attributes and operation definitions are kept. The classes are modified to inherit from the abstract class SnapshotItem to define a connection to the filmstrip core elements. Since the associations of the interface are defined on the abstract class SnapshotItem, the inherited type of the association ends is SnapshotItem. To replace these with the actual type of the transformed class, both associations are refined using the redefines keyword. With this UML feature, association ends can override other existing association ends of the class hierarchy, e.g. it is possible to specify a more precise end type for the navigation. The results are a type-safe access of the properties and another advantageous side-effect, which prevents links between objects of different types, e.g. between Scheduler and Process. In addition, the properties become well-defined even when using multiple inheritance. The refinement of the association SnapElement creates a property to access all objects of a specific class from the snapshot object, instead of all objects that inherit from SnapshotItem, which will be useful when transforming the OCL expression allInstances(). An example of a transformed class with all UML features visible is shown in Fig. 6. Association classes of the application model are included in this transformation step. These refinements were omitted in the class diagram in Fig. 2 for better clarity.

Lastly for every class that has operations with side-effects, a new abstract class inheriting from the abstract class OpC is created. This new class represents the base class for all concrete operation classes of this class and has an attribute aSelf of the type of the application model class to represent an object, that an operation call is invoked on. In the example from Sect. 2 this class is called SchedulerOpC.

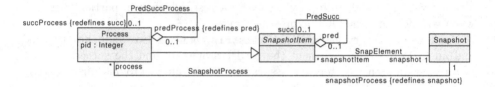

Fig. 6. Redefined association ends for class `Process`

3.3   Application Model Operations

The expressions of query operations remain with the application model class and can be used in the filmstrip model as well, since other elements probably depend on it. Only some OCL expressions, e.g. `allInstances()`, are transformed according to Sect. 4, since their effect is different in the filmstrip model.

Operations with side-effects are transformed differently. In the application model, the parameter values of these operation calls is only required at the time when the operation is invoked. On the contrary, in the filmstrip model, these operation calls are modelled statically with the class `OpC` and it is desired to validate the operation calls statically as well. Thus a new class is created for each operation with side-effects. It inherits the abstract operation call class of the operations owner class introduced earlier. The operation parameters are replicated as attributes of this class. The only variable left is `self` which is saved in the attribute `aSelf` inherited in the class (see class `SchedulerOpC` in Fig. 2). As a result, all variables required for the pre- and postconditions are provided by the concrete operation call class. These attribute values must point to the predecessor snapshot. Successor values can be accessed with the association `PredSucc`.

The pre- and postconditions are transformed into invariants and assigned to the concrete operation call class as well. The class is only instantiated when such operation call occurs. Therefore the invariants representing the operation pre- and postconditions only trigger once for every operation call invocation. This matches the exact behavior of the pre- and postconditions.

The OCL expressions of the pre- and postconditions need to be adjusted, when transforming them into invariants, because the variables inherently available in such expressions, e.g. `self` and parameters, have become class attributes. In addition, postconditions may contain unique expressions that are not available in invariants, i.e. `@pre` and `oclIsNew()`. These special expressions need to be transformed along with the other expressions that change their behavior in the filmstrip model. The details on these transformations are described in the next section. Finally the pre- and postconditions are removed from the operation as they are fully covered by the invariants and no longer needed.

4   OCL Transformation

In the filmstrip model, a clear separation exists between the filmstrip core elements and the application model elements. Therefore both parts are mostly functioning on their own after the transformation. As a result, most OCL expressions of the application model can be reused after the transformation. How the remaining aspects of the OCL elements are transformed, is described in this section.

4.1 Variables

Certain OCL expressions like operation pre- and postconditions have predefined variables, i.e. `self` and operation parameters, accessible in the expression. When transforming these pre- and postconditions into invariants, the parameters are lost. Also the variable `self` has a different value, since the OCL expression moves from the owner class of the operation to the operation call class of the filmstrip model. Thus each access of a variable is changed to point to the proper attribute of the operation call class. This includes the variable `self`, which is replaced with the expression `self.aSelf`. For postconditions, the values of the post state are required, which are accessed using the association `PredSucc`. For the application model invariants this is not necessary, as they remain at their corresponding class and the value of `self` does not change.

4.2 Expression Transformation

When transforming OCL expressions for the filmstrip model most of the OCL elements can be kept. As stated before, the expressions of the application model do not include filmstrip elements. Therefore, they will not use elements from outside of its originating snapshot.

However, the OCL expression `allInstances()` with its global property represents an exception to this rule. In the application model it is used to access all objects from one state, i.e. all objects in a single object diagram. In the filmstrip model a whole state is represented as one snapshot and multiple snapshots may be part of a single object diagram. Therefore the expression `allInstances()` needs a special treatment when being transformed. To replicate the functionality of the expression all objects of the requested type, that are assigned to one snapshot need to be accessed. The refinements of the association `SnapElement` are used for this task. To determine the correct snapshot the value of the variable `self` (`self.aSelf` for transformed pre- and postconditions) is used, again because the original expressions do not cross snapshots. As an example in the transformation process the OCL invariant expression `Process.allInstances()` becomes `self.snapshot.process`.

Other elements that need alternative representations in the filmstrip model are the expression `oclIsNew()` and the keyword `@pre`. `oclIsNew()` is a special expression only available in postconditions. Because the expressions of postconditions become invariants, the expression is unusable. It checks whether an object is created during an operation call, which equals to the statement: It was not existent in the predecessor state. In the filmstrip model this property is replicated by checking for the predecessor of the object using the association `PredSucc`.

```
context Scheduler::New( p:Process )
post: waiting = waiting@pre→including(p) and
      ready = ready@pre and active = active@pre
```

Fig. 7. Postcondition of the scheduler New() operation in the application model

```
context New_SchedulerOpC
inv: aSelf.succ.waiting = aSelf.waiting→collectNested( p1 |
         p1.succ )→asSet()→including( p.succ )
     and aSelf.succ.ready = aSelf.ready→collectNested( p1 |
         p1.succ )→asSet()
     and aSelf.succ.active = aSelf.active.succ
```

Fig. 8. Transformed postcondition of the scheduler New() operation

Thus an OCL expression p.oclIsNew(), where p is a process object, becomes p.pred.oclIsUndefined() in the filmstrip model.

The keyword @pre is also only available in postconditions. If an expression is postfixed by this keyword, the expression is evaluated in the pre state of the operation call. The keyword only affects one expression and can be used multiple times in an OCL query. In the filmstrip model the pre state is explicitly available for every operation call. To evaluate the expression in the filmstrip model, the association PredSucc is used. The expression switches to the predecessor snapshot of the current object, executes the postfixed expression and switches back to the original snapshot.

However there are a few pitfalls depending on the actual type of the current objects. Basic types, i.e. Boolean, Real, Integer and String, are stateless and do not need to be switched. For collection and tuple types the contents have to be switched to the predecessor state. Particularly collection types require caution, as the OCL operation collectNested, which is used to switch to the predecessor state, changes the type of collections from Set to Bag or from OrderedSet to Sequence. To counteract these changes, the OCL expressions asSet() and asOrderedSet() have to be added, to keep the original behavior. Also the types when switching to and from the predecessor state may differ, depending on the evaluated expression. Let sched1 be a scheduler object of the filmstrip model, the expression sched1.waiting@pre in a postcondition to access the waiting processes in the pre state, is transformed into sched1.pred.waiting→collectNested(succ)→asSet(). Note the type of the evaluated value: it goes from Scheduler to Set{Process} to Bag{Process} (during the collectNested() evaluation) and back to Set{Process} again.

To give an example for the OCL transformations, Fig. 7 shows the postcondition of the operation New in the scheduler application model. After the transformation the expression has become an invariant of the operation call class, the variable access changes and the keyword @pre is transformed. The result is shown in Fig. 8.

```
context Snapshot inv cycleFree:                                    (a)
  Set{ self }→closure( s | s.succ() )→excludes( self )
context Snapshot inv oneFilmstrip:                                  (b)
  Snapshot.allInstances()→select( s |
    s.pred().oclIsUndefined() )→size() = 1
  and Snapshot.allInstances()→select( s |
    s.succ().oclIsUndefined() )→size() = 1
context OpC inv assocClassBehavior:                                 (c)
  self.pred()→size() = 1 and self.succ()→size() = 1
  and OpC.allInstances()→forAll( op |
  (self.pred() = op.pred() and self.succ() = op.succ()) implies
    self = op )
context SchedulerOpC inv aSelfDefined:                              (d)
  not self.aSelf.oclIsUndefined()
context SchedulerOpC inv aSelfInPred:                               (e)
  self.aSelf.snapshot = self.pred()
context New_SchedulerOpC inv paramPInPred:                         (f)
  not self.p.oclIsUndefined() implies
    self.p.snapshot = self.pred()
context Scheduler inv validSnapshotLinking:                        (g)
  not self.succ.oclIsUndefined() implies
    self.succ.snapshot = self.snapshot.succ()
context Scheduler inv validLinkingActive:                          (h)
  not self.active.oclIsUndefined() implies
    self.snapshot = self.active.snapshot
context Scheduler inv validLinkingReady:                           (i)
  self.ready→forAll( c | c.snapshot = self.snapshot )
```

Fig. 9. Various invariants of the filmstrip model to ensure correct usage and behavior

4.3 Filmstrip Model Constraints

To complete the filmstrip transformation, additional invariants are added to the resulting model, in order to force correct interaction of the filmstrip model elements and being able to reproduce the application model behavior correctly. In a first step three invariants are added to the filmstrip core elements. The definitions are shown in Fig. 9(a)–(c). The first invariant is called cycleFree and ensures, that the filmstrip line is free of cycles. The second invariant is called oneFilmstrip which prohibits the existence of more than one filmstrip per object diagram. And the last definition is called assocClassBehavior and makes sure that two snapshots are linked with at most one operation call.

The next invariants are applied to the operation call classes generated during the filmstrip transformation. These ensure correct values for the attributes. At first the attribute aSelf must be defined, since it is the object, the operation is called on. Furthermore it must point to an object in the pre state of the operation call, i.e. it must be assigned to the snapshot accessible by the query operation pred(). The definitions are shown in Fig. 9(d)–(e).

Additionally the attributes covering the operation parameters need similar constraints depending on the type of the attribute. For those attributes, the value must be in the pre state of the operation call, the same as the value of aSelf. Unlike the attribute aSelf the parameters may have undefined values. An example definition of such invariant for the parameter p of the operation New of the class Scheduler is shown in Fig. 9(f). Collection and tuple type attributes must be covered accordingly. Types other than classes of the application model, like String and Integer, are stateless as they cannot be assigned to a snapshot and therefore do not need restrictions. This includes enumerations.

Lastly, a few invariants are added to the classes from the application model. The first of these is called validSnapshotLinking and is added to all classes transformed from the application model. It assures, that links of the association PredSucc are only established between objects from consecutive snapshots in the right order. An example for the class Scheduler is shown in Fig 9(g). This invariant only checks objects, that have a successor instead of every object of a snapshot, because objects may be deleted during an operation call and therefore do not necessarily have a successor. Furthermore objects without a predecessor are created during the operation call leading to its snapshot.

The next invariants affect associations from the application model. To represent a single state from the application model, objects of one snapshot may only be linked with objects from the same snapshot. The invariant validLinking does this by comparing the snapshot objects of the association ends. Figures 9(h)–(i) show examples for 0..1 and * multiplicity association ends. N-ary associations and association classes must be covered accordingly.

5   Examples of Use

This section uses the object diagram from Fig. 3 to detail some of the benefits of the filmstrip model. The state in the object diagram demonstrates a sequence of operation calls of the transformed scheduler as modelled by the filmstrip model. The object diagram contains a total of four snapshots connected with three operation calls. Thick lines indicate elements from the application model (compare Fig. 2). The other objects and links are elements of the filmstrip model. The order of the operation invocation is from top to bottom.

The object diagram shows a whole process cycle (as introduced in Sect. 2) of the process with pid 1 starting from the Active state. Since all information is available in the object diagram and therefore accessible with OCL, it is possible to create an OCL query, which checks the order in which the process passes the states and whether it hits every state or leaves any of them out. Other queries can e.g. list Ready processes of certain snapshots:

```
Sequence{ s1, s2, s3, s4 }→collect( s | s.scheduler.ready )
→ Sequence{ Set{p2}, Set{}, Set{p5}, Set{} }
    : Sequence(Set(Process))
```

The query lists all Ready processes for every scheduler of the given input snapshots. Compared to this example, starting from the snapshot objects, it is also possible to find snapshots, in which a given process is ready next:

```
Set{ p1, p2 }→collect( p | Tuple{ idProcess=p,
    snapshots=Set{p}→closure( succ )→select( pp |
      pp.schedulerReady <> null } )
→ Set{ Tuple{ idProcess=p1, snapshots=Set{s3} },
        Tuple{ idProcess=p2, snapshots=Set{} } }
    : Set(Tuple( idProcess:Process, snapshots:Set(Snapshot) ))
```

This query uses the order of the objects given by the association `PredSucc` to find all future incarnations of the processes and selects those snapshots, where the process is in the `Ready` state. A better overview of the resulting map is given in the following table:

idProcess	p1	p2
snapshots	Set{s3}	Set{}

The result shows that in this particular operation sequence the process `p1` is next `Ready` only in snapshot `s3`, whereas the process `p2` is never `Ready` again after the first snapshot.

Further test objectives include, whether an operation sequence exists, so that a certain process is never scheduled or if deadlocks exist in the system. These objectives can be expressed with OCL invariants. Some constraints can be expressed easier using OCL extended with linear temporal logic (LTL) [18]. For example, the temporal expression

$$\text{Unassigned} \wedge (\text{Unassigned } until \text{ Waiting})$$

on processes asserts that every process begins in the unassigned state and remains in that state until it finally gets into the waiting state after being assigned to a scheduler. In the filmstrip model this property is expressible with plain OCL. For the resulting expression it does not matter how many processes are part of the system state and in what order they are processed. Another test scenario is the reachability of a certain state from a given start state, which is done by constraining the last snapshot to the desired final state.

The example system state of the filmstrip model is built up without actually invoking any operation call. Those are only modelled using the new elements of the filmstrip model. All invariants of the transformed model are fulfilled by the system state. Extracting object diagrams, as they appear in the application model, can be done by removing all but the elements with a thick border in the state. Four distinct states remain that equal to four object diagrams from the application model. Sequence diagrams can be extracted by looking at the operation call objects and comparing the two snapshots linked with it. The delta between the objects linked to the snapshots are the actions taken place during the operation call.

Since no operation needs to be invoked to create these system states, verification and validation tools for UML and OCL models without support for model dynamics can be utilized to generate system states like the one in Fig 3. When enriching the model with further constraints, e.g. test objectives using temporal logic, those tools can be used to verify such dynamic properties in a bounded environment.

6   Implementation

The whole transformation process is implemented in Java as a plugin for the USE tool [11]. This particular transformation is intended to be an integral part of our validation and verification framework and therefore we have decided to implement the transformation in Java. Alternatively, we could provide a programming language-independent formulation in transformation languages like QVT-R or ATL.

The implementation follows the definitions of the transformation in this paper closely and has a high compatibility to different models. The plugin uses the setup described in this paper and therefore does not require a configuration. It transforms all UML and OCL features supported by USE and is compatible to all models, loadable in USE. The transformation is a linear process, which results in fast transformation times[1]. The plugin is available for download on the USE website[2].

7   Conclusion and Future Work

We have provided a widely applicable and automated way of transforming UML and OCL application models into filmstrip models and presented a fully functional implementation on the basis of the USE tool. Transformed models can, however, also be processed and validated with other tools. The approach forms a baseline for further verification and validation processes on the filmstrip model by being compatible to a maximum number of application models with only one generic transformation. Basic ideas of test objectives have been provided.

Future work should study automated test generation on the basis of the filmstrip model. Furthermore, the verification times of the approach needs to be analysed in a detailed case study. Improvements to the filmstrip model include compatibility to nested operation calls to allows for an even wider range of application models to be transformed and more detailed tests on them. Another field of study is the comparability of snapshot objects and the possibility to allow multiple operation calls from one snapshot. This introduces the reusability of snapshots to create snapshot graphs instead of linear filmstrips, similar to Kripke structures. Thus getting closer to the specification of CTL formulas instead of LTL formulas.

Acknowledgements. Thanks to the reviewers and Dániel Varró for their constructive comments.

References

1. Al-Lail, M., Abdunabi, R., France, R.B., Ray, I.: Rigorous Analysis of Temporal Access Control Properties in Mobile Systems. In: ICECCS. IEEE (2013)
2. Anastasakis, K., Bordbar, B., Georg, G., Ray, I.: On Challenges of Model Transformation from UML to Alloy. Software and System Modeling 9(1), 69–86 (2010)

---

[1] The scheduler example is transformed in less than a second.
[2] http://sourceforge.net/projects/useocl/

3. Bill, R., Gabmeyer, S., Kaufmann, P., Seidl, M.: OCL meets CTL: Towards CTL-Extended OCL Model Checking. In: Proceedings of the MODELS 2013 OCL Workshop, vol. 1092, pp. 13–22 (2013)
4. Cabot, J., Clarisó, R., Riera, D.: UMLtoCSP: A Tool for the Formal Verification of UML/OCL Models using Constraint Programming. In: Stirewalt, R.E.K., Egyed, A., Fischer, B. (eds.) ASE 2007, pp. 547–548. ACM (2007)
5. Clark, T.: Model Based Functional Testing using Pattern Directed Filmstrips. In: Proceedings of the 4th International Workshop on the Automation of Software Test, pp. 53–61. IEEE (2009)
6. Conrad, S., Turowski, K.: Temporal OCL Meeting Specification Demands for Business Components. In: Unified Modeling Language: Systems Analysis, Design and Development Issues, pp. 151–165. IGI Publishing (2001)
7. Dick, J., Faivre, A.: Automating the generation and sequencing of test cases from model-based specifications. In: Larsen, P.G., Wing, J.M. (eds.) FME 1993. LNCS, vol. 670, pp. 268–284. Springer, Heidelberg (1993)
8. D'Souza, D., Wills, A.: Catalysis. Practical Rigor and Refinement: Extending OMT, Fusion, and Objectory. Tech. rep. (1995), http://catalysis.org
9. Flake, S., Müller, W.: Past- and Future-Oriented Time-Bounded Temporal Properties with OCL. In: SEFM 2004. pp. 154–163. IEEE Computer Society (2004)
10. Gil, J., Kent, S.: Three Dimensional Software Modeling. In: Torii, K., Futatsugi, K., Kemmerer, R.A. (eds.) ICSE 1998. pp. 105–114. IEEE Computer Society (1998)
11. Gogolla, M., Büttner, F., Richters, M.: USE: A UML-Based Specification Environment for Validating UML and OCL. Science of Computer Programming 69 (2007)
12. Gogolla, M., Hamann, L., Hilken, F., Kuhlmann, M., France, R.B.: From Application Models to Filmstrip Models: An Approach to Automatic Validation of Model Dynamics. In: Fill, H.G., Karagiannis, D., Reimer, U. (eds.) Modellierung (2014)
13. Jackson, D.: Software Abstractions: Logic, Language, and Analysis. The MIT Press, Cambridge (2006)
14. Kanso, B., Taha, S.: Temporal Constraint Support for OCL. In: Czarnecki, K., Hedin, G. (eds.) SLE 2012. LNCS, vol. 7745, pp. 83–103. Springer, Heidelberg (2013)
15. OMG (ed.): Object Constraint Language, Version 2.3.1. OMG, OMG Document (2012), www.omg.org
16. Salas, P.A.P., Aichernig, B.K.: Automatic Test Case Generation for OCL: A Mutation Approach. Tech. Rep. 321, The United Nations University – International Institute for Software Technology (2005)
17. Snook, C., Butler, M.: UML-B: A Plug-in for the Event-B Tool Set. In: Börger, E., Butler, M., Bowen, J.P., Boca, P. (eds.) ABZ 2008. LNCS, vol. 5238, p. 344. Springer, Heidelberg (2008)
18. Soden, M., Eichler, H.: Temporal Extensions of OCL Revisited. In: Paige, R.F., Hartman, A., Rensink, A. (eds.) ECMDA-FA 2009. LNCS, vol. 5562, pp. 190–205. Springer, Heidelberg (2009)
19. Yu, L., France, R.B., Ray, I.: Scenario-Based Static Analysis of UML Class Models. In: Czarnecki, K., Ober, I., Bruel, J.-M., Uhl, A., Völter, M. (eds.) MODELS 2008. LNCS, vol. 5301, pp. 234–248. Springer, Heidelberg (2008)
20. Ziemann, P., Gogolla, M.: OCL Extended with Temporal Logic. In: Broy, M., Zamulin, A.V. (eds.) PSI 2003. LNCS, vol. 2890, pp. 351–357. Springer, Heidelberg (2004)

Reverse Engineering of Model Transformations for Reusability

Jesús Sánchez Cuadrado, Esther Guerra, and Juan de Lara

Modelling and Software Engineering Research Group
Universidad Autónoma de Madrid, Spain
http://www.miso.es

Abstract. Reuse techniques are key for the industrial adoption of Model-Driven Engineering (MDE). However, while reusability has been successfully applied to programming languages, its use is scarce in MDE and, in particular, in model transformations.

In previous works, we developed an approach that enables the reuse of model transformations for different meta-models. This is achieved by defining reusable components that encapsulate a generic *transformation template* and expose an interface called *concept* declaring the structural requirements that any meta-model using the component should fulfil. Binding the concept to one of such meta-models induces an adaptation of the template, which becomes applicable to the meta-model. To facilitate reuse, concepts need to be concise, reflecting only the minimal set of requirements demanded by the transformation.

In this paper, we automate the reverse engineering of existing transformations into reusable transformation components. To make a transformation reusable, we use the information obtained from its static analysis to derive a concept that is minimal with respect to the transformation and maximizes its reuse opportunities, and then evolve the transformation accordingly. The paper describes a prototype implementation and an evaluation using transformations from the ATL zoo.

Keywords: Model transformation, Reusability, Reverse engineering, Re-engineering.

1 Introduction

Reusability is a key enabler for the industrial adoption of Model-Driven Engineering (MDE). Some techniques have been proposed to reuse complete transformations, such as superimposition [19], phases [14] and genericity [13], but their use is still an exception. As noted by [1], one reason for this situation is the lack of repositories for selecting and effectively reusing transformations. Even the ATL Transformation Zoo [2], which is the closest relative to a transformation repository, consists of a collection of transformations not designed for reuse. This contrasts with the rich ecosystems of libraries in e.g., object-oriented languages like Java or C#, which successfully promote development with reuse.

D. Di Ruscio and D. Varró (Eds.): ICMT 2014, LNCS 8568, pp. 186–201, 2014.

In previous works [13], we proposed a technique for transformation reuse based on generic programming. In our approach, reusable transformation components encapsulate a transformation template developed against so-called concepts, which resemble meta-models but their elements are variables. Binding these variables to concrete meta-model elements induces a rewriting of the template to make it compatible with the meta-model. Thus, we obtain reusability because the transformation component can be used with any meta-model that can be bound to its concepts. However, this technique implies developing transformations with reusability up-front, by designing suitable concepts for the input and output domains and then writing the transformation template accordingly. Thus, it is not possible to profit from existing transformations beyond their use as a reference to manually implement a generic, reusable transformation. While concepts need to be concise to facilitate reuse and include only the elements accessed by a template, transformations are developed for concrete meta-models (e.g. UML) which reflect the complexity of a domain and may include accidental complexity from the transformation point of view. Hence, making an existing transformation reusable requires both a simplification of the meta-model into a truly reusable concept, and an according reorganization of the transformation.

In this work, we propose a semi-automatic process to reverse engineer existing transformations into generic, reusable transformations. It has been implemented for ATL as this is one of the most widely used transformation languages. Our aim is to foster reuse by facilitating the transition from existing, non-reusable transformations into reusable components that can be offered as transformation libraries in a repository. The process starts by extracting the effective meta-model of a transformation, which implies its static analysis to derive typing information. Then, the effective meta-model is evolved towards a concise concept through a series of refactorings, and the transformation is co-evolved accordingly if needed. The approach is supported by a prototype tool, and has been evaluated using transformations of the ATL zoo.

Organization. Section 2 presents our previous work on reusable transformations. Then, Section 3 overviews our proposal to the reverse engineering of existing transformations into reusable components, which is detailed in the following two sections: static analysis of ATL transformations (Section 4), and extraction and customization of concepts (Section 5). We evaluate our approach in Section 6, review related work in Section 7, and draw conclusions in Section 8.

2   Reusable Transformations

In order to build a reusable transformation, in previous work [13] we proposed the notion of *transformation components* with a well-defined interface called *concept*. Fig. 1 shows a generic transformation component to calculate metrics for object-oriented languages, as well as its instantiation for a specific meta-model. The component (label 1) includes a transformation template from a hand-made concept characterising object-oriented languages to a metrics meta-model. We only show an excerpt of the template, which calculates the Depth of Inheritance

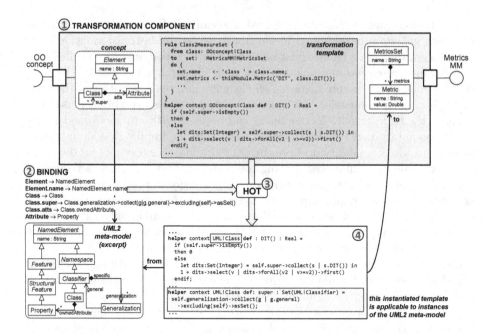

Fig. 1. Example of definition and usage of transformation components

Tree (DIT) metric. The concept, which is the component interface, gathers the structural requirements that a meta-model needs to fulfil to qualify as input meta-model for the transformation. The concept should be as simple as possible to facilitate reuse, excluding elements that are not needed by the transformation. In the example, the concept includes class Attribute even if it is not used in the excerpt of the ATL template, because other rules do it.

The way to reuse a component is to bind its concepts to meta-models (label 2). While it is possible to have concepts as source and target of a transformation template, binding only the source is more common in practice [13]. If a concept is not bound, it is simply treated as a meta-model. By default, each element in the concept must be bound to one meta-model element. This can be adjusted for each concept element by attaching a cardinality that indicates how many times it may be bound. By space constraints, we do not discuss this feature further.

In the figure, the source concept is bound to the UML2 meta-model. The binding is performed through a dedicated domain-specific language which allows defining correspondences. The left of each correspondence refers to a concept element, like Element, Class or Class.super. The right may include either elements of the bound meta-model or OCL expressions defined over the meta-model. For example, Element is bound to NamedElement, Class to Class, and reference Class.super is bound to a collection of Class obtained through the OCL expression Class.generalization->collect(...). We use a structural approach, so that abstract classes in the concept may not need to be bound, in which case, any feature defined in it should be bound in its concrete subclasses. Thus, if Element were not bound in the example, then name should be bound in both Class and Attribute.

The binding induces an adaptation to the transformation template (label 3), yielding an ATL transformation applicable to the instances of the bound UML2 meta-model. In this case, the adaptation modifies the context of the helper, and adds a new helper that calculates the superclasses of a given one (relation super in the original concept), as given by the binding of Class.super.

Altogether, building a reusable component involves the development of a transformation template and its associated concepts from scratch. In the example, we developed a transformation to calculate metrics and a concept for object-oriented languages. However, the ATL zoo already contains two transformations that calculate object-oriented metrics for KM3 and UML2. Unfortunately, these meta-models (especially UML2) contain a lot more elements than the transformation needs, thus not being suitable to be used as concepts. If we would have been able to make reusable one of these transformations, we would have saved a lot of effort, as the resulting component would be applicable to any object-oriented modelling language. Thus, in the rest of the paper, we present a proposal to automate the reverse engineering of existing transformations into reusable components. As running example, we will reverse-engineer the transformation excerpt of Fig. 1, defined over the UML2 meta-model.

3 Making Existing Transformations Reusable

Promoting existing transformations into reusable components poses several challenges. First, we need to simplify the used meta-models (e.g. UML2) into concepts. This process can be automated by calculating the effective meta-models of the transformation (i.e. the classes and features accessed by the transformation code). However, the effective meta-model might not be the ideal concept, as we may like e.g., to merge classes or reorganize the inheritance hierarchy. Doing this manually can be cumbersome, since it must be checked if the change breaks the transformation behaviour (i.e., adapting the transformation would imply removing a rule), and then changing the transformation accordingly if needed. In this section, we introduce our proposal to automate this process.

Fig. 2 shows the steps in our approach. First, the transformation to be made reusable is selected. This implies looking up potential sources of interesting transformations, such as in-house developed transformations, transformation repositories (e.g. the ATL zoo) and open source MDE tools that include model transformations (e.g. MoDisco and Fornax). However, not any transformation is adequate to be generalised into a generic transformation (although they still can profit from the process to improve its quality and be deployed in a repository). For example, the *Ant to Maven* transformation fully depends on the Ant and Maven semantics, and thus it cannot be generalized to other build systems. Intuitively, we say that a transformation is amenable to reuse when there are variants of the meta-models it uses (e.g. variants of UML class diagrams, different versions of it, or meta-models for related notations, like Ecore).

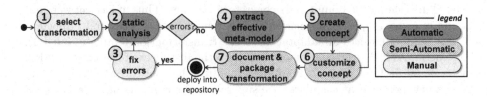

Fig. 2. Main steps in the reverse engineering of transformations into reusable units

The second step performs a static analysis of the transformation. This is particularly needed in ATL because ATL does not enforce type correctness, hence transformations may be ill-typed. Moreover, the creation of a suitable concept for the transformation requires precise type information. If the analysis detects errors, the developer is required to fix them (step 3), otherwise, the effective meta-model of the transformation is automatically extracted (step 4).

Starting from the effective meta-model, a concept is derived, which includes the *minimum* structural requirements that a meta-model should fulfil to be used with the transformation (step 5). The concept is more concise than the effective meta-model, as it is refactored taking into account the static analysis of the transformation, e.g., to remove unused features and intermediate abstract classes, or to move features up or down class hierarchies. The aim is having a concept as simple as possible to facilitate its reuse. The suitable refactorings are automatically computed and the user is only requested to approve them. For example, if we start from a transformation defined over the UML2 meta-model, the system may suggest replacing class Generalization by a reference parents, as this will facilitate future bindings. Additionally, it is possible to customize the concept through user-selected refactorings allowing, e.g., merging two classes into one, or changing an enumerate attribute by a set of subclasses (step 6). In this way, designers can include tacit knowledge of the domain in the design of the concept. A common example is the renaming of classes to assign names more akin to the domain. Both the creation and the customization of concepts may imply the automatic rewriting of the transformation to keep it consistent, and they are iterative since the application of a refactoring may enable another one.

The final step (label 7) is to document and package the concepts and transformation template. This can be done using a variety of formats, including text- and contract-based documentation. Currently, we use the PAMOMO language to describe the transformation contract via pre/post-conditions and invariants [6], enriching the transformation with documentation and an automatically generated test suite. For space constraints, we leave out this step of the process.

4   Static Analysis of ATL Transformations

Our reverse engineering procedure needs to extract the *static meta-model foot-print* of a transformation. This requires static type information regarding the classes and features used by the transformation. In strongly typed languages

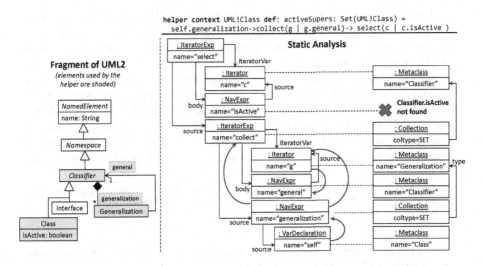

Fig. 3. Analysis of a helper

like Kermeta [15], the type information is available in the abstract syntax tree, but other languages, like ATL, do not provide this information. Hence, as a prerequisite to apply our approach, we introduce a static analysis stage to gather as much type information as possible from the ATL transformation. This section presents the static analyser that we have built for this purpose.

In the simplest setting, our analyser performs a bottom-up traversal of the abstract syntax tree, propagating types from leaf nodes to the root of the expressions (i.e. using synthesized attributes). In some cases, particularly for parameters, types also need to be passed top-down (i.e. using inherited attributes).

Fig. 3 shows the analysis of an ATL helper which gathers the "active" direct superclasses of a class. Each node of the abstract syntax tree is annotated with its type (boxes to the right linked with dashed lines to the nodes). These types are propagated along the nodes, as depicted by the red, curved lines (we only show some of them). For nodes corresponding to a property access or operation invocation, the existence of the property or operation is checked.

Even though the helper is accepted by the ATL engine, the analyser reports a warning because the isActive property is defined in Class but not in Classifier, which is the type of the variable c. At runtime, this expression will fail if the model includes classifiers different from classes, like Interface objects.

Reporting these issues is important to help improving the quality of the transformation and understand its constraints if they are not documented. Moreover, the analyser should avoid raising false warnings and errors which may lead to low-quality type information. To this end, we have enhanced the basic analysis with the following features:

- **Multiple Type Collections.** In OCL, it is possible to mix objects of different, unrelated types in the same collection, typically through the use of union and including operations. Our analyser keeps track of these operations in order to: (a) infer common supertypes, or (b) assign multiple potential types to the same expression node. This provides more accurate typing information for the effective meta-model extraction and concept creation phases.

- **Implicit Casting.** ATL does not support the oclAsType operation, which complicates the analysis as there is no explicit way for downcasting. Thus, our analysis looks for oclIsKind/oclIsTypeOf expressions that implicitly downcast a reference. For instance, the following variants of the expression in Fig. 3 are deemed correct by our analyser, because the usages of oclIsKindOf ensure that the type of c will be Class when used in the c.isActive expression.

```
self.generalization−>collect(g | g.general)−>          self.generalization−>collect(g | g.general)−>
  select(c | c.oclIsKindOf(UML!Class))−>                  select(c | if c.oclIsKindOf(UML!Class) then
  select(c | c.isActive )                                        c.isActive else false endif)
```

- **Structural Type Inference.** As explained above, a property access may not be resolved due to the lack of downcasting (either explicit or implicit). In such a case, our analyser looks for the property in the subclasses of the receptor's type. If it is found in one or more subclasses, they are tentatively assigned to the expression, and a warning is raised.

This list is not exhaustive, and we aim at improving the analyser since, the better it gets, the more accurate the reverse engineering process will be. Indeed, any other ATL analyser could be used instead of ours, whenever it provides the meta-model footprint of the transformation. The meta-model footprint refers to the meta-model elements involved in the transformation. This corresponds to the set of used types, in the example {Class, Classifier, Generalization}, and the set of used features, in the example {Classifier.generalization, Generalization.general, Class.isActive} (see Fig. 3). For practical purposes, we distinguish two kinds of used types: *explicit types* if they are explicitly mentioned in the transformation, and *implicit types* if they are indirectly reached through navigation expressions.

Additionally, our analyser outputs information about *call sites*, which are the locations where an operation or feature is accessed. This is the concrete class that receives the feature access, which may be different from the class defining the feature. Thus, for each call site, we store a pair of concrete class and feature. In the example, the set of call sites is {⟨Class, Classifier.generalization⟩, ⟨Generalization, Generalization.general⟩, ⟨Class, Class.isActive⟩}. This provides more information than just the accessed features, since it is possible to know that the Classifier.generalization feature is only accessed by Class objects.

5   Creation and Customization of Concepts

From the information extracted in the static analysis phase, we infer a concept that will act as interface for the reusable component. For this purpose, first we prune the meta-model to keep only the elements needed by the transformation.

```
rule Class2MeasureSet {
  from class: UML!Class
  to set: MetricsMM!MetricsSet
  do {
    set.name <− 'class ' + class.name;
    set.metrics <− thisModule.Metric('DIT', class.DIT());
  }}

helper context UML!Class def : DIT() : Real =
  if (self.super−>isEmpty())
  then 0
  else
    let dits:Set(Integer) = self.super−>collect(s | s.DIT()) in
    1 + dits−>select(v | dits−>forAll(v2 | v>=v2))−>first()
  endif;

helper context UML!Class def: super : Set(Classifier) =
  self.generalization−>collect(g | g.general)
    −>excluding(self)−>asSet();
```

Meta-model Footprint

Explicit types:
- Class

Implicit types:
- Classifier
- Generalization

Features:
- NamedElement.name
- Classifier.generalization
- Generalization.general

Call sites:
- ⟨Class, NamedElement.name⟩
- ⟨Class, Classifier.generalization⟩
- ⟨Generalization, Generalization.general⟩

Fig. 4. ATL transformation over UML2 meta-model (left). Source meta-model footprint obtained after the static analysis (right).

Then, we convert the pruned meta-model into a concept which may be simplified through the application of several refactorings, and customised to take into account specific knowledge of the domain.

5.1 Extraction of Effective Meta-model

To calculate the effective meta-model, we use a pruning algorithm like the one presented in [15], using the meta-model footprint obtained in the static analysis as input. The algorithm keeps in the meta-model the implicit and explicit types, and respects the inheritance hierarchies.

As an example, Fig. 4 shows a transformation defined over the UML2 meta-model, and the footprint that our static analysis returns. This footprint is used to extract the effective meta-model of the transformation. In particular, Fig. 5(a) shows an excerpt of UML2, while Fig. 5(b) shows the effective meta-model that results from applying the pruning algorithm to the transformation in Fig. 4.

5.2 Concept Creation

The effective meta-model is refactored into a more compact concept by removing or simplifying non-essential elements for the transformation, for which we take into account the call site information. On the one hand, the concept is the interface for reusability, and hence large inheritance hierarchies are discouraged because they affect comprehensibility [3]. On the other hand, concepts should be as simple as possible to facilitate their binding to meta-models. For example, the effective meta-model in Fig. 5(b) is not a suitable concept yet, because it contains some classes (like NamedElement) which may be not found in every object-oriented notation. This class appears in the effective meta-model because it is a container for name, which is only used by Class in the transformation.

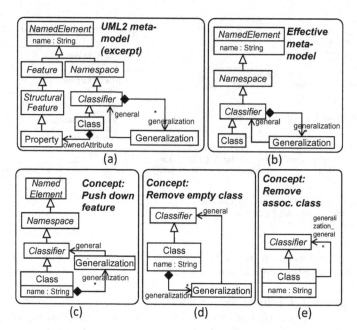

Fig. 5. Sequence of operations to convert the UML2 meta-model into a concept

To help creating the concept, we make available a number of refactorings automating the identification of simplification opportunities, their application, and the co-evolution of the transformation whenever it is needed. The system automatically suggests refactoring opportunities to the user, along with an explanation of the rationale of the proposal and its consequences (e.g. the transformation must be co-evolved). The user only needs to approve their application, since the refactoring locations are automatically gathered. Some of the refactorings are likely to be always accepted, such as removing empty classes. Hence, our tooling allows the user to configure which refactoring opportunities should be applied automatically. Moreover, the refactorings are applied in an iterative fashion, since the application of a refactoring may yield new refactoring opportunities.

– **Push Down Feature.** It moves a feature defined in a class to one or more of its subclasses, if only the instances of such subclasses use the feature. This information is taken from the call sites computed in the analysis phase. The refactoring is parameterized with the maximum number of subclasses to which the feature can be moved, in order to prevent duplication of the same feature in too many subclasses. For example, according to the call sites, the NamedElement.name and the Classifier.generalization features are only used by Class instances, thus they are moved to Class (see result in Fig. 5(c)).
– **Remove Empty Class.** Classes without features are removed if they do not belong to the *explicit types* set (i.e. they are only used in navigation

expressions). If the removed class is both a subtype and a supertype, the inheritance relationships are rearranged (this is called *pull-up inheritance* in [4]). The goal of this refactoring is to collapse inheritance hierarchies to enhance the comprehensibility of the concept and facilitate future bindings. In the running example, Namespace is removed, as well as NamedElement because the previous refactoring "pushed down" its only feature (see Fig. 5(d)).

- **Remove Unused Feature.** Any feature appearing in the effective meta-model but not in the footprint is removed. This is needed because the pruning algorithm [15] leaves opposite references even when they do not appear in the effective meta-model. Thus, this refactoring refines the pruning algorithm.

- **Make Leaf Abstract Class Concrete.** The effective meta-model may include leaf abstract classes, if their subclasses do not belong to the set of explicit types. In such a case, this refactoring makes such classes concrete, thus enforcing their binding to some class in the bound meta-models.

- **Pull Up Feature.** If several subclasses with a common parent share features, these are pulled up to the parent. This situation can arise initially in the effective meta-model, or due to the application of other refactorings. The refactoring can be parameterized with the minimum number of classes that should define the feature in order to pull it up.

- **Remove Association Class.** An association class acts as a reference that is able to carry properties. A typical example is Generalization in the UML2 meta-model. If a transformation does not use the properties of an association class (except the reference to the target class, like general in UML2), and the class does not appear in the *explicit types* set (except when used in *allInstances* operation), then the association class can be replaced by a simple reference in the concept. In such a case, the transformation needs to be co-evolved, replacing the navigations through the association class by references. The benefit of this refactoring is two-fold. Firstly, the concept becomes simpler. Secondly, the binding will be simpler if the meta-model also represents the same element as a reference, whereas if not, binding a reference in a concept to a class in a meta-model is easier than the other way round (we just need an expression like the one in Fig. 1 for Class.super). Fig. 5(e) shows its application to the concept, which implies co-evolving the transformation template. The details of the transformation rewriting are left out due to space constraints. In the running example, the expression self.generalization->collect(g | g.general)->excluding(self)->asSet() gets rewritten into self.generalization_general->excluding(self)->asSet().

5.3   Concept Customization

The previous process yields a concept, simplified to make it concise and reusable. However, this concept still retains the nomenclature and some design decisions from the meta-model from which it was derived. At this point, domain expertise can be used to customise the concept so that it reflects tacit knowledge of the domain. A typical example is the renaming of classes and features using the terms most frequently used in the domain. Similarly, some design options may be more common in a particular domain than others.

Next, we enumerate the domain-specific customizations currently supported, some of them inspired by standard object-oriented refactorings [5]. Some refactorings induce an adaptation of the transformation template, or use the information extracted from the static analysis of the transformation:

- **Renaming of Classes and Features.** It changes the name of classes and features, rewriting the transformation to accommodate the new names.
- **Extract Sub/Superclass.** This is a pair of related refactorings. *Extract subclass* splits a class into a superclass/subclass pair, the former optionally abstract. *Extract superclass* creates a new abstract superclass for a given set of classes, pulling up their common features. In both cases, the transformation does not need to be adapted.
- **Collapse Hierarchy.** This refactoring merges a class and a child class. It can only be applied if the parent class is not an *explicit type*, and it has just one child. This refactoring does not rewrite the transformation. However, if the concept includes some reference to the superclass, then the user is warned that if the superclass is bounded to a meta-model class with several children, collapsing the hierarchy excludes those children from the reference. For example, this refactoring is applicable in Fig. 5(e) because Classifer is not an explicit type and has a unique child Class. The result is a concept with a single node Class and a self-reference generalization_general. In this case, a warning is issued because Classifier received a reference. This means that if the resulting concept is bound back to the UML2 meta-model, mapping Class in the concept to Class in the meta-model, the reference generalization_general will only contain Class objects. Instead, if we keep the concept in Fig. 5(e) and map both Classifiers in the concept and the meta-model, then the reference may hold any subclass of Classifier (Class objects but also Interface objects).
- **Replace Enumerate with Inheritance.** An enumeration attribute used to distinguish several class types is replaced by a set of subclasses, one for each possible value. This refactoring is applicable if the enumeration literals are only present in comparisons, getting substituted by oclIsKindOf(...).

This list is not exhaustive, as we are working on additional ones, taken from [5]. As a difference from the refactorings presented in the previous section, the identification of the customization opportunities is not automated as it is difficult to deduce, e.g., whether the name of a class is appropriate in a domain or if a certain notion is better represented using two classes instead of one. Thus, users must select the locations where a customization should be performed, and then the concept is changed accordingly and the transformation is automatically adapted when possible.

6   Evaluation and Tool Support

We have evaluated our approach along two dimensions, described by the following two questions. First, *can we obtain a reusable component from a transformation not designed to be reused?*. Second, *to what extent is the effective meta-model*

	Process	DSC	NOH	ANA	ADI	NAC
	Initial meta-model	247	246	6.91	5.60	48
	Compute effective meta-model	31	30	0.77	0.47	23
UML	Ref. remove empty class (14)	17	15	0.59	0.36	9
	Ref. make abstract class concrete (1)	17	15	0.59	0.36	8
	Ref. push down feature (5)	17	15	0.59	0.36	8
	Ref. remove empty class (2)	15	13	0.53	0.27	6
	Ref. remove association class (1)	14	13	0.57	0.29	6
	Initial meta-model	16	16	0.31	0.07	2
KM3	Compute effective meta-model	11	10	0.45	0.01	2
	Ref. remove empty class (1)	10	9	0.4	0.01	1
	Ref. push down feature (1)	10	9	0.4	0.01	1

DSC: design size in classes
NOH: number of hierarchies
ANA: average number of ancestors
ADI: average depth of inheritance
NAC: number of abstract classes

Fig. 6. Metrics taken at each step of the process, for UML2 and KM3. The number of applications of each refactoring is shown between parentheses.

simpler than the original one, and the concept simpler than the effective meta-model?. To answer these questions, we have made an experiment based on two transformations from the ATL zoo, which calculate object-oriented metrics, one for UML2 (UML2Measure) and the other one for KM3 (KM32Measure).

To answer the first question, we applied our reverse engineering process to UML2Measure. We obtained a concept which we were able to bind to other object-oriented notations like KM3, Ecore, Java/Jamopp and METADEPTH. The bindings have less than 40 LOC, whereas the original transformation has about 370 LOC. This shows that our technique is effective, and yields reusable transformation components with concise concepts as interface for reuse.

To answer the second question, we reverse engineered both transformations and measured the effective meta-models/concepts obtained along the process. We used the object-oriented metrics proposed in [3], related to understandability and functionality quality attributes. High values of these metrics influence negatively the understandability. Fig. 6 summarizes the results. For UML2Measure, computing the effective meta-model removes all classes not related to class diagrams; however, the metrics relative to hierarchies and abstract classes indicate that the effective meta-model still has complex hierarchies. Our refactorings reduce this complexity to the half, obtaining a concept significantly simpler than the meta-model. In the case of KM32Measure, the computation of the effective meta-model and the refactorings have less impact because KM3 is a very simple meta-modelling core, almost a concept.

We also evaluated the gain from using the final, refactored concept as interface for reuse, w.r.t. using the effective meta-model for that purpose. Thus, we reused UML2Measure for Ecore, KM3, Java/Jamopp and METADEPTH. In all cases, the bindings from the concept were simpler than from the effective meta-model. For instance, abstract classes can be left unbound in our approach; but since the effective meta-model contained lots of them, the burden to decide what to bind to what was much lower for the concept. The *push down feature* refactorings improved the comprehensibility of the concept, because features were no longer hidden in the middle of hierarchies. The *remove association class* refactoring was particularly useful, as none of the bound meta-models had the notion of Generalization present in UML2. Thus, we had to define fairly complex bindings from the effective meta-model to emulate the Generalization class, but the bindings from the concept were straightforward. Altogether, this experiment shows that the obtained concept favours reuse more than the effective meta-model. A more extensive evaluation to confirm this intuition is left for future work.

Additionally, we validated the correctness of our implementation, binding the concept obtained from the UML2Measure transformation to the original UML2 meta-model. Then, we executed the original transformation and the adapted template using several third-party UML models as input, checking with EMF Compare that the results were in fact the same.

To support our reverse engineering process, we have built an Eclipse plug-in integrated in the Bentō[1] tool. The tool is interactive. As an example, Fig. 7 shows part of the interaction for the KM32Measure case: (1) the original transformation and the component information is configured, (2) the analysis phase detects warnings and errors in the transformation, (3) the refactoring opportunities are listed and can be easily applied, displaying the result in a tree-based visualization. Step (3) can be repeated if the system finds new refactoring proposals due to the application of a previous refactoring, or to apply domain customizations. To support this step, the tool allows computing metrics and showing information about the use of the concept in the transformation (4). Interestingly, the metrics facility has been included by reusing the oo2measure component obtained in the evaluation, and binding it to Ecore. Finally, the component is packaged by generating meta-information for our Bentō tool (5).

7   Related Work

Proposals on model transformation reuse can be type-centric or type-independent. The former include reuse mechanisms for single rules, like rule inheritance [11], and for whole transformations, like superimposition [19] and phases [14]. Regarding type-independent approaches, there are fine-grained techniques like parameterized rules [8,10,17], and coarse-grained ones aimed at reusing complete transformations [16]. Among these proposals, only [16] supports the reuse of transformations for arbitrary meta-models, as in our case. For this purpose, the authors extract the effective meta-model of the transformation as-is, and adapt the meta-model where the transformation is to be reused by making it a subtype of the effective meta-model. In contrast, we use concepts as reuse interface, we simplify the effective meta-model to facilitate its binding, and we do not modify the models/meta-models to be transformed but we adapt the transformation.

Our approach performs a static analysis of the original transformation. Even though the ATL IDE includes a static analysis engine that proposes feature completions, this only provides basic information which is not very accurate. The static analyser presented in [18] allows navigating ATL transformation models. The analyser, which is a facade to the ATL meta-model provided as a Java API, does not provide type information or advanced analysis support.

---

[1] The tool and a screencast are available at http://www.miso.es/tools/bento.html

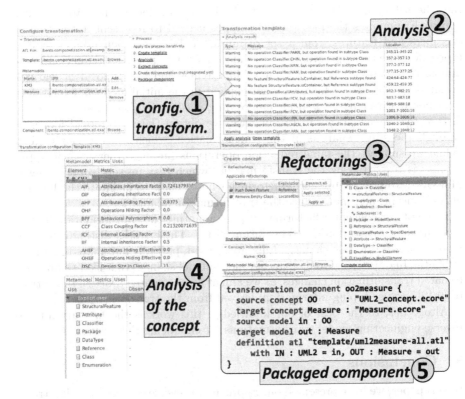

Fig. 7. Process followed to reverse engineer the KM32Measure transformation

Our meta-model extraction procedure relates to works on meta-model slicing and shrinking, though our goal is to simplify a meta-model to make an associated transformation easier to reuse. This poses additional challenges, like the need to identify whether a meta-model refactoring does not break the transformation.

Meta-model pruning is usually structure-preserving. For instance, the algorithm presented in [15] takes a set of elements of interest of a meta-model (in our case the meta-model footprint of the transformation) and returns a pruned version of the meta-model containing the minimum set of elements required for the new version to be a subtype of the original. Our approach is similar, but we simplify the resulting meta-model, e.g., by flattening hierarchies and removing opposite features unless both ends belong to the meta-model footprint. In [7], static meta-model footprints are obtained from Kermeta code in order to estimate model footprints. Kermeta includes type information in the syntax tree, hence no explicit static analysis is needed. The meta-model pruning phase is in line with [15], except that it includes all subclasses of every selected class.

A few works propose simplification techniques for meta-models, mostly based on refactorings for object oriented systems [5]. For instance, in [4], the authors present some type-safe meta-model reduction operations which guarantee extensional equivalence between the original and the reduced meta-model (i.e. the set of models conforming to both meta-models is the same). Their approach computes the meta-model snippet needed to represent a selection of classifiers and features from a set of initial models, and then applies several type-safe reduction operations to the meta-model snippet. As reduction operations, they support the flattening of hierarchies and the removal of features declared by classifiers which were not explicit in the initial models. Type-safety is achieved through the *pull-up inheritance, push-down feature* and *specialize feature type* refactorings [5]. In our case, we obtain the meta-model footprint through the static analysis of the transformation, which is more challenging. While we support the same reduction operations (among others), their applicability is restricted by the transformation, which may prevent some changes. Moreover, we provide further refactorings whose goal is to facilitate the binding of the concept, and may induce the transformation adaptation.

Some of our concept refactorings require adapting the transformation, like in meta-model/transformation co-evolution [9,12]. These works distinguish three kinds of transformation changes: fully automated, partially automated and fully semantic. In our case, we only consider meta-model changes that lead to fully automated transformation changes, as we aim at an automated process. In contrast to [9,12], we use typing information derived from the transformation.

Altogether, to the best of our knowledge, this work is the first attempt to reverse-engineering model transformations for enhancing their reusability.

8 Conclusions

In this paper, we have presented our approach to reverse engineer existing transformations into reusable components that can be applied to different meta-models. For this purpose, we first perform a static analysis of the candidate transformation to extract typing information and identify type errors. Then, we use this information to build a concept, that is, an interface optimised and customised to facilitate the reuse of the transformation. In this process, the transformation may need to be adapted to make it conformant to the concept.

We have demonstrated our approach and supporting tool by performing the reverse engineering of an existing ATL transformation to calculate object-oriented metrics. The results show that the obtained concepts tend to be more concise than meta-models, and therefore suitable for our purposes.

In the future, we foresee having a repository of reusable components that can be navigated and integrated with other components, thus speeding up the development of MDE projects. In addition to support reusability of whole transformations, we will also consider extracting slices of an existing transformation, and its subsequent re-engineering into a reusable component. We would like to consider other kinds of components, like components for code generation or in-place transformation, as well as further transformation languages in addition to ATL. While we support the manual definition of PaMoMo specifications for documenting transformation components, we plan to work on their automatic derivation from existing transformations. Such specifications could be used as composability criteria for components and for testing.

Acknowledgements. This work has been funded by the Spanish Ministry of Economy and Competitivity with project "Go Lite" (TIN2011-24139).

References

1. Kusel, A., et al.: Reuse in model-to-model transformation languages: Are we there yet? SoSyM, 1–36 (2013)
2. AtlanMod. Atl zoo, http://www.eclipse.org/atl/atlTransformations/
3. Bansiya, J., Davis, C.G.: A hierarchical model for object-oriented design quality assessment. IEEE Trans. Software Eng. 28(1), 4–17 (2002)
4. Bergmayr, A., Wimmer, M., Retschitzegger, W., Zdun, U.: Taking the pick out of the bunch - type-safe shrinking of metamodels. In: SE 2013, pp. 85–98 (2013)
5. Fowler, M.: Refactoring. Improving the Design of Existing Code. Ad.-Wesley (1999)
6. Guerra, E., Soeken, M.: Specification-driven model transformation testing. SoSyM, 1–22 (2013)
7. Jeanneret, C., Glinz, M., Baudry, B.: Estimating footprints of model operations. In: ICSE 2011, pp. 601–610. ACM (2011)
8. Kalnina, E., Kalnins, A., Celms, E., Sostaks, A.: Graphical template language for transformation synthesis. In: van den Brand, M., Gašević, D., Gray, J. (eds.) SLE 2009. LNCS, vol. 5969, pp. 244–253. Springer, Heidelberg (2010)
9. Levendovszky, T., Balasubramanian, D., Narayanan, A., Karsai, G.: A novel approach to semi-automated evolution of dsml model transformation. In: van den Brand, M., Gašević, D., Gray, J. (eds.) SLE 2009. LNCS, vol. 5969, pp. 23–41. Springer, Heidelberg (2010)
10. Wimmer, M., Kappel, G., Kusel, A., Retschitzegger, W., Schoenboeck, J., Schwinger, W.: Surviving the heterogeneity jungle with composite mapping operators. In: Tratt, L., Gogolla, M. (eds.) ICMT 2010. LNCS, vol. 6142, pp. 260–275. Springer, Heidelberg (2010)
11. Wimmer, M., et al.: Surveying rule inheritance in model-to-model transformation languages. JOT 11(2), 3:1–3:46 (2012)
12. Di Ruscio, D., Iovino, L., Pierantonio, A.: A methodological approach for the coupled evolution of metamodels and atl transformations. In: Duddy, K., Kappel, G. (eds.) ICMT 2013. LNCS, vol. 7909, pp. 60–75. Springer, Heidelberg (2013)
13. Sánchez Cuadrado, J., Guerra, E., de Lara, J.: Flexible model-to-model transformation templates: An application to ATL. JOT 11(2), 4:1–4:28 (2012)
14. Sánchez Cuadrado, J., Molina, J.G.: Modularization of model transformations through a phasing mechanism. SoSyM 8(3), 325–345 (2009)
15. Sen, S., Moha, N., Baudry, B., Jézéquel, J.-M.: Meta-model pruning. In: Schürr, A., Selic, B. (eds.) MODELS 2009. LNCS, vol. 5795, pp. 32–46. Springer, Heidelberg (2009)
16. Sen, S., Moha, N., Mahé, V., Barais, O., Baudry, B., Jézéquel, J.-M.: Reusable model transformations. SoSyM 11(1), 111–125 (2010)
17. Varró, D., Pataricza, A.: Generic and meta-transformations for model transformation engineering. In: Baar, T., Strohmeier, A., Moreira, A., Mellor, S.J. (eds.) UML 2004. LNCS, vol. 3273, pp. 290–304. Springer, Heidelberg (2004)
18. Vieira, A., Ramalho, F.: A static analyzer for model transformations. In: 3rd International Workshop on Model Transformation with ATL (2011)
19. Wagelaar, D., Straeten, R.V.D., Deridder, D.: Module superimposition: A composition technique for rule-based model transformation languages. SoSyM 9(3), 285–309 (2010)